A BARRICADE CULT CLASSIC
SEX AND THE OFFICE

A BARRICADE CULT CLASSIC
Sex and the Office

Helen Gurley Brown

BARRICADE
BOOKS
FORT LEE, NEW JERSEY

For my sister Mary

Published by Barricade Books Inc.
185 Bridge Plaza North
Suite 308-A
Fort Lee, NJ 07024
www.barricadebooks.com

New Introduction Copyright © 2004 by Helen Gurley Brown
Original Copyright © 1964 by Helen Gurley Brown
All Rights Reserved.

No part of this book may be reproduced, stored in a retrieval system, or transmitted in any form, by any means, including mechanical, electronic, photocopying, recording, or otherwise, without the prior written permission of the publisher, except by a reviewer who wishes to quote brief passages in connection with a review written for inclusion in a magazine, newspaper, or broadcast.

Library of Congress Cataloging-in-Publication Data

Brown, Helen Gurley.
    Sex and the office / Helen Gurley Brown.
        p. cm.
    Originally published: New York : Avon, 1983
    ISBN 1-56980-275-0 (pbk.)
    1. Single women 2. Women--Employment. 3. Success. I. Title.

HQ800.2.B7587 2004
650.1--dc22

2004043723

First Printing Barricade Edition
Manufactured in Canada

CONTENTS

INTRODUCTION

T HE BOOK you're now reading—or *thinking* of reading—was written four decades ago. Yikes! Can it possibly hold up its little head now or is it as dated as the Triceratops and Lindy Hop? Well, when Barricade Books said they would like to republish *Sex and the Office*, I asked myself the same question: Is the book viable this minute or is it too "yesterday"? I meticulously re-read every word (*a kind of dense little number*) to find out, and you know what? I think it *isn't* just an historic document which stirred people up a bit at the time of publication. It is a small volcano of information and good advice for *now* women who want to have more interesting relationships with men, both bosses and associates, in places where they work. The information and advice in this book will add a little sparkle and dazzle to their days without screwing up their careers or the functioning of the company. Work is where we *are* eight hours a day, five days a week, right? Even sometimes over the weekend. Wouldn't it be dopey not to think of our workplace as a possible source of souls and bodies with whom to make a romantic connection? I think so.

When we speak of offices, we aren't talking just about offices, of course. Special friendships can be formed at a construction site, museum, convention hall, television studio, or department store, any place where men and women work together. And, no, we aren't talking about actual *sex*, of course, but about friendship and loving relationships, possibly with a sexual *tinge* (that may become more deeply hued later on, if you like).

The role of women in the workplace has significantly changed in the last few years, of course, with so many women now primary household providers, some single mothers, and hardly anyone working just to help with the bills or to pass time until she is married. Companies *need* women to be brilliant and capable and will reward us accordingly. But does this new recognition change the way women interact with men in the workplace? In today's business world, where women are still fighting for total equality with men, especially when it comes to pay, should we play up our sexiness and femininity or try to act more tough and masculine? Tough we can surely be—work hard, stay true to our convictions, turn away distractions when deadlines loom, no headaches or menstrual blues from *our* crowd, exercise the little body like a linebacker—but more masculine? I don't think so. I strongly believe that neither men *nor* women need to lose their ability to relate to and attract one another on the job no matter how noticeably any of us may be clamoring to the top.

Of course, when the subject of "sex and the office" comes up nowadays, we are aware that in the past several years a number of women have registered complaints, even brought lawsuits against companies or specific men within the companies, for what is known as sexual harassment—more accurately—sex discrimination. In many cases, the complaint had nothing to do with an actual sexual encounter or a man's hope for one but with a woman being refused access to the top-echelon job she felt she had earned and deserved just because of being female. Some of these lawsuits were undoubtedly justified. The litigant had worked her brains out for years, was a cracker-jack whiz at her work, due the promotion to superstar status only to be denied it because of having breasts instead of balls, if you'll pardon the expression. That kind of "sexual harassment" in an office should certainly be dealt with, legally if necessary, but there is less and less of it as companies every day reward the person, male or female—forget gender—who is the brainiest, hardest-working, and most profit-producing.

Okay, since the book was first written there have been actual lawsuits—or formal complaints to management—brought by women who claimed they were being harassed/pestered by Mr. Not Wonderful in a disagreeable personal way (i.e., he made a pass at them). I suggest using flattery to get him to stop. Tell the harasser you find him attractive—we don't have to deal with unvarnished truth around here, do we?—but that your good judgment tells you this kind of "playfulness" between you and him in the office isn't a good idea for either of you so let's *stop*! If you feel you need more ammunition, you could mention a person in your life—husband, boyfriend, father—who would give you a bad time if you were to respond to the office person's advances, particularly the man who is buying you a mink coat for Christmas, so thanks for the compliment, pussycat, but no thanks and, oh yes, would you please stop touching my breasts and patting my backside! At any rate, in this book we are talking of *consensual* attraction in the office, not harassment.

There *are* a few antiquities in the book—carbon paper, telex machines, only glancing mention of computers—they didn't exist for general use when the book was written, but the computer hasn't changed our feelings about each other in the workplace. Has Internet dating cut back the necessity of *having* more friendships and dating activity at work? I don't think so. Online dating possibilities are good options for women whose offices (or other work sites) do not offer a decent supply of men but outside "possibilities" are surely no reason to eschew office folks with potential. Regarding my enthusiasm for fraternizing at Lunchland, few people these days have the luxury of taking one and a half hour lunches and may simply eat at their desks. Prices for meals? I have quaintly mentioned somebody being irked because of having spent $4.00 in a restaurant for "a fancy lunch." That investment today might get you egg salad from the deli but I don't want to wade through the lunch chapter and change prices; lunching with a male associate is still happening this very second and, yes, it is a wonderful way to further sink *in*.

Is it antique to extol office parties for boy/girl connecting when many companies have eliminated office soirees for the sake of cost cutting? I think there are still enough parties to justify including them. My own company, with its component parts of magazines, newspapers, television and radio stations, still has numerous get-togethers and so do other companies. Oh yes, the better you are at your job, the more often you'll be included in the party.

Office wardrobe recommendations in this book could be a little brought up-to-date, what with me originally suggesting trim business suits, blouses unbuttoned one extra button, and high heels for office allure. Many offices have switched almost totally to casual attire—jeans, T-shirts, sneakers—but formfitting sweaters and T's, and jeans hugging the right hips can be just as sexy as more traditional office clothes. I have quaintly suggested pants and the basic little black dress as occasional good selections for the office. Occasional? Can you imagine a time when women didn't wear pants, trousers and basic black as a virtual office uniform? Well, I'm leaving the wardrobe section in.... I don't want to rewrite the book and feel wardrobe is one of the few "dated" places.

The "plain-girl power" I mention you may not need to invoke, though it's not dated. If you're Uma Thurman or Catherine Zeta Jones, all you need to do to get a man's attention at the office or anywhere else is just show up but some of us less spectacular ones may need to develop federal-case listening skills, award-winning responsiveness to what's being said and, yes, we hope *charm*, in order to sink in more successfully at the workplace and make off with prizes. A few suggestions are here.

While delineating all the delicious possibilities of love that started at the office (or other workplace), I haven't neglected to acknowledge that men—wherever you meet them—can give you a bad time. They're not always as loving, tender, devoted (or faithful!) as we'd like them to be. There's advice here about coping with the aggravation, plus, he may be married and you're not, and you would like the situation rearranged. Well, this isn't a book about marrying somebody you met at work, but the advice for coping with an unhappiness-causing man is pretty much sound as ever, I think. I've coped with a few.

Now, because of my thinking (and having seen it proved to be true) that the better you are at your work, the sexier and more attractive you are, there is lots of be-good-at-your job stuff here, all from the original book, but I think it firmly stands. Few men are attracted to the office birdbrain, particularly if she is on their team. Being wonderful at your job simply helps make you attractive and produces those better male friendships. If you are not yet one of those high-echelon women mentioned earlier, being a secretary or an intern will still get you *in* to a company, especially in today's downtrodden economy and, if you wish, you can climb up from there. There's stuff here—still viable—to help you be a shiny little star at meetings, and to sell your ideas. I suggest you take work home, to basically endear yourself to the max to the company which will subsequently reward you with a flashier job. Secretaries also deserve spiffy men in their lives if that is the work that defines you and what you want to do. Being good at *whatever* job you have is recommended for attracting the attention of male co-workers.

Office politics? Yes, jungle warfare is as prevalent as ever, I'm afraid, and the book offers suggestions on how to play it wisely. Don't take sides too noticeably despite how you *really* feel, don't be one of the vicious gossipmongers though you *listen* up a storm. As intrigue, factions, and chicanery swirl around you, absorb, listen, be as natural as possible and do your work as well as you possibly can—this will benefit everyone. I think the office-politics advice in here is still viable.

Finally, this book offers a few thoughts on what to do when you're *fired*. Maybe we all ought to go through a firing once so we can empathize with those now going through it. Being asked to leave a company basically strengthens your guts (I know, I've been fired several times). You have to find a new post pretty soon to not only get on with your career, perhaps in a better place, but to meet some new men as well.

Enough! I think I've mentioned the few places in the book that might not be quite of the moment office-wise, but there aren't that many. I want you to go on reading. I *think* there's some stuff in here you're going to enjoy, even find helpful. Please go!

COME FLY WITH ME

H AVE YOU a drop of sporting blood? Then come with me to
the office. You don't have to buy. Just look!

There's such a lot to see and do. We'll start by learning how to
love your boss . . . absolutely essential if you're to participate in a
rich, full office life. Then we'll find out how to dress for the office—
selecting gowns that look high-necked to the office manager and
low-necked when you lean over. After that, we'll start sneaking up
on the boys career-wise (don't worry, we'll be so gentle and ladylike
they won't mind a bit. In an ideal world we might move onward and
upward by using only our brains and talent but, since this is an imperfect world, a certain amount of listening, giggling, wriggling,
smiling, winking, flirting and fainting is required in our rise from the
mailroom). We'll learn how to look gorgeous while all this is going
on and how to deliver a modest acceptance speech as we're handed
"the key to the men's room" in recognition of our achievement.

There'll be a short survival course in Jungle Warfare (the office
politics which sometimes riddle and decimate an establishment).
We'll learn how to remove a piece of furniture from a reception
room in daylight and how to survive a firing.

Next we'll visit Lunchland—and what a lot goes on *there!* You'll
learn how to get a man to take you to lunch who thought he was
only riding down in the elevator with you and how to get *eight* men
to ask you to lunch who thought you were only taking notes in their
meeting. There'll be instructions for the preparation of tea-for-two,
laced with brandy, for icy January days or an icy January boss,

3

learning how to sleep on the floor of your office (alone) and games for grown-ups to play on coffee breaks. (Yes, grown-ups play too, *especially* in offices.) We'll go to an Office Party and, among other things, follow the financial vice-president into the men's room with the office nymphomaniac in hot pursuit. We'll also entertain beloved and deserving co-workers in your apartment.

We'll travel on business—practically the *sexiest* of all office spoils. (We must learn to track *other* men, since they've stopped letting Your Sky Captain saunter back through the cabin. Here's a hint: Hotel lobbies are no longer out of bounds for ladies to track in.)

Wives, widows and divorcees will be invited to join us in *all* this fun and will be told how. We're very sharing and democratic!

When you've had a good night's sleep, we'll plunge to our clavicles in other sexy tides of office life . . . the folksy kind you can participate in or just observe from the sidelines. (We'll probably all prefer to observe the Girls Who Get Paid for It, but some of you naughty girls may want to attend The Matinee.) Three Little Bedtime Stories may just bring back memories—who knows?—and, if you haven't been bagging your full quota of office men lately, note the specific instructions for stalking and capturing without leaving a single black or blue mark on the body.

Enough promises! Enough titillation! Are you ready? Then slip into your mink life jacket, fasten your pink alligator seat belt, put on your jeweled goggles and come with me to the office.

CHAPTER 1

HOW TO LOVE A BOSS

To HAVE a lovely work life you don't have to have fantastic drive or looks or brains or be a nymphomaniac or have the hide of a Burmese elephant or sacrifice any of the joys of having a normal healthy husband and normal healthy children. To have the best of all possible times in the office you *do* have to work hard, however!

Work? YOU? Hard? AT A *JOB*? I can see you laughing right into your dimpled little hand. Working hard on a job is for sallow spinsters with nothing *else* in their lives. If you're eighteen and pretty, any company should be happy to have you just as an ornament. If you take a job at all, it's just for Easter-in-Honolulu money . . . or to wait for *him*. You certainly don't intend to get your brain all sweaty.

My dear, you must stop reading (if you can read) right now! This book is not for you. You'll never have a speck of fun if you think you're doing somebody a favor just by filling a posture chair (even though most offices are crying for helpers). You don't have to be driven and compulsive, but you must try to do better and better in your job if you are to have this rich, full daytime life . . . the hours filled with surprise, excitement and, among other attractions, wonderful male companions. Forget the fact that working hard in a job seems kind of antique . . . something girls did only during the Great War or the Great Depression. Girls who want to have fun in offices do it *now*.

The better job you have and the better you are in it, the better the men you get to fraternize with (instead of just stealing hungry looks at them from your file-girl perch). And though it may seem to the untrained eye that you are selflessly working on office projects together, what you are really doing is sinking into them like a cobalt treatment so that you may make off with them after work—if that's your pleasure. (Of course I think getting married to the *first* man you make off with in an office or anywhere else is so *dull*. You ought to sample several before you make up your mind.)

There are other prizes for high-voltage workers. As one girl I respect very much says, "If a girl doesn't have all the money she needs to do *everything* she wants—including buying clothes, taking lovely vacations and furnishing a beautiful apartment—I can't for the life of me understand her not moving toward a job that will pay for *most* of it. Not to do so is not only unsexy—it is unholy."

Are career girls—the ones who *get* those lovely things—different from other women?

Not usually.

You'll find not half so many successful girls were inner-directed or told-to-by-voices as they were simple fluffheads who started working because they *had* to. Then the fun and games began and they stayed.

But men hate career girls! Really, dear, you probably still believe storks bring babies! Do men hate Elizabeth Taylor, the glamorous columnist Suzy, Barbra Streisand, Queen Elizabeth and Sophia Loren? Raging career girls all! The men who hate career girls hate the career girls who hate *men*. These girls really don't like men *or* sex very much and use their jobs to hide out. Some of the most sensational career girls I know career all day, then whomp it up all night with the men they've collected during the day (at least until they've settled on *one*).

Let's list the ground rules for having the most fun in the office; i.e., access to the most men and the most money. Some of the rules won't sound like anything but drudgery. Well, the details of doing a good job are *not* particularly glamorous. Neither is the whale oil that goes into Arpège (except to another whale) or the metallic thread that makes a silver lamé dress—it's the wearing of those things that makes them sexy. On an attractive girl a great job looks and smells good too, even though certain mundane choring goes into the making of that job.

First though, we must have the job, and most jobs are found in offices.

WHAT'S AN OFFICE, MOMMY?

Every place a girl works is an office—the opera house, the Boeing 707, the laboratory, the movie set, the fashion show runway, the ad agency. I'm afraid there isn't room to put down the rules for all offices even if I knew them. Most offices are more alike than different, however, and most of the ones where girls get a crack at success are conventional business offices rather than the more exotic varieties. So we're going to talk about business offices.

BEING A SECRETARY GETS YOU IN

There you are with your M.S. in Political Science, but does Adlai really *need* a lovely girl to chin with about Mao and Nikita? (After what happened to British War Minister John Profumo over the girl *he* chatted with, it's a wonder any political dignitary is chatting with *anybody* female.) What is more likely needed by Mr. Stevenson or anyone like him is somebody to turn out about thirty pounds of correspondence a week.

The personnel director of a company that has delicious jobs for girls says, "Pretty, degreed and pedigreed Vassar and Radcliffe girls are always streaming through here asking what opportunities there are—in other words what we can do for *them*. They all want the big break. The catch is, none of them has a single thing in mind she can do for *us*. We can always use a good stenographer, and furthermore we *do* give her a chance to get ahead."

Nobody is asking you to forget your college education or what you really want to do in life. But maybe the way of achieving what you want is offering to do something somebody actually needs *now*. (The way to becoming a man's *wife* may be skinning halibut with him on a live-bait barge, even though you don't expect to be doing that when you're Mrs. Halibut.)

A cosmetics company tycooness once told me, "Some very important men will throw their arms around you if you're a good secretary but they wouldn't let you in the place if you did something else. Once you're in, you look around and plot." Mrs. Nelson Rockefeller worked in *his* office, but we're not talking about marrying the boss. That could be merely a fringe benefit compared to the other splashy rewards of a happy work life. Anyway, there's no better known "in" than being a Miss Girl Monday through Friday. (Probe below the surface, and you'll find about 72 per cent of all female tycoonesses have a secretarial job somewhere in their past.)

LONG-RANGE PLANNING

If you plan to use secretarial work as a wedge to get elsewhere, there are two ways to go about it:

1. *Do* tell them what you have in mind for later.
2. *Don't* talk about later but just get in.

Sometimes advertising your goal makes people nervous, and it's better just to get in on any basis and be your own lookout. If you do take Route 1 and agree to be a secretary temporarily, don't pin them down . . . "Yes, but *when* will I start writing editorials?" That kind of dialogue before you've even started the filing is a sure sign of a malcontent. Who needs a sour face at the file cabinets?

Always remember that as a beginner you need them more than they need you. Sure, they require typists and run lots of ads for them. In fact, I never saw anything *like* the ads for secretaries in *The New York Times*—"Glamorous job with magazine publisher. Beautifully decorated offices. Short hours." . . . "Be an integral part of top television show. Meet interesting, famous people." . . . "We guarantee two trips to Europe a year—all expenses paid. Teach you a foreign language." For a girl who got her first secretarial job when lines were still forming for them, this kind of talk sounds like a white-slave invitation. But never mind that they're begging you to come in. You need their *arena* to work out in if you're to become a full-fledged gladiator.

WON'T YOU GET STUCK?

Some people think that once you're a secretary a company will never think of you as anything else. I'm convinced the only people who get stuck in secretarial jobs are happily or willingly stuck. Would you believe it—good companies prowl like tigers to find people they can move upward. Secretarial work isn't a bad thing to be "stuck" in, anyway. Executive secretaries are close to some of the most glittery men in the world and have great lives.

Very well, you may use this spot to stay happily "stuck in" or to spring forward from, depending on your tastes and talents.

LEAPING UPSTREAM

I asked the fashion director of one of America's biggest fabric companies how to make secretarial work your tool. (It was an important one for her.) "While you're a secretary," she said, "learn as much as you can about whatever the company does, whether it publishes books or packs sausages. Snoop and study and volunteer to work on any kind of little project they'll let you in on. Be everybody's helper. When you go to look for another job, you may not have the actual title to your credit, but you can say, 'Look, my name doesn't appear on this report, but I actually interviewed most of the people in it.' Save every scrap of paper that will authenticate your participation."

More about moving out of secretary-hood later. First, let's say you *are* a secretary, with or without other plans in mind. How do you get the sexy most—which is to say the *successful* most—out of this job?

REQUIREMENT NUMBER ONE

If this is to be that most satisfactory of all man-woman relationships—the one that transcends all others—the first thing to do is hire the right boss. You may hire several wrong ones while you're young, but after you're experienced, you certainly should be able to hire a rich, successful, beautiful, kind, wonderful, lovable employer with fabulous friends. This eliminates most bosses under thirty-five (who are so selfish, nervous and irritable most of the time that about the only way you can get along with them is to keep them under sedation), but it still leaves a rather large field to choose from.

If after careful screening you've still managed to hire a loser—and it's long after the time when you should have to put up with such a thing because you yourself are now efficient—the kindest thing to do is fire him. Give him a couple of weeks' notice and a set of character references that he can show to his next secretary if she wants them.

DO BOSSES MAKE LOUSY LOVERS?

What about actually falling in love with or *being* in love with your boss? It's heady for a while—being in his arms all night and in his good Eames client chair all day taking dictation and exchanging soul-looks. The trouble is that this sort of thing so often ends badly. You either marry each other—not the *worst* disaster but it can spoil the best boss-secretary relationship—or he *is* married and you can't stand booking *their* steamship tickets, or he *doesn't* marry you and you're depressed by the other girls who call him up. I think it's better to keep this darling as a friend, someone who may from time to time advise you about *other* men. (A divine boss of mine once gave a very good cocktail party so that I could impress a beau.)

You *may* succumb to a boss or two—they *are* attractive—but once you've finally picked one to be your dearly beloved *friend,* how do you care for him so that your office life will be all the lovely things we've promised?

You must love him like crazy. Denying love and devotion to a good boss who spends eight hours a day with you would be like a yellow-breasted mother swamp finch denying worms to her yellow-breasted swamp-finch babies. Other people give the man trouble. You must be there to help him gird on his armor for battle and then bind up his wounds when he returns. You can't be as aggressive about this when you're a shy baby worker but you can at least seem to be *concerned.*

I don't feel there's any justifiable cause to criticize a boss ever. The fact that he is somewhat overextended at Alfred Dunhill and every bar in town is really none of your business. If he wants to *make* it your business and discuss these indulgences with you, you are his conspirator, not his caviling Aunt Sarah.

You are *for* all his schemes, up to and including his taking over the company. It's easier for you than for his wife, who may see his power play costing her the cabanas, the flagstone *and* the swimming pool.

Adrienne Sausset, devoted secretary to California's Governor Pat Brown, sent out five thousand letters over her own name, on her own time and with her own postage, telling other secretaries to vote for her boss in the last election. That—among other things—got him re-elected.

Another friend of mine has had her bags packed, her apartment sublet and new homes found for her cats six times, on the strength of her boss expecting a presidential appointment. No action yet but there's always another election, and she's staying *packed.*

A chic Beverly Hills secretary I know found herself hawking avocados one spring. She had shown such enthusiasm for her boss's ranching ventures, he decided she was just the person to unload his bumper crop of little cuke-size fruit at the Farmer's Market. She was relieved of duty when she backed his station wagon full of little cukes into a bakery truck one afternoon. He reluctantly decided she was more use to him at the office.

You shouldn't think twice about embracing any cause dear to your boss provided it won't land you under federal investigation. I became a Republican to impress my boss, advertising executive Don Belding. It was either that or go underground. Actually, I liked the party so well I only switched back to being a Democrat last year.

Other girls have embraced Zen Buddhism, the International Kite-Flyers Society and World Federalists without any harm to their psyche or integrity.

COMMON COURTESY

Bosses get their feelings hurt just like hostesses when nobody comes to their parties. Encourage your boss to over-invite for all cocktail soirees and luncheons. Try to get him to give the party at the poshest place instead of economizing on second poshest. More people will show. If an invited guest turns you down, see if he'd like to send somebody else from his company.

Many bosses are on a diet. He'll adore you if you slip him almond mocha roll and Danish crullers, but that's a good way not only to fatten him up but also to kill him *off*. Even though you may rather fancy a Big Daddy boss weighing close to three hundred, I think you have to choose in favor of having him around for a while.

Don't assume that because a man is just sitting in his office staring out the window that he is available for conversation or can even be interrupted. My friend Ernest Lehman, who wrote the movie version of *West Side Story* and nine other film hits, once overheard his secretary tell someone on the phone, "No, Mr. Lehman isn't busy. He's just thinking."

BE THE BEARER OF LOVELY TIDINGS

Most bosses are insecure (along with the whole human race) and need to be told *somebody* loves them. It doesn't necessarily have to be you. Reassurance that management cherishes them (based on inside poop from chatting with the girls) could be exactly what's needed. If you can imply that the prettiest girl in the filing room has a secret crush on him, your profit-sharing might really amount to something by Christmas. A very young or newly-hired secretary may not be able to execute these blandishments immediately, but she'll soon learn how.

Once, when things were extremely sticky for my husband at Twentieth Century-Fox studios (because of the death of the studio head, the old regime was out and the new regime was hacking away at the "leftovers"), a lovely steno-pool girl got to be a kind of legend in her time by soothing the beleaguered and once-powerful.

David was a leftover. He had been creative head of the studio and No. 2 man in the old regime. That made him a mud-pie in the new. At the time Laura (not her name, but close) came to him, the glacial freeze was about two yards thick. Hardy old-timers were getting pneumonia in the executive gymnasium. Along with every other executive who had been with the studio more than two weeks, David's telephone calls and urgent memos were going unanswered. Pamela, David's regular secretary, left for vacation just then. She was a once-powerful leftover herself, and the snubbing was getting her down.

The very first day Laura reported to work, she shut the door to David's office, leaned against it and said breathlessly, "Mr. Brown, I shouldn't tell you this but as you may know, last week I was working for—and she named the new head of the studio—and I heard them talking about you. They couldn't say enough wonderful things about you and have something fabulous in mind for you."

It was like water to a parched Bedouin. David barely restrained himself from shaking her like a peach tree as he demanded the details.

"I can't tell you any more this minute," she said, "but I'll be getting other bulletins."

During the week, Laura continued to develop her original story into a very fancy needlepoint which kept her boss soothed, entertained and contented by the hour—so much so that he hardly noticed Laura wasn't bringing any new bulletins. In about a week, he came out of his trance long enough to ask Laura if she didn't think perhaps he should just go in and ask the new regime exactly what it had in mind. No, Laura said, that would be precipitous. It was in the very hush-hush planning stage.

Well, Pamela returned from vacation, the plans apparently never got off the drawing board—or whatever movie moguls plan on—and lovely Laura floated away to cheer up some other beleaguered executive. Did David hate her? No, he wistfully used to ask Pamela if she'd had any news of lovely Laura, and why didn't *she* have bulletins. "Oh, for God's sake," Pamela said, "*I* can always fill your head full of lies if *that's* what you want."

"They weren't lies," David said. "That girl knew something."

She knew how to please a boss, that's for sure. And she probably did know something. The conversation she overheard just wasn't the final one on the subject.

Maybe you haven't Laura's cliff-hanging technique for telling a story, but you can see that under certain circumstances a little encouragement from a secretary goes a long way.

LITTLE PITCHERS MUST HAVE BIG EARS

Aside from delivering discreet personal compliments, it is your bounden duty to collect the best gossip the office has to offer—rumors of mergers and firings too. Pass them on each day as a little love offering.

How do you keep from informing *on* your boss while you gather choice gossip *for* him? (Other secretaries naturally demand something in return for any big nuggets.) Well, you toss in something not too incriminating every so often—such as the fact that his nose bleeds have been tapering off since he's been taking Vitamin K.

One slight warning. Since bosses love gossip, they also pretend that anything that comes in the mail is for them. They will even go through your desk on the pretext of looking for a rubber band and then read all your old valentines and love letters. If there's anything really private, you can hide it between the pages of the telephone directory. Hardly any boss will ever look up a number himself.

SECRETARIAL SKILLS

It seems quaint for a girl to have any now, and I know men don't really expect much. One chap I know actually gets *tears* in his eyes when he finds long, freshly-sharpened pencils in his desk drawer, and the sight of a brought-up-to-date address book chokes him up completely.

Never mind how cavalier other girls are with their bosses. You have to be efficient. Your goal is a sexy office life with marvelous things happening to you and these don't accrue to girls who are *slugs.*

If you can't spell, and hardly anybody can, look it up. You can get away with fowell for foul and stratejic for strategic for ages (half the time bosses can't spell either), but one day some busybody letter-recipient is going to circle the thing with red grease pencil and send it back to your office. The daddy of the letter is going to raise the roof.

Never give anybody a messy erasure—at least not a big bluish, purplish, blotchy, bruised-looking one. If you do, he'll simply set a wet Pepsi-Cola bottle or burning cigar down on it. Then he'll feel free to re-dictate the whole last section, which is what he wanted to do all the time because his thinking had since become crystallized. If you bring in a perfect copy to begin with, you gain character and don't run the risk of having to transcribe a brand new letter.

If he writes a really nasty letter, have him sign it and think it mailed. Show him the monster next day and say, "I'm afraid this didn't make yesterday's mail. Would you like to look it over again before it goes out?"

I wouldn't suggest such drastic action except for the fact that I've never known anybody who wasn't horrified on re-reading one of his own hate letters. Perhaps he'll restate his case less petulantly and more effectively.

MANNING THE PHONES

Tangle with the Mafia if you like but stay clear of his switchboard girls. Most bosses cherish these ladies if only because they know so much. Uncrossed they are very nice people. However, if you say things like, "Pauline, for God's sake you cut me off again" (and you *know* it was she because you were doing your nails with both hands and had the phone under your ear), a chill can set in between you and Pauline and between you and your boss, but never between *Pauline* and your boss. (I tell you she has her methods!) At the very least, you will wind up "losing" most of your personal calls.

If you get somebody on the phone for a man who has since picked up a call from London, apologize profusely. You are *genuinely* distressed. "Isn't this dreadful, Mr. Tate? Mr. Fubershaw has picked up another *call*." Skip where the call is from, London-dropping will only blacken the rage.

To get somebody out of the john for a phone call, don't hang around and wait. Seeing you propped up against the wall with an anxious look on your face will make for self-consciousness among the new arrivals and may even drive some of them to different floors. Send somebody in to get your man out.

TO LIE OR NOT TO LIE

This is an individual choice, but if you decide in favor of it, the watchwords are, "Don't get caught."

I don't want to make a liar out of you, but sometimes there is no explanation for your mistakes other than you've gone clean off your rocker. In that case it's better to hush up than confess, if you can get away with it.

My boss, Don Belding, used to remember clients' birthdays, and what a passel of birthday presents we used to send out—music boxes, wooden bears, plates and saucers . . . honestly! Well, one day we got a thank-you note from a man in Honolulu saying, "Dear Don, I loved the ashtray, but can you tell me why it came by way of Osage, Arkansas? We used to know some people in Ozona, Tennessee, but don't believe we know anybody up in the Ozarks, etc., etc."

Well, you know whose family lived in *Osage*. Apparently I had written his name, then my mother's address, then his address. It was very cozy!

Since I read the mail first, I could act. "Dear Mr. Von Weatherham," I wrote. "You don't know me, but you could certainly do me a big favor. You remember that letter you wrote Mr. Belding about the ashtray. I wonder if you could please write back and say you like the ashtray a lot only not say anything about it coming to you by way of Osage? Etc., etc., etc." It was a calculated risk, but he did it, the lamb!

YOU KNOW SOMETHING BIG

A fellow employee, possibly somebody higher up, is stealing . . .
or maybe it's nothing that bad . . . he may just be fumbling. You've
seen him do it.

You really have to be careful whom you rat on—not only out of
fear of reprisal, but also because you may not be the world's most
accurate judge of who's fumbling. I saw a pretty girl get contu-
sions from her own confusions one day. She told a fascinated room-
full of executives that a particular account executive was gumming
things up badly at the client's. (She was sleeping with the client
and ought to have known.) An immediate check was made to con-
firm or deny her story, and it turned out the A.E. did pull a mild
bumble occasionally but nearly everybody in the organization
adored him. He made them feel smart. The client who "talked
in his sleep" but who apparently was not quoted accurately did
not feel smart, however, and he broke up with the girl. (This is a
true story. They all are. I couldn't begin to make up this stuff.)

If you possess some other kind of knowledge (like a tip on a
customer your company could go after, picked up from overheard
party conversation), it will usually be appreciated. March right in.

OTHER PEOPLE AROUND THERE

Never alienate the mailroom boy. He probably reads your mail
or, if it's too boring, he at least scans the last three paragraphs to
see who sent the letter he just got back marked "Addressee unknown." (Sending personal mail unidentified in the hopes you
won't get docked for postage is too risky! Put your initials on the
envelope.)

Aside from his knowing too much for you to antagonize him,
this mailroom child can play Columbus to your Isabella. Send him
exploring for a fan during the heat wave, and he'll come back with
two—provided you've launched him properly (i.e. chocolate fudge
for his birthday and walnut brownies for Valentine's).

Of *course* you are a little mother to *all* the growing boys around
the place. You dispense Band-Aids and smiles to anyone who is

wounded on the job, aspirin and Bromo to those who got the wounds the night before.

I recently heard about a waiter pushing through the swinging door of an executive dining room just as a group vice-president started through the other side. The executive's forehead was dented in like a tinfoil sailboat. At the very same time his friends called the doctor, they sent for a twenty-nine-year-old bookkeeper who had a reputation for great kindness. While they stitched up his head, she held it in her lap, murmuring, "There, there." He's been reported in love with her ever since.

You know, of course, that you listen when men talk. You compliment them when they do well. You are charmed by them much as you would be by a date. What's so difficult about that?

THE DEEP SEA MONSTERS

A special word about lady bosses and other lady executives around the place. They're supposed to be a pretty horrible bunch—putting burning matches under the fingernails of little female underlings and all that. I never worked with or for such a lady but I've met some of them at luncheons. Usually the women are over forty-five, and the reason they act the way they do is because it was harder to succeed when they succeeded. Men in the office were very mean to them. Most lady bosses under forty are as nice as anybody. If you happen to have drawn a female Tartar, young or old, I'd suggest you learn everything you *can* from her—some of them are pretty smart. Work as hard for her as you would for a dreamboat, and, when you've had all you can take, move on to the next job.

FEEL SOMETHING

You're going to hit me with an iced mackerel, but I have to tell you that the way you *get* the most out of your job is to *give* the most. You should feel empathy in your bosom—it doesn't tickle or anything—if you are to get better and better jobs and go on to where the money and deep-piled fun are. When you're trying to get a number for your boss and it's busy, busy, busy, you're as vexed as he is. When you help another girl type some reports, you *care* that she has a deadline. When the company gets a new client, you're thrilled.

Some of your girl co-workers may jeer. Look at little Goodie Two-Shoes. You'd think it was *her* firm. Keep feeling this empathy in your bosom and it could *happen.* At least you'll enjoy the loving friendship and high regard of a lot of men.

To win at *anything* you must not be too withdrawn or negative or fearful. I'm not suggesting you do anything that causes you to feel brassy or embarrassed, but an over-fastidious, never-take-a-chance attitude about little challenges can stymie your chances for fun and success in business. Of *course* it can be done and yes, of *course* you'll help. "Look, you take this end of the desk and lift and I'll scootch the rug under" is far better dialogue than, "I'm not straining my back—the stupid building ought to tack the carpets down."

Men adore enthusiastic girls. Think about that!

Summing it up, I'd say *give it to them!* Whatever anybody wants, dig it, find it, make it, mint it, scrounge it, grow it or crochet it— but never say no! A top secretary should have sources for everything from ringside seats for the bloodthirsty to *lomi lomi* massage for the weary. (A secretary friend of mine "borrowed" four elephants from Ringling Brothers Barnum & Bailey Circus for a client who wanted to photograph them for an ad.)

THE DURATION

How long do you stay a secretary? Forever, if you like. Some women who work for important men get to be almost an extension of that person and wield more power than they possibly could in a different kind of career. A good executive secretary may have the feeling the place would practically fall apart without her because it practically would! Besides being dusted with power crystals, working beside a man you admire and adore who is smart and exciting is quite satisfying in itself.

Secretaries who don't work for anybody nearly that glamorous may not wish to get on the launching pad and orbit to a different job either. Their husbands wouldn't like it, they're only working to help with bills or until they get married, or they don't want their water-skiing weekends gummed up with satchels full of work.

But suppose *you* hear the sound of distant drums calling you to the kind of job in which someone puts *you* on an airplane and hands you *your* brief case.

Before you start marching, we'd better make sure you're dressed for the parade. Let's march straight to the next chapter for advice on the loveliest uniforms for an ambitious, sexy girl.

CHAPTER 2

UP TO HERE

AND DOWN TO THERE

How SEXY can you look in an office and still be appropriately dressed?

Or never mind being appropriately dressed. How sexy can you look and still further your career? Lovely as cleavage is (if you're lucky enough to have it), we don't want it—or them—spoiling your chances to succeed. Don't scoff! One executive I know may be speaking for many when he says that he loves seeing acres of raw bosoms on the stage or at cocktail parties, but across a crowded desk he gets that "wet flounder" feeling.

If you're clever, however, you can have it all—success, the look of a lady and an air of devout sexiness right in the no-nonsense precincts of an office.

First, let's define what a sexy look *is*. For a girl, *being* sexy is simply a matter of liking men enormously and being glad she's a girl. That's all there is to *that!* Yes, of course, certain little squiggles and squaggles contribute to a sexy look and we'll get to those, but if people can say about you, "She dresses beautifully," that's tantamount to their saying, "She dresses sexily."

Some girls are sexy who don't dress beautifully, of course, but I believe they're sexy in spite of the way they dress. They'd be even more alluring—tight sweaters and forgotten bras notwithstanding —if they also dressed in elegant taste. Lady sexpots—Balenciaga-gowned movie stars, society girls and the like—are in far greater demand than trollopy-looking girls.

Your aim, then, is to dress beautifully. Within that framework, what can you and what can't you get away with in an office? Aren't there some never-nevers? Yes. Rhinestones, sequins, slinky-slinky black, tiers of organdy, miles of lace, clankety-clank jewels, the fragiles, the wispies and the see-throughs are out. What do you care when gone-mad colors, sensuous silks, huggy-bear wools, starchy piqués, maddening plaids, shocking chic and clothes that fit like hot wax are in? Who needs rhinestones?

There was a time, of course, when all managements preferred a little brown wren at every desk. Around 1908 it was thought daredevil enough for girls to be *in* offices without calling attention to their faces and figures. Things really have changed since then, though some people aren't aware of it. In her book, *Manners in Business,* Elizabeth Gregg McGibbon advises the executive secretary, "Make yourself as inconspicuous as possible." Really! What boss, pray, who has gone to the ends of the earth to hire the most dazzling girl he can find wants to have to locate her with a divining rod when he's ready to dictate? If a striking appearance really disturbed him, a girl with large mammary glands would have to wear a suit of armor, and you *know* any boss with a secretary who did that would shoot himself—or spend his entire day keeping track of his can-opener.

Of course we don't want you to be the girl about whom men poke each other in the ribs and say, "Hey, Charlie, you ought to drop around and get a load of Bertie Lamson today . . . leopard culottes!" What we do want them to say or think about you is that you're delicious and chic and that you look good enough to eat—or to take to eat at Perino's or "21." How can you look this way? Gerry Stutz, the entrancing president of Henri Bendel, says, "First you have to figure out what you really look like. I'm convinced half the women who shop frantically for clothes on their lunch hours haven't any idea." If you can't quite catalog yourself, Miss Stutz suggests that you ask a close friend or loved one to help you. No letting them gloss anything over, however. An editor of the *Ladies' Home Journal* even suggests you put a sack over your head with two holes cut out for eyes when you do this figure analysis.

This is what you have to discern. Are you a short, curvy little cat, a boyish elf of a girl (some of them are the sexpots of the world), a statuesque, womanly woman like the kind carved on Grecian boat fronts? Do you have short legs, long legs, short torso, long torso, bulky rib cage, small rib cage, slopy shoulders, square shoulders— or what *do* you have? It's important to know. If you're 5'1" and hippy, you shouldn't be prowling around with a leggy, Diana-the-Huntress vision of you in your head because you'll buy all the wrong things. Once you understand your figure—what you really look like—you're more apt to reach for the clothes that will flatter it. Then, within the range of clothes that are great for your figure, you may also begin to buy with an "image" in mind. Depending on whether you naturally reach for Alex jersey, heathery tweeds, or Bianchini silk, you can evolve as a temple temptress, misty-moors and Great Danes creature or sixteenth century drawing-room charmer . . . yes, even at the office. There is just no end to "image" possibilities.

After you know what you look like and have picked an "image," Miss Stutz says there are endless people and things that will help you acquire taste—fashion magazines, newspaper fashion pages (getting better and better), the well-dressed women you see and copy, plus store windows and fashion shows, even museums, movies and theater costuming. Anne Klein, designer of some of the sexiest but most elegant working-girl clothes in the world (Junior Shopisticates), thinks a great salesgirl is a working girl's best friend. If you can find one who understands you and your needs and who also has taste, she'll call you when your kind of clothes come into the store.

But what's all this about following fashion when you're supposed to be dressing to please *men?* Please believe me, the way you please *men* is by dressing to please *you,* provided your taste is good. Following fashion keeps your taste honed—it just works out that way!

As for the claim that fashion isn't sexy because designers are all mincing homosexuals who hate women and try to make them look like little boys—hogwash! Marc Bohan of Dior did a jeweled bodice last season scooped out so low in front one reporter said the bosoms could not only be seen but heard. This is looking like a *boy?* (Besides, the homosexuals I know *adore* girls—they just don't want to go to bed with them.) Speaking of bosoms, if you look fashionably chic and dress like a lady nearly every day at the office, you can, on occasion, get away with murder! One fine April day you can appear in a peek-a-boo Restoration Period neckline that would have them thinking any less well-dressed girl had flipped her lid. Thanks to your year-round reputation for impeccable taste, on you they figure the neckline is simply the latest! Ladies get away with things. Let me illustrate.

THE LADY'S REWARD

A young advertising executive I know was being wooed by another agency and had dinner with the wooing agency's head at his sumptuous home. As the men sipped cocktails and talked of split commissions and creative media buys, the wooing agency head's wife sat quietly in a wicker chair sipping her own Pimm's Cup No. 3. All of a sudden, the chap being proselytized said he nearly fainted mid-discussion as he glanced over at his hostess and found he could see straight up her dress. She was wearing tangerine lace underthings. "If she'd been a hoyden . . ." he said. "But Mrs. Sinclair (we'll call her) is fourth-generation Sinclair banking stock. Furthermore she looks like Grace Kelly." When he looked again, he said, the show was over. The lady's legs were pristinely crossed at the ankle, and that's the last such glimpse he's had from that day to this. He took the job, of course!

Lady Thunderbolt Number 2: A young Radcliffe-graduate copy-cub came to lunch with some men and me in Chinatown one day. We were used to seeing her in her good little Lanz cottons, but this particular day she had belted one of her good little Lanz's tightly in to her twenty-two-inch waist and left the dress-top unbuttoned to one and a half inches above the belt. The bodice fit snugly and she was small bosomed so you couldn't really *see* anything, but what pandemonium! She had the fellows falling into their lobster Cantonese.

These may sound like the desperate measures of latent nymphomaniacs to you. I think these were ladies enjoying the prerogatives of being ladies . . . raising temperatures without raising eyebrows.

In twenty-two years of being a working woman, I've never doubted that dressing beautifully for the office is worth it. Many a man in the office has just left his wife at home in a wrapper. It may cheer him two thousand per cent just to look at you, and some of that cheer may rub off on your career.

Now for a few specifics.

Color

Men adore color. They respond to it like the Moiseyev Ballet at the first blast of a good chardas. As Bruce Clerke, managing editor of *Ladies' Home Journal* and a former editor of *Harper's Bazaar,* says, "Think how often men describe you in terms of color— the girl in the red dress, the one in the blue suit." Wear lots of color. Wear *more* color in winter. Miss Clerke sometimes wears a mustard skirt, cranberry blouse and powder-blue cardigan.

Suits

Suits are much overrated for working girls! They're expensive. Most offices are too warm to work in with your jacket on, so what are you left with—a blouse and a skirt! Besides, fifty-two per cent of the suits seen in offices say to a man, "I want you to understand that I'm a nice girl . . . a nice *dull* girl!"

Suits square you off—boxy little jackets, boxy little skirts. And goodness knows, they usually fatten you. If you're a suity type have suits. Every girl should have one or two good ones in her wardrobe for important luncheons and such. If you aren't altogether the suity type, however, as many rounded girls aren't, stop feeling you've failed Coco Chanel. Whether you have many or a few suits, I think each one should be a "really something" that you can wear for at least five years. Little dressmaker suits are for little dressmakers!

Dresses

Dresses are much more becoming to rounded girls than suits, in my opinion, and with a coat or jacket they make an important ensemble. A career girl who also deprecates suits describes her fabulous working wardrobe: "I have a clutch of wool dresses that would get me by anywhere . . . little nothing wools, bell-skirted wools, no-sleeve wools, leotard-sleeve wools, simple, printed, plain, sophisticated, sleek, fluffy-puffy and casual wools. I have them in all colors and they all cost more than a little dress should! In summer the 'clutch' consists of no-crush linen, cotton and silk."

The Basic Dress

It's a myth that grew up in the Depression that you can make one dress look like thirty-two different ones. There's usually one best way to accessorize a dress or suit—so you keep right on doing it that way with the same emerald pin and long pearls. The "dress" girl we just heard from says, "My basics are things that are always ready to stand on their own and go—my five-year-old black and white tweed suit, an olive Italian knit, a tiger-print linen with matching chiffon scarf." My own favorite "basic" is a red and green plaid wool dress from Jax (who makes madly sexy dresses) with empire lines. It's five years old but always says, "Put me on. I'm becoming. I'm sophisticated. I'm your 'image.' I don't show dirt or wrinkles. I'm warm and you know how cold you get." How much more basic should anything be?

The Understated Look

Many a girl in recent years has dedicated herself to the cult of understatement. Not a button, not a bow, not a collar, not a cuff, not a sleeve, not a pocket, not a welt, not a belt, not a gather. As the perceptive Hearst columnist Suzy says, "You can understate yourself right out of business."

Simplicity and dull colors may be your cup of tea. I happen to adore little charcoal wools and unadorned black myself, but I hope they all say, "You Tarzan, me Jane." And I hope, for the love of heaven, you *do* come out in something colorful once in a while! Men usually respond wildly. "Why don't you wear pink all the time?" they beg. Or, "I love your crazy zig-zag dress." A dress never overshadows a girl who isn't shadowy to begin with.

There are days, of course, when you don't feel like blossoming out in your cherry-blossom and mango silk print. You feel more like wearing a pall. Don't force! There should be a couple of things in your wardrobe in which you can "hide out" and still be reasonably chic.

Skirts and Blouses

Ann Pearson, Special Events Director of Burdine's Department Store in Miami, says, "I don't believe any woman admitting to twenty and a half should be caught dead in the city in a skirt and blouse. They give you that little-office-drone-that-nothing-good-is-going-to-happen-to look. The possible exception," says Ann, "might be a hand-loomed Irish Tweed skirt and snowy linen shirt with every baby stitch put in by hand. Even so, the outfit would be better for Sunday afternoon at the chateau."

Amen! If you're a blouse and skirt or sweater and skirt addict and can't break the habit, at least have some good little jackets—velveteen, paisley, cotton brocade—to go along and complete you.

Coats

I think one reason many coats are so boring is that girls buy them too *big*. Then they just sort of mush around in them looking like Napoleon's men at St. Petersburg trying to keep warm. I always buy coats a size smaller than my dress size. That way they are as short, spare and peppy as coats ought to be. I suggest you try it too.

Jewelry

There's nothing wrong with junk jewelry usually, only the junk collector's arrangements! What you do with jewelry is often what separates girls with taste buds from girls without any. When you're all dressed up, made up and ready to go, add the pin or the beads. Look coldly and slant-eyed at yourself in the mirror. Did you look better before you added them? You aren't sure? Take the pin and beads off again. Put them on again. If they get to go with you, they should be pulling their weight in chic.

Don't be afraid to throw out nearly all the jewelry you own and stick with a few things that are great. This gets to be a particularly good idea when you're over thirty-five. Wearing one great pin four days in a row is better than changing to nothing-burger clinkers. If a particular color of jewelry isn't becoming—even something as basic as silver, gold or rhinestones—rule it out.

Men complain about girls who clank, so be careful about bracelets banging together when you work.

If you can't afford a beautiful wristwatch yet, I suggest keeping your Mickey Mouse or sweet-girl-graduate black and gold one in your purse to be used to tell time only. High school class rings and crumby wristwatches say you aren't ready for lovely business-world things to happen to you.

Shoes

What could be sounder than several pairs of black leather pumps for winter (and who cares if they all look alike), several black patents for summer, and that's it! Shoe-fetish girls are going to think this pretty dull, but really you need long-stemmed American-Beauty legs and dazzling feet to warrant calling attention to them with buckles, baubles and bows. You *could* make one of your winter black pairs black *alligator* and one of your summer pairs bone if you're that bored.

All your shoes should be kept in first-rate repair. As one elegant career girl puts it, "Girls knock themselves out to wear sexy dresses, and their shoes look as though they'd been hoeing potatoes in them.

They pretend nobody notices, but *everybody* notices." Agreed. Black leather shoes are the easiest of all to make new again. Once the silken toes of blue and green striped silk sandals are slubbed, they're *slubbed.* If you're a green-, blue-, red-, or fuschia-shoe girl to the death, however, the new little bottles of dye correct scuffs in these colors.

High-heels or mid-heels are about as low as you should go in the office. I would never wear anything lower from portal to portal. You *do* have an audience. If you're going to be on your feet all day, bring flats to change into (if your office doesn't frown). Forty-nine cent Japanese straw scuffs are comfy.

Stockings

Something about a run says, "Naughty, careless, slovenly girl," when you had *nothing* to do with it but supplying the legs for the hose to run on. Keep an extra pair of stockings in your desk and change quickly. If you chase around a lot, a pair in brief case or glove compartment is handy too.

If you're paying more than ninety-nine cents a pair for hose, you're a spendthrift.

Purses

Most purses stay in, on, or under a girl's desk all day. Why, then, do they have to be sensational and different every day? Even if you visit the outside world, I think one good black leather bag for winter and a patent for summer are sufficient. Who has time to re-equip a new purse every morning?

Hats

Men are a little suspicious of hats, either because they're jealous (I'm serious—they never get to wear anything nearly so fancy or beautiful) or because hats say garden parties and ladies' luncheons to them. You have to watch too *much* hatting in the office—still I think every working girl should have one or two hats about which people can say, "Oh, my word, let me *see* you," when she strolls in in it, a little squashy emergency beret for funerals and rain, and an all-embracing turban for hair disasters. I shouldn't wear a hat in the office all day, even if you're entitled. It looks as though you had more important things to do than play with your playmates there.

Slips and Girdles

Most skirts and dresses are lined so that you don't really need a slip, do you? I'm for leaving off everything possible in the interests of being less bulky, feeling more free and having more money to spend on what shows. If you're going to wear a slip at all, it should be luscious—lace-loved, wild-animal patterned or whatever. (Some major department stores have a permanent counter of marked-down name-brand lingerie.) I can think of one special reason to wear a slip. When you take dictation or sit in a meeting, a bit of lace peeking out below a slender sheath skirt is fascinating—probably in better taste than a great expanse of leg-above-the-knee showing.

Girdles make me want to jump out the window, so I can't tell you anything very constructive about them. I do know Olga girdles are good because I worked for that company for a year. They are sexy, simple little garments that other companies are always copying. Olga is a real live woman.

Bras

There should be all kinds of bras and all kinds of colors in your bra wardrobe—for plunge necks, scoop necks, shirts, sweaters. It isn't any cheaper just to have one bra and wear it every day until it dies.

I believe nearly everybody pads. Even if you're plentiful, you pad below to push everything up and out on occasion, and the occasion may be the office. Don't feel guilty! You don't have to be consistently padded or plain either! Keep them guessing.

Most people I know are hysterical about showers . . . they just can't get *enough* of them and have to be dragged out. I would suggest a lot of girls ought to drag their bras into the shower *with* them. Tattle-tale-gray-looking bras look *terrible* when a strap falls down below a sleeve-line or a sleeveless dress armhole is so wide you can peek in and see the tattle-tale. Miracle fabrics tend not to look dead white after a while anyway, and that's another reason to own colored bras and keep the white ones as clean as possible.

An extra pair of panties should be in your desk drawer along with the extra stockings.

YOU'RE GOING OUT RIGHT FROM THE OFFICE

For cocktails after work there's no need to change. Your daytime wardrobe may be your most beautiful anyway if you love your job. If you have a date for dinner and don't live too far away, it's always nice to go home and get spruced up. A business associate may savor you in something Grecian for the night if he's seen you in twill all day. If there isn't time to go home and you know about the date in advance, bring clothes and change in the office. (I can't count the times I've slid into an evening dress to go on to a movie premiere with David. The elevator man helped zip.) *Bringing* a cocktail dress is better than wearing it and being too gussied for the office all day *or* trying to make do in gingham at the Hilton.

If a big date blows up like Hurricane Cindy and there isn't time to go home to change, you know perfectly well what you're going to do. You're going to go out on your lunch hour and buy something regrettable. I did it too, but I'd like to suggest three alternatives: 1. Go home on your lunch hour and pick up something you already own instead of shopping for something new. 2. Get your hair done and forget the dress. Fantastic hair does everything for you. 3. Borrow clothes from somebody who lives closer to the office than you do. (I'm for borrowing and lending because dresses rarely get worn out before they get boring.)

THE OFFICE PARTY

Now why would you want to insult the office party by going in your carbon-paper-smudged seersucker? Don't you expect to have *any* fun?

The Christmas party certainly rates a special dress. If you don't want to wear a party dress all day, bring one along and change. If nobody else is doing that, at least wear a dress that says, "Yes, I am taking this party seriously. I think it's going to be a great party. I expect to enjoy myself." Men appreciate your high spirits. One girl I know who is a mad twister sews her blouse to her petticoat the morning before she leaves home for an office party in the evening.

WHAT TO WEAR TO BE ESPECIALLY SEXY

Sometimes secret weapons are called for. *You* know when these conditions exist. The following modes of dress have been known to move immovable objects.

1. As I pointed out, a blouse and skirt will usually not get you *anywhere;* however, there is one exception: A long-sleeved, severely tailored, button-down collar boy-shirt that hugs the bodice without any folds or pleats, worn with an equally figure-hugging skirt, makes you the "id" girl. It seems to work on the same principle of a girl wearing a man's pajama tops. The contradiction of boy-tailoring on a girl's curvy figure is arousing. Incidentally, you have to throw acid on a Brooks Brothers shirt to wear one out. They're a fine investment in white, blue, yellow, pink, green and biege.

2. Wear beautifully fitting pants to the office on Saturday overtime assignments. An attractive man I know says he can resist *any* girl in a dress but goes absolutely to pieces when girls wear pants. Another one hired his secretary because he saw her flitting around the office in skinny bluejeans one Saturday. She turned out to be brilliant, but he didn't know it at the time.

3. You remember the discussion of turning from lady-into-witch twice a year. Here is the witching-costume of one lovely Deborah Kerr type I know: fragile grey wool with wide bertha collar and a deep V neck. Nothing happens as long as she stands up. When she leans over, a man thinks he's won the Irish Sweepstakes, died and gone to heaven. Have a "joy dress" in your wardrobe but remember, you can only get away with it if you've been a lady for about 150 days running.

4. If you're small-bosomed, wear a pretty, lacy bra and leave your blouse unbuttoned one button below where it usually is.

5. A little pull-over blouse that just barely skims the top of the skirt in the same fabric—in other words, a two-piece dress with a short un-tucked-in top—can cause excitement. When a friend used to wear her black and white paisley one to work, the men were always trying to get her to reach up to top shelves for layouts and things. They couldn't see a darn thing when she did except her midriff covered in a nylon slip, but this seemed to titillate them.

6. In summer, have a tan that doesn't stop. One of the stunningest career gals I know (a ladies' club lecturer) tans in a bikini. Then she puts on a white pique dress that buttons all the way down the front with big black buttons. The dress is lined so she wears no slip—and no stockings. Somehow the tan that doesn't stop, the "nothing on but this little dress" look, the thought that buttons unbutton and all that is devastating to men.

7. This style isn't "in" right now, but consider sacrificing chic for sex just this once. A formfitting wool dress with wrist-length sleeves, plain high, round neckline, tapered-in hemline, hugging the figure everywhere but with no waist-seam or belt, makes you sexy as a seal (they are too so!). This dress would zip all the way down the back, from which it is a great angle for your co-workers to view you. (I hope you check all of your clothes for their back intrigue.) When you walk out of his office, you know very well his eyes won't make contact with that report you left on his desk until you're well out of sight.

8. Go choir-girl occasionally with a chalk-white collar and cuff set. It could be worn on the dress just described. Nothing pleases some men more than thoughts of deflowering innocence.

9. Select a fragrance as your very own and have it wafting from you at all times. You think you do, but I'll bet you don't! You put on a dab in the morning, another dab at lunchtime, and by 4:00 you figure it's too near time to go home for another dab!

The fragrance-girls keep dabbing *all day*—it's the only way. It's also a good idea to start out in the morning with a big double dab of perfume on cotton, backed by more cotton to keep it from soaking through, then tucked in your bra.

Does the fragrance have to be expensive? Not necessarily. Catherine di Montezemolo, fashion director of Interpublic and a marchesa to boot, uses a fragrance called Pot Pourri—English and quite inexpensive. She sprays it around her office too. Another dream girl I know uses a men's after-shave lotion.

10. This isn't something to wear, but when a man is seated at his desk reading a letter, stand just behind him, very close, smelling wonderful, of course, and read along with Mitch—or Mack or Sam. *You'll* finish the letter, but there's no guarantee he can keep his mind on it, especially if you nudge up to him kind of close.

11. If you have bushels of hair, I assume you keep it in a French twist or tucked away most of the time. In that case, let it down like Rapunzel some rainy morning. You can say you're drying it out, but what you are actually doing is proving that unleashed hair has an unleashing effect on men.

TO BE USED ONLY IN CASE OF DIRE EMERGENCY

I won't put this down as a recommendation—I don't want the responsibility! I'll just tell you about a friend who unintentionally nearly finished off one of the executives in her office one day. It was a hot August Sunday afternoon, and several people were catching up on work in the building. Leslie was working alone in her own office, however. The air conditioning was off, and the place got hotter and hotter. Finally, Leslie said, she walked over to the door, locked it, took off her blouse and bra and started to work al fresco. She had been happily in this dishabille or *no* habille for some time when the door burst open, and a co-worker—male persuasion— burst in. (*Any* girl can make a mistake and take the night lock *off* when she *thinks* she's putting it *on*.) Leslie's friend backed out of the room, saying, "Whoops, terribly sorry," but he has never been the same since. Leslie says he drops by her office four or five times a day and looks longingly in at her. The day after the "show down," he told her, "It's our little secret, Miss Woods. I'll protect you." But apparently what she needs protecting from most is her friend's inner man.

In summing up clothes for the office, young artist Patty Oldenberg had some very sound advice in her New York *Herald Tribune* column. Patty said, "Don't listen to the experts too closely. Wear the wrong thing here and the right thing there and the wrong thing at the right place and so on, but wear it if it pleases you and you'll feel good and look good too."

Now let's talk about your sunny, funny face and how to have a scrumptuous office. No rest for the wicked . . . or the sexy.

CHAPTER 3

MAKE-UP AND LIVE

M<small>ANY AN</small> "EXPERT" advises working girls to keep make-up to a bare minimum. An office, they say, isn't the place to razzle and it isn't the place to dazzle, and the only thing to smell like is a bar of Fels Naptha (no Nuit de Longchamps, Joy, or any of that nonsense). Well, I'm convinced the experts must all be left-at-home wives who, if they had their way, would also have office girls wear shrouds and nettles. Of *course* you don't keep your make-up at the office to a bare minimum! For the love of heaven an office is where the *men* are!

Men like girls to look natural. Of course they do, but that doesn't mean *truly* natural—eyebrows strolling straight across the nose-bridge or not showing up anywhere (some girls don't *have* any, poor darlings). *Au naturel* would mean saffron-colored skin, mop-water colored hair . . . really, I can't go *on!*

Advising a girl to keep her make-up to a bare minimum is usually hooked in with that nonsense about letting your beautiful soul shine through—especially if you are a plain girl. Fooling with make-up is supposed to be only for narcissistic beauties. The truth is, a plain girl frequently has a wretchedly unattractive soul but her soul takes on luster when she uses make-up or has her nose fixed or puts on her wig. I know all about what fixing can do for the average girl. When I'm on a television show in my padded bra, capped teeth, straightened nose, Pan-Cake, false eyelashes and wig I may not be natural, but I'm absolutely *glorious!*

If you want to feel princessy and have things happen to you at the office, I suggest you wear *plenty* of make-up but put it *on* naturally. (I'll tell you how.) If you are only dabbing on the merest dab of powder and daubing on the merest daub of lipstick to wear to work, you should face it. You're *hiding out!* You're afraid to be a beauty! Wearing make-up does put you "on" all right. Men notice you, men strike up conversations with you, and men even get the idea you're interested in them and they respond. You can't lie low and be squashy and safe and comfortable and unnoticed the way an un-made-up girl can.

All right, how do you get the "naturally" beautiful look that men love? You get it by using a foundation, make-up, two kinds of rouge, lipstick, eye shadow, eye liner, eyebrow pencil, mascara and powder. And I'm going to tell you right now how to use them "naturally."

HOW TO DO A PERFECT MAKE-UP JOB

This is the works. From beginning to end. It was taught to me by Jane Rasché at the Max Factor make-up salon in Hollywood, where I have often seen Jane and her boss, Hal King, transform the faces of fifty-year-old frumpy ladies into quite pretty faces, as well as take ten years off of celebrities! If you're just a regular plain girl, these particular techniques can make you radiant.

Perhaps you feel you can't handle the entire procedure every day before you go to the office. (I don't see why *not*. You could get up at 5:00 A.M. and go to bed right after sundown!) It *is* possible to get in most of the steps every morning but just not do them as painstakingly as if you had lots of time.

1. Start with a clean face. *Liquid cleansers* are great. Cold cream has to melt on your face to get to the stage liquid cleanser is when

you pour it from the bottle. That makes cold cream slower. Soap and water are thorough but *soapy* . . . and drying.

2. Pat on a *lotion* or *astringent*. This feels nice; that's the main thing you can say about it. It is also supposed to close pores, and you don't want to go running around with your *pores* open! Of course you don't.

3. Put on a *moisturizer* (I'll tell you about a great inexpensive one in a minute). The moisturizer is said to keep the moisture in your face all day, and I'm sure if it does that, that's *good*. I really don't know. Anyway, it makes your face creamy-smooth to start putting your make-up on top of, and a moisturizer feels nice to your skin, too.

4. Put on your favorite *make-up* (liquid, cake, whatever). Smooth it over your face everywhere. Don't be a scaredy cat about under the eyes. That area's part of your face too. The idea is to smooth on a second skin. Blend the make-up down to just below the jaw-line, not clear over the throat.

5. If you have heavy shadows under your eyes, use Max Factor's *Erace* over this area. Choose one shade lighter than your own skin tone because you want to lighten the shadows. Also use *Erace* on nose-to-mouth lines.

6. Dab *fluid rouge* high on cheekbones just under eyes. Blend it across these bones with your fingers and down just a little on the cheeks, but don't have a lot of rouge in the fleshy part of your cheeks unless your face is very full. Rouge causes shadows and will make you look sunken-cheeked if placed too low.

7. Now powder over everything with *translucent powder*. Your make-up will have supplied the color for your face. Powder over lips and eyelids too because this sets your make-up. If you use loose powder, transfer it to a bottle with holes in the top and shake it out onto a puff or cotton ball. Powder lashes too. All powdered? Brush powder from your face with a powder brush.

8. Draw a ribbon of *eye shadow* from the inner corner of your eye to the outer edge, tilting the shadow up just a bit at the outer corner so your eyes won't look droopy. Stroke the shadow close to the lashes. Shadow looks best on most girls when it goes up over

only half the lid. You can experiment with it all the way up to the eyebrow, however, and look at yourself.

If your eyes are deep set, a light shade of eye shadow—pale blue or green—will bring your eyes out to meet the man who's looking at you. If your eyes aren't sunk in very deeply, a darker shade of eye shadow will give them depth. If you use shadow from a tube, powder over it to set the color. Powdered eye shadow from a bottle is already "set."

9. Use a tiny brush to outline your eyes with *eye liner*. Start from the center of the upper lid and, staying fiercely close to the lash, draw a line to the outer corner of the eye. Then go back and fill in from the center of the lid to the inner eye. Use the side of the brush to do this—you'll get in trouble trying to use the very tip. When the brush is practically dry, line your lower lashes. You want only a breath of color for a shadowy effect. Go *under* the lashes, dear. Don't daub on top of them.

Fluid eye liner which comes in a little bottle usually dries up rather quickly. Max Factor's *Black Pan-Cake* is great for eye liner and doesn't. Moisten an eye-liner brush with water and just run it over the cake of *Black Pan-Cake* as though it were mascara. One cake—$1.50 plus tax—should last easily a lifetime. I sometimes brush on eyebrows with it instead of using a pencil. Any Max Factor counter should be able to order *Black Pan-Cake* for you if they don't carry it. (No, this company doesn't pay me.)

10. This is the point where you put on *false eyelashes* if you're wearing them. The secret to putting them on without trauma is to get just the merest whisper of a line of the glue across the top edge of the lash. After the lashes are on, line the upper eyelid again with liner. Just paint right over the strips of lash—it won't hurt them.

11. With a razor blade sharpen your *eyebrow pencil* to a wedge-shape (not round like from the pencil sharpener). Now draw tiny little strokes that look like hairs to fill out your eyebrows. The part of the brow closest to the nose should be the lowest point. The very center of your eye is the highest—you can go a little heavy with pencil there. Then pencil on out to the outer edge of the eye. You can lift a little at the edge if you like. Never curve the brow downward or you'll look like a beagle.

All eyebrow pencils are good as far as I know, but I'm mad about a pencil you buy in the stationery store—an *Eagle Chemi-seal* #315 *veri-black*. The color is actually a soft charcoal grey that's very flattering to brunettes. The pencils are seventy-five cents for a box of a dozen. Six girls could go in together and own two pencils apiece for just thirteen cents a girl.

12. Apply *mascara.* Brush it on top of the lash as well as under the lash and add mascara to false lashes too. It combines fake and real to look *all*-real.

I think a regular big eyebrow brush about half the size of a tooth-brush (instead of the teeny-tiny brush that come with the product) is best for applying mascara. I also like cake mascara because you can work up a really good case of eyelashes! While you do one eye, the other lashes will dry from *their* application. You can do as many as six applications to each eye if you want to build really beautiful lashes (and get to work at twelve noon!). A working-girl friend of mine washes everything off her face but mascara and leaves her "lashes" on from one month to the next. "You protect your nails with three coats of polish," she says. "Why not your lashes?" She may have a point. Anyway, it's fun to go to bed with big, black fringy Elizabeth Taylor eyelashes when you're used to seeing your-self with naked Elizabeth I eyes at bedtime.

13. Put on your *lipstick.* Since "colorless" lips are chic, you may want to outline your lips with a darker shade—and use a brush, for goodness sake—then fill in with a lighter shade. If your mouth goes down at the corners, give it a bit of a lift with a tiny upward line of your brush. You know all about drawing in a completely different mouth than the one you own—beefing up here, minimizing there. Of *course* you do!

14. For *the* royal *coup* to make you look like a glowing angel, dust cheekbones ever so lightly—but *lightly*—with *dry rouge* stroked on with a powder brush. Try it! It looks heavenly.

15. Lily gilding: If you are not using *Erace* or another product to cover under-eye smudges and they still seem to show a bit through your make-up, take a ⅝″ brush, dip it in your make-up foundation and paint lightly over the shadows. Do you realize what

a wicked woman you are? You are *painting your face*—and is it ever fun and flaw-hiding!

16. Final Touch! Dampen a small silk sponge with water and gently pat it all over your face. This gives you an alive little glow no matter how much make-up you're wearing . . . *voilà*, the natural look!

These instructions work with anybody's cosmetics. As a matter of fact, I find it hard to buy bad ones, including those from the dime store. I won't bore you with any more of my personal choices. I will tell you about just one that does the work of at least three so that you can save maybe twenty dollars a year. A little jewel called *Lubri-Derm* (made by Texas Pharmacal Company and usually located in the drugstore) is a hand and body lotion, a great moisturizer (as good as any high-priced ones I've ever used) to go under make-up, and can also be worn overnight as a light night cream. A roomy pint bottle is about $2.50.

I was going to give you a recipe for making your own cold cream to keep in your desk drawer. After assembling all the ingredients and locking myself in the kitchen for three days, I got a yield of one tiny jar, two scorched palms, and I don't know how many naughty oaths to my record for a cash outlay of $3.89. Obviously it wasn't worth it! I am jotting down the recipe for a dandy mask, however, that will send you radiant and wantable to the office if you use it the night before.

PROTEIN MASK

Mix ¼ box rosemary leaves—the dried ones—with three cups of water in a saucepan. Boil until the color of strong tea. (It turns green at first and then brown.) Strain and discard leaves. Store liquid in the refrigerator.

To use: Mix three teaspoons of liquid with one egg white, stirring to incorporate thoroughly. Apply to face. Leave on thirty minutes. Wash off with cold water. Use twice or three times weekly to refine large pores and improve skin texture. Immediate results are a better skin tone. Three weeks will show a noticeable difference in texture and clarity.

OTHER PARTS OF YOU TO KEEP NICE

Fingernails

I don't think most offices care *what* color polish you wear—Ape Red, Peach Berserk or Mad Mauve—as long as your nails are beautifully cared for. Any shade of *peeling* polish is the wrong shade.

If your nails are too scruffy to take polish, take heart . . . and take liver! Weak, snively little nails grow hard as boards (and men play right into your hands) if you get lots of liver into your system. Other good things happen inside you and outside you, too. It's a mighty rough go eating all the fresh liver (aaggghh!) you need to be super-healthy and beautiful—at least a pound a week—but there's a way out. You can drink powdered liver in fruit or tomato juice. I don't think you can continue to do *anything* very long if the potion gags you, but powdered liver in the following recipes is *almost* tasty. (If your office has an ice box, you could whip these up every afternoon. They only take a minute.)

LOVELY NAILS COCKTAIL #1

Start with one heaping teaspoon, work up to three or more, of *powdered yeast-liver* in bottom of a giant old-fashioned glass. Sprinkle in *seasoned salt.* Squeeze in a big squeeze of *fresh lemon.* (One lemon should last for four cocktails.) Mash the lemon juice and powdered yeast-liver together. Fill up the glass with tomato juice. Stir and mash some more until the powder is all dissolved. Eat with a cracker—and grow splendid nails!

LOVELY NAILS COCKTAIL #2

Start with one heaping teaspoon, work up to three or more, of *powdered yeast-liver* in bottom of old-fashioned glass. Add a heaping teaspoon of *frozen orange juice concentrate* (or any other flavor). One can will last a week or so. Squeeze in a big squeeze of *fresh lemon juice.* Mash all these things around. Fill up glass with *canned grapefruit* or *pineapple juice*. Stir and mash some more until the powder is all dissolved. Here come the fingernails!

If you can't find powdered yeast-liver in a store, and I haven't seen it very many places, order it from: Gladys Lindberg, 3946 Crenshaw Boulevard, Los Angeles 8, California. A one-pound jar is $1.75, two-and-a-half-pound jar—$3.95, five-pound jar—$7.85. It lasts a long time.

Hair

Now that beehives and bouffants are practically out, I guess we don't have to argue about whether they are appropriate for the office! I think any hair style that is flattering and makes you feel scrumptious is appropriate except long hanging-down hair. (Pearson's Law of Abundant Affinity states: The girl who wears too much of anything usually has not had time to keep all of it clean, and that usually goes for long hair.)

If you don't have particularly pretty hair, may I remind you again of a remedy you've been hearing about since baby days. Brushing. Just brush and brush and brush. You really don't need a comb except for setting. A small brush should be in your desk drawer.

Wigs

A brunette who has always had thin hair says, "If I had to choose between my car and my wig, the car would have to go!" It isn't to be believed what a beautiful wig can mean in your life. Though dreadfully expensive if they're good, wigs are often prettier than a girl's own hair. Shop hard. Even the $250 ones vary in quality.

If you're a wig girl, I suppose you have to go through buying a different color than your own hair—it's such fun to shock people. But do you really want to look like Harpo Marx? That's the effect of blonde hair on most deep-dark natural brunettes. Ebony-tressed blondes look just as peculiar.

If you choose a wig to match your own hair, there's no need to blabber about it at the office. It isn't a shameful secret or anything like that, but once girls know you're wearing a wig, they're so impressed with its naturalness and beauty they're always feeling the merchandise and wanting to try it on.

Dying doesn't usually hurt strong hair. Miss Bruce Clerke of the *Ladies' Home Journal,* dyed her hair twenty-seven different shades twenty-seven days in a row trying all the products that came into her office, and she still has a full head of hair. I mix the dye and peroxide in a plastic mixing bowl and swab it on with a long pencil which has cotton stuck on one end with colorless nail polish.

Teeth

If you can't brush after every meal, use dental floss! Once you finally acquire the habit of either brushing or using dental floss after you've eaten something, you'll wonder how you ever stood yourself any other way. The dental floss can be used at your desk surreptitiously.

If you brush, leave a box of baking soda in the girls' room. It's the only dentifrice I know that won't get stolen. One brave girl I know brushes with the yellow soap out of the wash-basin container. She says it's the best dentifrice she ever used (she says this while foaming at the mouth of course).

Figure

The only way I know to have and keep a beautiful figure for the office is through exercise. So go home and exercise! For inspiration I'd suggest you read Bonnie Prudden's *How to Keep Slender and Fit after Thirty* (Bernard Geis Associates) and *Easy Way to a Perfect Figure and Glowing Health* by Debbie Drake (Prentice-Hall). The program I've had the most luck staying *with* is the *Royal Canadian Air Force Exercise Plan for Physical Fitness* (Pocket Books). It only takes twelve minutes a day and I've found you can last month after month.

Some girls keep a chinning bar across the door of their offices. Men love to use it when they swing through the door, and it's good for you *too*. You can get one with green stamps (two books).

Desk Drawer Supplies

It's fine to keep a little beauty kit in your desk drawer, but the best-groomed girls I know carry their supply kit right in their purse. A 6½ x 3½ inch zipper bag holds lipstick, brush, pressed powder, mascara, eyebrow pencil, eye liner and brush, perfume flacon, safety pins, bobby pins, nail file and comb.

Should you go to the girls' room for all touch ups? The company would lose a hundred million woman-hours a day if all girls did that. You can do quick checkups at your desk. If a man sees you, don't panic. He knows you don't glow entirely from inner fires. Naturally you only do checkups, not major overhauls, at your desk.

When you arrive at work in the morning, it's nice to be fully put together. In an emergency, however (you've washed your hair at six A.M. and need the extra thirty minutes of bus-time to help you get dried) you can arrive in curlers if they're under a big chiffon scarf so the effect is like that of a 1919 lady in a duster. The way you get away with this occasional casualness is by being an efficient, hard-working, dedicated girl worker who usually looks chic. That makes up for everything.

THE SEXY OFFICE

Now that we have you looking like a strawberry-vanilla bonbon, let's see about an office to match.

Some girls don't believe in sprucing an office or their cubicle or corner of an office. They feel it reveals the nesting instinct. What's wrong with the nesting instinct? You're a *girl!* And you spend more daylight hours in your office than any place else, so of course you want it to be homey. You'll be entertaining *men* there, too. I don't have in mind bringing in hand-crocheted antimacassars or jars of jelly to catch the light on the window ledge or anything like that . . . just a few colorful touches that say "you" and give the place a little warmth and welcome. If you don't have an office of your own, you will (if you've started to follow the instructions in this book).

Certain companies are not for sprucing either, of course . . . they prefer virginal stainless steel and unadulterated fluorescent. Piffle poofle to that! Interesting surroundings make interested workers. Most managements, to give them credit, will let you spruce as long as it doesn't cost *them*. I know one company that tolerates a surf board, two shrunken heads and bongo drums in the corner of a mahogany-paneled room to keep a statistician happy. Most of what is done is up to you, however. The company may slap on a coat of paint, but hiding the radiator pipes with built-ins is out! Sometimes they seem to overlook the bare minimum for survival. Two girl copywriters and I shared an ex-dental suite for some time that was fungus green from top to bottom, had sinks, lavatories, basins and outlets for Bunsen burners (they made their own false teeth) but no light, air, rugs or draperies. The whole effect was rather mossy, if you want to know the truth, and you can't tell me it didn't affect our cosmetics copy.

If you happen to start out without any draperies at all, that's bad! Many companies use the hand-me-down system. The executive V.P. gets the *new* draperies. *His* draperies go to a senior vice-president. The veep's draperies go to a *junior* veep. Junior's go to the traffic department. Anything that comes down the line for *you* is apt to crumble right in your hands. In the matter of scanty furniture, I'll just mention that furniture does change offices sometimes on a dark night when the office is moving to a new building. There's no guarantee the rightful owner won't march in and have the couch carted away, of course, but you can always throw yourself down on it and refuse to get off. The ensuing scuffle will point up your need for more furniture. It's probably simpler, however, to scrounge about and legitimately acquire some odds and ends of furniture that please you. Naturally, you won't do any major decorating—who has the money to glorify a home *and* a home away from home? These are a few suggestions that call for only a modest investment:

1. If the office paints and also by some miracle gives you a choice of drapery fabrics, remember that neutral walls and draperies (beige, grey, ivory, greige, etc.) and draperies without a pattern aren't so easily tired of. You are the square-cut emerald: the room is your setting. If in desperation you decide to slather on a coat of paint yourself or stitch up some curtains, the same neutral theme should apply. It's a temptation to paint a scruffy little office orange,

shocking pink or hot lemon to cheer it up, but those warm-blooded hues have a tendency to close in on you in about six weeks.

2. Have a wall of pictures. I am forever plumping for walls of pictures in apartments, but they are just as attractive in offices. The more shapes and sizes, the better.

You can pick up pictures from the junk shop for two, five, or seven dollars apiece. I have an original 3 x 6 (that's *feet*) oil of two peacocks munching grapes in a Spanish courtyard, a blockbuster at $9.75. A friend has framed a 2½ x 3 (that's still *feet*) silk scarf map of Paris. One inexpensive method of amassing a wall of pictures is to buy dollar prints, back them with heavy cardboard or corrugated wrapping paper, "frame" them by running black masking tape all around the edge.

Get most of your pictures together before you hang so you can make one mighty splash. Lay them out on the floor of your office in a space exactly the size of the wall they'll be hanging on. Rearrange and regroup until they look great. Then get them on the wall exactly as they are on the floor. Hah!

3. Pick up a couple of cheap chairs—black lacquer high-backed with woven straw seats (about ten dollars) or basket chairs, also woven (five dollars). Paint them or leave them straw.

I'm for throwing out the regular fluorescent office desk lamp and replacing it with something more attractive. (There are some pretty ten-dollar lamps.) You can always use it in your apartment later.

4. A few cushions and pillows show the office is female. A fashion coordinator I know has three moss-green velvets and three mulberry damasks, plus a petit point footstool which can be sat on in case of crowds. Just those three touches are not bedroomy but make it a woman's office.

5. It's fun to have a plant. You feel all motherly when it gets new leaves. My own six-foot-high rubber plant has been lugged through nine different officers—nerves of steel—and across the country. John Carsey, associate producer on the "Tonight" show, has one that reaches from his desk to the ceiling . . . a living monster. Some people say that several executives who were thought to have gone to CBS are probably growing right inside its trunk.

You could have a row of potted geraniums on the window sill—

much more chic than those scraggly, sexless philodendrons that seem to be the official office plant. Philodendron is okay, but it must be loved.

6. Draw a window in a windowless office. If an artist does this, he can draw it right on the wall, complete with Paris street scene. My friend Marilyn and I drew one for our friend Mary Louise on regular brown mailroom wrapping paper. It was stapled together in three sections—office wrapping paper comes just so big. We painted on curtains, panes of glass, flower pots on the sill, trees, birds and butterflies outside.

7. Campaign for a bulletin board—a big one. This is one thing your company might put up because it sounds so businesslike. Aside from office memoranda, etc., you'll also tack up cartoons, interesting mailing pieces, travel posters and pictures of Albert Finney. One girl I know did a collage across her entire board with color pages from fashion books. She started with pink ones on the left side, branched into reds, purples, blues, greens and yellows. It was gorgeous!

8. Have something visible that's related to client functions— marketing textbooks, charts, surveys, a map of distribution. Even if you aren't on intimate terms with this material, just having it there is impressive. One public relations girl I know has her client's U.S. distribution map tacked up, an Algerian dagger quivering right in the heart of Florida, his biggest market.

9. Books look marvelous and say good things about you. (Anybody who owns books can't be all dumbbell.) Five dollars should buy ten to fifteen books in a second-hand store. (It's better if they are books you've really read and liked.) Paperbacks look nice too. If you have magazines about, keep current. Throw out the 1953 *Newsweeks*.

10. Desk accessories should be female . . . sharpened pencils in a blue Delft jar, a Can Can dancer's bronze boot for a paperweight, a cigarette box that is glass and gilt. Any small trophies you've won at tennis, badminton or the bossa nova could be used for paperweights too. Japanese stores are loaded with lovely baubles for offices—red lacquer trays on which you can keep two pretty tea-

cups and a pot, a scroll for your wall, silk tassels to attach to any cord that turns on a light.

If your company supplies desk blotters, persuade whoever orders them to buy egg yellow, valentine red or blue next time instead of office-y green and brown.

11. Have fresh flowers on your desk. Anything sticking out over a back fence into the alley is for borrowing. Lemon leaves and eucalyptus branches at a dollar a bunch stay fresh for ages if you clip the stems. Girls who display flowers sometimes get brought them.

12. Keep an apothecary jar of hard candies on your desk. Gumdrops and jelly beans are delicious but disappear awfully fast. Some girls solve the expense problem by just letting the jar remain empty until the biggest eater takes the hint and refills it.

13. It's okay to let your office achieve a well-cluttered look of "art objects." An austere, businessy office wearing a girl inside suggests she's pretending not to be one or else has no imagination. Well-cluttered with papers and junk is something else again. You can work better once they're gone—so every now and then tidy the place like Mr. Clean.

If you're a smoker, empty your ashtray. A girl I know saw her boss standing by her desk one day looking as though he'd been hit by a poisoned dart. Her eyes followed his eyes and saw four half-finished cups of coffee, all imprinted with a bright red lipstick smear, with cigarette butts floating in each. No fair throwing the coffee in the plants (murderess!) or in the waste basket. The janitors' union will be up to see you.

The ashtray on my desk says "I'm sexy" in six languages all around its rim. I'm sure you can find one just as interesting.

All right, there you are—your face, your figure and your office all gussied up to absolute perfection so that lovely things can happen to you. Let's go on now to what you can make of your job— by working *very* hard and looking *very* delectable.

CHAPTER 4

SNEAKING UP ON THE BOYS

How do you switch over to the job with the taffeta-rustle sound?

One of my successful friends says that from tiny tothood straight through all your slavey jobs, you have to imagine yourself opulent. While transferring files to the basement in sneakers and coveralls, you have to keep feeling mink around your shoulders and smelling Shalimar rising from the valley of your bosom. That way, she says, you inexorably slither toward a high-powered job.

She's not kidding *me*. Annie is talking about Positive Thinking (and it worked for *her*—she's a department store wheel now). I, however, couldn't positive-think myself out of bed in the morning if the mattress were on fire.

Are you too a molasses-foot? Do you have so little vision or confidence you think the gods would roll over and die laughing if you aspired to a fancier job? Join the club! We meet Tuesdays and Fridays, have the secret handshake, and then pass around a pitcher of martinis. Our trouble is that we're ready for the bigger job every way but emotionally.

There is hope for us molasses-feet, however. First, no matter how modest and un-go-gettum you are, a far-sighted management may literally force you to do something bigger if it thinks you're capable. (It happened to me.) Also, there are other helpers—a few bouts with a psychiatrist, for example!

I'm not bouncing this psychiatry recommendation around lightly. I know you don't drop in to be shrunk as casually as you would visit your friendly neighborhood saloon, but it *is* possible to talk with a psychiatrist without signing away years of your life.

When I was plucked from my secretarial post to write copy at Foote, Cone & Belding, a major advertising agency, I was utterly terrified. Though I could afford just one half-hour session a week, a patient, adorable psychiatrist used to prop me up and spoon-feed me my ego ration every Saturday morning until I'd begun to score a few points in my new job.

Why am I plumping for a better job for you if I found taking one so painful myself? Because the only thing painful about it was the fear of failing. Aside from that, the better job, with its new men, more money and more prestige was a pleasure dome.

Sometimes people have reasons for not wanting to get on with a career which are not the real reasons at all. A glamorous young woman I know showed extraordinary talent in the University of California drama department but decided not to pursue an acting career "because of the wolves." Wolves do pursue actresses, of course, just as they pursue models, typists and campus representatives in stores. The only way to be safe from wolves is to disguise yourself as a lamppost and stand very, very still. (I'm not even sure you'd be safe *then!*) I doubt that my young actress friend was really afraid of wolves—I think she just didn't want to work as hard as you have to work to be an actress.

Other girls are frightened of the life that success can bring . . . very dangerous and threatening, with people and men and involvements sifting through it. Therefore, though smart and able, some girls remain slobs. NO management is going to pester a slobby girl with threats of promotion.

FAST AND SLOW STARTERS

What about people who aren't scared—who are ready for bigger things but can't seem to get a crack at them? (Some cooks—and some managements—just don't know when to take a cake out of the oven.)

Don't worry too much. A retarded beginning is better than taking off like a jet and having your tail drop off. Take the case of little Terry Jane Moss. Terry Jane and I worked together at radio station KHJ in Los Angeles as stenographers. The child was only seventeen but what a pusher! The day Pearl Harbor was bombed, little Terry Jane realized with her child's mind that something Big was up. She popped on the bus, got herself down to the station and worked through the night with newscasters, AP and UP representatives, engineers and executives. She was even out on the roof spotting bombers for them. On Monday morning when the rest of us nincompoops showed up for work, Terry Jane was being driven home in the station manager's limousine with a hundred dollar bonus in her purse. Now by all rights, Terry Jane ought to have her own broadcasting company by now. The last time I saw her (she would be about 41 now) she was working in a laundromat. I figure she burned herself out as a teen-ager.

SOLID BRASS

All right, you didn't start too early! You're eager for a real break, and you've done more than your share to show management you're ready. What do you do *now?*

Don't do anything against the grain!

I believe it takes a very special kind of girl to brazen her way into a spot where nobody's invited her. If you feel spooky and uncomfortable about what you're going to ask them to let you do, maybe you shouldn't ask them. This has nothing to do with being a molasses-foot but simply shows you have perception about what's right for you.

A $40,000-a-year department store buyer told me what happened to her when she was a secretary at CBS. They were interviewing girls for the ingénue role on a top network show. She'd never even had the lead in a high school play, but suddenly visions of fame, money, and marrying one of the brothers from One Man's Family crowded her head. Why shouldn't I march in there and read for them too, she asked herself.

She just couldn't do it. Every time she got up from her desk her knees buckled. "You know I was right," she says. "I'd had no acting experience. I have no acting talent now. It would have been a humiliating and embarrassing experience. A real actress probably wouldn't have felt that way, and this break would have been exactly what she needed."

Not everyone is so wise.

A beautiful and ambitious young clerk at Kenyon & Eckhardt (the second ad agency I worked in) had been told by one of our nine successive creative directors that she could attend a creative meeting and submit copy ideas. This was important to her, because it would be the first step toward leaving her clerk's job to become a copywriter.

Unfortunately the creative director left on a trip without having made arrangements with us meeting-attenders for the girl to be present. This was only a technicality to her, so she just marched in to the meeting and started bombarding us. Every time she said Soap de Champagne or Suds-Sational (we were naming a shampoo) we regular copywriters acted as though we'd just got some in our eye. The kinder ones just hadn't heard her.

Super bitches? No, just run-of-the-mill. The girl may have been worthy, but she didn't have proper sponsorship and sank without a trace.

FIRE AWAY!

But suppose it's the right time and the right place, and you're in the right frame of mind to move up. You've done everything you can for a firm for more than a year—worked with what you had to work with, asked for more chores when you weren't busy, got junk out on time, seemed to have cared about management and other people in the company (not just whether *you* lived or died) and nobody has rewarded you with a chance to advance. What do you do now?

First, you ought to have a heart-to-heart talk with whoever is in charge. Hopefully, you know of a specific job you could take over. Ask for it. You've earned the right. If who's-in-charge is deaf, I think the thing to do is move out—at *your* convenience. Don't let anyone force you to quit then and there.

You can go to another company, start as a secretary, work hard again and hope *they* won't be so dense. Or you can try talking your new employer into letting you start at something other than secretarial work. (I'm assuming now you're not a beginner but a mature, seasoned secretary.)

There's another route you can take. Perhaps you have a little money saved, quite a lot of courage and would like to take the plunge into something that has nothing to do with secretarial work. Just on the chance these ideas may spark others for you, here are some possibilities. (Incidentally, each one of them has been tried by somebody I know and it worked.)

Approach the new venture with the idea that if you fail, it isn't the end of the world. A chap named Ed Howe—I don't know who he is, but he sounds wise—said in *Forbes* magazine recently, "I try to have no plans the failure of which would greatly annoy me. Half the unhappiness in the world is due to the failure of plans which were never reasonable and often impossible."

With this in mind:

1. Get a job selling a product—not in a store where they come to *you* and commissions are paltry but door to door, office to office or by telephone from leads supplied by a company. Your product could be reducing equipment, insurance, freezers, encyclopedias . . . anything. Maybe the company you're in would let you take a whack at *their* product—or you may have to track down a new one. Some firms will take you with virtually no experience if you're eager. The prestige may not be great, but the money *could* be, and someday you may have salesmen who work for *you*.

2. Be a decorator. Any bona fide A.I.D. (American Institute of Interior Designers) decorator will spit at the idea that a girl with little more than good taste to qualify her can sneak up on this

profession, but I've seen it done. Suppose you worked as a secretary for W. & J. Sloane or any other good furniture store. During that time you should have, with your little pitcher ears and big green eyes, seen and heard a lot about fabrics, woods, periods, decors, scaling furniture to rooms, etc. You could augment this knowledge with reading in depth, decorating courses, friendships with decorators and manufacturers, haunting museums, visiting antique stores and touring famous homes when they're open. You could start with just one client who's willing to take a chance on you (perhaps while you're still a secretary). Charge a minimal fee, do a good job and you're off and running.

3. Become a couturier. Your taste is superb. The clothes you make yourself look as good to most people as Givenchy's (though you know better—Givenchy seams could be worn on the *outside*). Perhaps you could interest one or two women in letting you design and make a costume. They might even want something copied they've seen on you. Add a few more customers; then you can hire an assistant to sew and open a small boutique shop. You'll buy some of the things and design others yourself. Easy does it. Start tiny.

4. Do research for a successful writer. One important novelist I know has experienced none of the adventures he writes about. His research girl has ferreted out everything from the conduct of an archeological survey in Crete to the performing of a lobotomy. You could combine your survey work with secretarial work for a writer, or keep your regular secretarial job and do free-lance research until you gain experience. A girl who hopes to become a writer herself would find this experience profitable (though of course to write, you must *write!*).

5. Become a photographer. A recently-fired secretary I know owned a Leica camera (worth about $800 but bought from a distressed party for $100). For years she had been taking pictures in the park of mothers, children, dogs and trees. After she was fired, she got a magazine-editor beau to set up appointments for her with the picture editors of his magazine—food department, fashion department, etc. She took her portfolio, consisting entirely of her Sunday afternoon amateur stuff, around to each editor and got her first assignment—to photograph the Columbia University campus.

She expects to work up a lot more pictures and a regular clientele by the time her unemployment insurance runs out.

6. If you've a great face and photograph well (some pretty girls don't), become a model. For photography, you need some terrific pictures of yourself. You might go to work for a photographer as a secretary and take part of your salary in merchandise. Maybe he'll use you as a model sometimes. With your pictures you will go visit other photographers, magazines and art directors of advertising agencies. Actually amateur pictures of you don't do badly if somebody talented takes them and blows them up big. Naturally, being signed by and working with a model agency helps.

I'm not going to suggest kinds of modeling other than photographic because they don't pay any better than secretarial work and girls are made to feel very crepey-necked and ancient at age thirty-two.

7. Be an entertainer. You sing. You play the mandolin. You do flamenco. Start by entertaining at parties for a small fee. You may get enough experience and confidence to audition for clubs or a show. (Ethel Merman did while she was still a secretary.)

If you have looks and stamina, get a job as a Playboy Club bunny. You'll make about as much money as a good secretary, but a producer may spot you for a show.

8. Become a tour conductor. If you've been to Mexico nine times and know more about bullfighting than anybody but the bull and the matador, you might as well take people south of the border and get paid. If you know that much about other places, you could open your own travel agency or take tours *there*.

9. Cook with your cooking. Write a recipe book. (Yes, there's always room for one more.) Peg Bracken's *The I Hate to Cook Book* has sold over 100,000 copies to date, and she was a busy wife and mother when she wrote it. (She might have been a secretary.) At least send in your best recipes to women's magazines. They often buy from outsiders.

10. Open your own secretarial service. You simply rent space in a hotel and hang out a shingle. The public stenographer at the Statler Hotel in Los Angeles wears glorious hats while she types and makes bundles of money.

NEGOTIATIONS ARE ON

Perhaps you're not quite up to these plans yet, but you're damned if you'll do secretarial work one more year without some guarantee of a chance at something else. Okay . . . strike a bargain with the people who have a job open.

The public relations director of *Ladies' Home Journal*, Charlotte Kelly, was "still a secretary" at thirty, though a good one. When she applied for the job of secretary to the then-publicity director of the *Journal*, their filing was piled up to the rafters. Memos were backed up like bills in Congress.

"Look," Charlotte said, "I will work like a robin red-breast as a secretary and make this a smooth-functioning department. Then in return I hope you will let me have a whack at writing publicity releases some time. I won't badger you about it night and day or consider that *that's* my job and not secretarial work, but perhaps you'll give me some extra ones you're too busy to do."

Two years later she was making the same bargain with other young girls.

The trick, Charlotte says, is that you *must* keep your end of the bargain almost to forgetting what they promised. You have to do *more* than your share to get them to do any of theirs.

You could try this kind of bargaining in an interview even if you don't know of a specific job to aspire to. "Look, I'm ambitious," you say, "and I will do whatever you need me to do and work like a potato bug. But I want to do something besides secretarial work, and I hope there'll be a spot for me." (This is a little different than coming in as a baby and demanding your big chance. Now you have poise and experience to offer them.)

After you make this pact and they say yes they'll try, don't stay longer than a year if things aren't working out. If they don't live up to their bargain or ever let you do anything but secretarial work, make another bargain with somebody who keeps promises. Remember, though, you must pitch in and do the dirty work with enthusiasm as though that were all that mattered.

Of course, there are dozens of companies who won't bargain. They want a secretary with no fancy notions in her head. Well, there are dozens of companies that don't even want a secretary. You have to "interview" a lot of impossibles to find the company and job for you. I have no doubt you can find it.

MISS FATHEAD

Now . . . what if you get the fancier job or the promise and find yourself saying as follows: "And I'll have my own office and my own secretary and probably an assistant and three phones of my own (with your voice bearing down heavy on the 'my own')." That means you probably won't know what to do with any of these things when you get them (if you should, which is doubtful). The only important consideration is whether the new job lets you give more, *be* more, fulfill more of your promise. Never mind whether you've got a secretary and several phones to lord it over—the big thing is whether it provides you a more exciting day and a closer relationship with men on *their* level.

Now on to fraternizing with men on the level where things happen—glamour, travel and romance.

CHAPTER 5

THE KEY TO THE MEN'S ROOM

Being great at a terrific job is sexy. You are far more intriguing than a drone or a slug. Men don't like drones or slugs in offices any more than they like having them around the house. By being a deliciously successful career girl you can collect fabulous men as lovers and friends. A pal high up in the television business says, "I'm constantly impressed with the durability of business-rooted friendships with men. I'm still dating, writing to or chatting on the telephone with a couple of dozen such men. I recently wrote a chap I hadn't seen for seventeen years that I was coming to Miami on business. He got me a single reservation at his beach club, set up interviews for me, sent his car to drive me around. Do you think for a moment he'd have put out the red carpet if I'd been retired to suburbia these seventeen years?"

Another tycooness, now married, says, "I've found nothing to compare in duration and fervor with the friendships you make with men in business. You have to be a full-scale embezzler or get into a fist fight with the guy's wife before he drops you, and even then it's with tears in his eyes."

You do want wonderful male friends, don't you . . . to date or marry or whatever you have in mind? Then let's talk about things to do to be a sexy whiz in a job somewhat above the secretarial level.

PULL OUT THE STOPS

Once you're in scoring position with this great job, it's no time to guard your precious weekends from vandals. Give them gladly. Take work home. *There is no exception to this rule.* A few years from now you may want to summer in Rio. Make up your mind *this* year to put the company hopelessly in your debt.

To accomplish this you must do what is due each day *that* day and a few things that aren't. Of course every girl has moments when she wants only to lie close to the eaves and breathe just enough to keep alive. I don't think it pays to go against natural rhythms but if you lie bat-like in a torpor for twenty-four hours, you must work on the double to make up!

Doing "what isn't due" may be as simple a thing as submitting unasked-for ideas. One beaver who is moving up in retailing says, "Every sixty days without fail I head up a sheet of paper, 'Why Don't We?' Then I give it to my boss. The company hasn't used any of my ideas yet, but I know they sometimes get passed onward and upward. The important thing is this: they know I'm out here."

Bone up and soak up! Study whatever business your company is in. Read all the trade journals, the Wall Street Journal, letters to the salesmen, the stockholders' report. Take people to lunch who know more than you do and pump them. A girl I know at the Yale Lock Company has learned how to pick a lock. Said she figured it would come in handy whether she succeeded or failed in the job.

MELT THE BUTTER, USE LOTS

It's okay to butter up *anybody* . . . boss, client, visitors, brass, workers, even people who are a little creepy.

I can see your mouth corners turning down . . . being nice to people you hate is phony. All right, Miss Pure Motives, have it your way—but in my opinion, a business office is *not* the place to discriminate between the worthy and unworthy recipients of charm. You can draw the line in your personal life if you wish, although I never do. (I positively *slather* over the milkman to get certified raw skim milk delivered to my door, and he looks more like a tugboat than a dreamboat.)

Send the congratulatory wire. Take the vice-president's wife to tea. Carry on over a new crew-cut. Carry on and carry on. No matter what your motives are, you'll make people feel nice and that's always good.

THE LOVER'S TOUCH

Listening, babying, flirting (except when it would embarrass the object of your attention) are all things you should do with impunity . . . and a little style. And there just may be room at the top for you to cheer a Chairman.

You have to make up your own mind about sleeping with people to get ahead, but there's nothing wrong with *talking* to a man. Long, probing, business-friendship talks are delicious, whether they improve your perch or not.

I could name ten corporation executives whose real business confidante is a woman—not a secretary, in these cases, but some girl who has a terrific grasp of executive problems.

STEP INTO MY PARLOR

The smart tycooness entertains, even if it's just a twice-a-year cocktail bash. Dinner party, brunch, bridge and "stop by for a drink" are all perfect little affairs to show you off. (We'll get to the other affairs later.)

One of the most successful ad girls I know (a late rival) was so maniacal a hostess you had to start booking people in January if you wanted them for a treasure hunt May Day. Anybody who waited until only a reasonable time in advance to ask them found that Perle Mesta had everybody important at the office tied up for all the prime time.

It's definitely smart to show how well you cook, what a pretty apartment you live in and how feminine you are at home (as well as being brilliant at work). You're the new girl success who bears no resemblance whatever to that tweedy, walrus-shaped thing of the past.

WHY DON'T YOU WRITE?

According to her associates, an ex-Broadway chorine has orbited in public relations in two short years by putting everything in writing. "Janice never goes out for a hamburger without getting an idea while sopping on the mustard," says a friend. "Then she comes back and sends it to *someone*. A full-blown lunch date gives her enough material for twenty memos."

You know how seeing a story in print makes it seem "official." There is also something impressive about neatly typed ideas, reminders and requests for information. Keep them short.

DON'T THROW ANYTHING AWAY

Your office may look like headquarters for the scrap drive, but saving things is another trick I have seen parlayed into shimmering success.

One of the girls I worked with on the Max Factor account brought along every cosmetic idea she'd ever thought up at other agencies . . . lipstick that tasted like strawberries, a ballpoint pen that wrote perfume to make letters smell good, shampoo in champagne bottles, cologne that was half gin to attract alcoholics. Each new creative director (and we had nine) would be introduced to Marjorie's brain children as though they were brand new babies, not teen-agers. I used to go nearly mad knowing she was in there bowling over still *another* creative director.

Whether anybody does anything about your ideas doesn't matter. As I suggested earlier, showing them and your thinking off is sufficient.

USE YOUR FRIENDS

You should have a long list of people who can be useful to you. And you should be on a few long lists yourself. (Being useful is different from being used. It's quite moral.)

I could always get heaps of information for a project from the librarian in the history and geography department of the Los Angeles Public Library. Ditto an adorable chap at the *Los Angeles Times* who would read old news stories to me over the phone and even spell the names. I also had a panel of wife-and-mother girl friends who would tell me how mothers felt about aspirin, oranges, adultery or anything I needed to know.

Your secretarial background should come in handy here. You're used to coming up with what people need, but now the requests may be tougher.

OTHER THINGS TO USE

Every girl has just so many things going for her . . . good cheek-bones, sense of humor, terrific backhand, etc. Yes, they all fit into business. If by some incredible stroke of luck you're loaded (diamonds, money, tax-exempt bonds), there's no reason not to let it show in a nice way.

By all means have lunch with your father, the oil tycoon, and tour him through the office. Wear your Traina-Norells to work. Have your own Piper Cub. Only use of your talent will eventually provide you any real fun on the job, but for some weird reason certain people in charge are impressed by who and what belongs to you and may give you more of a break if you're well-possessed.

ARE YOU A HURRICANE OR A TRADE WIND?

In your new spot you can play it two ways: You can be a crispy, crunchy, starchy, bristly, high-heeled clickety-clacking girl wow, slaving the livelong day to turn your molehill into a mountain (then running around and showing it to everybody); or you can relax (to the naked eye).

I think stirring up a big fat hurricane around yourself was probably necessary for a business woman in 1923. If you didn't, men looked right through you like glass. I think hurricaning now is only practiced by the phonies and people who are not very sure of themselves.

Let me give you an example. Last spring I was on a panel television show at a Midwestern university. The kids had their own studio and transmitter and telecast shows into town. I never saw so much going on, fervor-wise. The producer was producing, the coordinator was coordinating, the cameraman was rolling around getting angles. It was like a submarine after a hit.

How was the show? We were all so over-rehearsed that everybody's lines came out like grey flannel.

By contrast, over at NBC they get the "Tonight" show on five nights a week without any fuss. It *seems* to be the most casual, informal, easy-going little jewel of a show you've ever seen with everybody's lines sounding like silver bells. It only takes fifty *pros* working quietly and without showing off to make it look and sound that way.

No, of course you aren't *really* casual about your work, but it's probably better to start sooner rather than later being a pro. The best of them—Frank Sinatra, Margot Fonteyn, Lyndon Johnson, Bob Hope—make it *look* easy, don't they? You should too. Incidentally, men hate loud-mouth, show-off dames. Those are the ones they're really prejudiced against in business.

TO IMAGE OR NOT TO IMAGE?

A lot of women in business have images. A girl who later started a magazine and became a hostess to royalty used to trail mink on the floor behind her when she was a mere slip of a secretary. She also used to move her two good Louis XV chairs down to the office to impress a lunch date, then have them hauled right back home to wow the cocktail trade. Her image was Opulence. (Don't ask *me* how she did it on her salary! I've heard some conjecture, of course.)

Another powerhouse I know can't be got to without a visa and a letter from three congressmen . . . the Exclusive Type. Another one wears only leopard *everything* from the skin out . . . Jungle Goddess. A fourth eats just a few grapes and a gram or two of crystallized ginger for lunch. Fragile, About-to-Float-Away image.

If you feel an image cropping out, probably there is no reason to run for the fungicide. Images, however, don't do much for you unless they are solidly backed by talent and hard work. I think it's better to have the talent and hard work come first. Then let an image gradually emerge out of your natural idiosyncrasies.

BITCHINESS

I'd be burying my head in the ostrich to pretend there weren't highly successful bitches in business—but, oh, how everybody detests them. It isn't at all necessary to be one to make good. *Really* it isn't.

On a fashion magazine a new young editor is as pretty as carnations and wildly ambitious. Nobody can beat her in to work in the morning and nobody can outlast her in the evening. She's informed in depth. So far so good. The other day an older editor was showing some new merchandise to an important department store executive. "And this is the sportive cocktail suit," she was saying. "And the boots. . . ."

Enter the carnation girl who tucked in her tummy, underslung her fanny and went to work. "Oh, isn't that a heavenly suit, Mr. Mudd? We just love it at Dazzle, but has Miss Finch shown you . . ." and she pulled out a tweed evening coat which happened to be the next item on Miss Finch's list. "Isn't it divine?" she burbled. "The minute I saw it I said that's for Mr. Mudd."

Miss Carnation kept right on slithering, darting around, being a bitch and, let's face it . . . charming . . . while the older editor watched in fascinated horror. The buyer was bamboozled all right— men can't always tell who is being bitchy if they are the recipient of a lethal dose of charm. One of these days, however, Miss Carnation will find a hatchet in her neck.

Another young lady I know who is exactly the same age as the carnation girl works for a book publishing company selling subsidiary rights to magazines, paperback companies, book clubs, foreign publishers. It's a responsible job. She has two girls working for her. I have never been in her office when I haven't heard, "Carol, you can handle this. Take him to lunch if you like." Or, "Elizabeth, you know the *Post* people. Will you see what you can do about this?" She doesn't have to grab authority. She gives it.

The carnation girl rarely dates . . . afraid the night lights might wilt her for work. (She probably also dislikes or is afraid of men anywhere but in business.) The publishing girl has a heavy date schedule and two of the men she dates want to marry her.

IDEAS PLEASE

A project is giving you trouble. The deadline is nigh. Very well, you must borrow some ideas!

A young copywriter friend in California telephoned me in New York recently, and said, "Help! I've got to think of twenty ways to increase the sale of avocados, and I've got to think of them in twenty minutes."

I came up with six, including a contest to describe the taste of an avocado. (I planned to enter "An avocado tastes like cashew-flavored green cold cream" myself.) David, my husband, thought of several more ideas. My friend reported that all but two of our schemes were voted by the group to be totally impractical, but at least she didn't go to the meeting empty-minded.

Another copywriter I know was given the assignment of developing a singing commercial about margarine. He couldn't carry a tune, much less *rhyme* anything. His forte was straightforward prose about batteries and generators. He called home, and his thirteen-year-old daughter bailed him out.

Naturally if you had to borrow all your ideas you'd be in the wrong job. Your company would soon know and so would you. But in emergencies and when you're learning, it's okay.

THE CREATIVE MEETING

Suppose a brilliant idea comes to you smack, first thing in the meeting. Do you spring it?

Not necessarily! It may well be your casually tossed-in thought is The Answer, but nobody will recognize it because it came on such little cat feet. If there's to be a second meeting, you might do well to retain your jewel and return with it mounted in a more Tiffany setting.

I believe a company soon learns whom it can count on for the good stuff, regardless of whether you present it with showmanship. Nevertheless, if you make enough of a federal case out of your plans, it's at least harder for three other people to say it was *their* idea.

Men sometimes claim women are too emotional. (They love it when you get all soggy and dramatic about *them*, but not when you get that way about an idea.) Girls aren't any more emotional than men, really, but accompanying your idea with some unemotional charts, graphs and figures is wise. Statistics are marvelous for backing up your visceral convictions. One girl I know makes her convictions match the statistics. If she comes across some hair-raising figures on the population boom or insecticide poisoning, she'll manage to get around to those subjects and sound as smart as Kiplinger. Other people make up their statistics as the need arises, which may be the soundest plan of all!

WHAAAAT?

They've been talking about the double framostan with the transitional support for about twenty minutes, and you don't whether the discussion is about bridges, girdles or elevated shoes. When you're an old pro, you can come right out and ask, "What *are* you talking about?" As a wobbly amateur, you have to tread on dainty little feet. Listen raptly and if it "feels" kind of like something you ought to know, play it owly. (They don't talk much.) If other people are asking questions, ask one or two yourself—but not too many. Little girls with too many big questions are usually just showing off their ignorance. They want to be "on" in the meeting but have nothing to get on *with*.

MORE MEETING NOTES

If you honestly believe everybody in the room is wrong about something except you—and it's possible they are—then sweetly, firmly say so, but don't get mad.

If you've had trouble getting the floor, it's tempting to be vehement, inflamed and hysterical when you get it (especially if you're arguing with men who tend to think women in business are vehement, inflamed and hysterical). Quiet does it. You know how the least emotionally-involved arguers at dinner parties win everybody over and the impassioned ones lie there bleeding and ignored. The more you keep the edge out of your voice and the petulance out of your mood, the better your chances to change minds.

How long do you fight for your cause? Only so long. You may not really change your mind, but the time comes when you stop saying, "I'd rather die first." It's only a business decision at stake, not your virtue.

What about tears to help convince people?

Tears are very impressive, but then so is a derailed Pullman with cut-off arms and legs sticking out of the windows. Some people just aren't too keen about getting impressed that way. Besides, it's very hard to turn tears on and off at random. I know. They usually well up when you have the least use for them. As an old cryer from way back, I'd recommend that when you feel the little devils forming ranks, you hide out and stay hidden until they disperse.

THEIR IDEAS

You must compliment other people's ideas when they're good no matter what the agony. "That is a fantastic idea, Eloise. It's just sensational," will get you credit for being a perceptive and a warm, wonderful human being. Hah! Clamming up and staring at your pencil will get you credit for being the jealous piker you are.

Suppose they're now giving the hoof, the ears and the tail to somebody for an idea you thought of yourself last week but it was so miserable you threw it out. If you mention you thought of it first, nobody will believe you. Do not hari-kiri. Know that your fertile brain will come up with other ideas, and next time they'll be riding *you* around on their shoulders.

PROPS PLEASE

One girl executive tells me she never totes anything to a meeting except a little red alligator notebook in which she writes smashing little red alligator notes in red alligator ink . . . *only* if what's being said is important.

How chic! I used to need a wheelbarrow to haul my paraphernalia in.

It's my opinion that auxiliary material can be very helpful to your cause because it relieves a meeting's boredom. Anything people can pass around, sniff, touch, fondle, shred or stroke is great. If they can eat it, that's the greatest.

My finest prop of all time was my mermaid picture. I tore it out of a back issue of the *Saturday Evening Post,* took it to a meeting and suggested Max Factor might feature eyes that summer wearing the Mermaid Look. The idea was so well-received that in three days five people had forgotten whose mermaid idea it was and were under the impression it was *theirs.* Poor darlings. They didn't have the one, the original mermaid picture to keep flashing in the meeting, and so they couldn't make the theft stick.

THEIR GRUBBY LITTLE FINGERS
AND THEIR FAT HEAVY HANDS

Once an idea of yours goes into the works, it will nearly always be tampered with and made worse by a boss, a group, a committee, a rival. This group grabbiness just can't be helped. Though one person's *anything* creative is usually better than a group effort, management—which doesn't always understand creativity—is nervous if it doesn't throw in a bunch of experts (often including management's wife, girl friend, golf buddies and haberdasher). Someday you'll be important enough to demand that everyone keep his G.L.F.'s and F.H.H.'s off your work.

It's a wonderful thing to be able to *move* with your ideas (i.e., they have to follow your plan and nobody can interfere). Any time you see a resounding success in business it's usually because one gifted person has got hold of the full responsibility for the store, the airline, the magazine, the ad campaign; and his concept is carried straight through to completion. (He has plenty of helpers but no other quarterback.) This kind of spot takes some working up to and little bit of luck. More than one tycooness says, "I just happened to be in the right place at the right time." I never had the thrill of having unlimited responsibility in business myself, but I had the thrill of the results when I wrote a book. I was the only quarterback.

What if you don't want full responsibility but you can clearly see that somebody up there is wrecking the company. You'd at least like a hearing to tell them how to straighten things out.

It's quite true that a fresh junior executivess can sometimes see straight through the morass and muck things are in and know in her bones what ought to be done. She may see clearer in her neophyte hours than she ever will again. Right or wrong, however, you can't often get people to listen seriously to your plans to revamp the company unless you're on the management team. (There must *be* Joan of Arc cases where a slip of a girl led the company out of bankruptcy, but I never heard of one.) Do your own job fiendishly well, keep looking for the Main Chance—mainer than the one you already have—and two years and several dead bodies later when they get around to doing what you knew ought to be done in the first place, you can crow (to yourself). This doesn't mean you can't always try in your ladylike way to interest people who are in power in your schemes. You may also get a crack at some of these men un- officially through dates, affairs, friendships. Smart girls sometimes get to be confidantes of important men. No reason not to talk about business when you're on his yacht.

If, unlike the girl who "hears voices," you're inclined to think something is so just *because* somebody in power says it is, it *ain't* necessarily! Don't be too impressed. You have a brain. Listen to it and do what it tells you as often as you possibly can.

PEOPLE-HANDLING

The Hand Shake

Some girls think it's unfeminine to show any enthusiasm shaking hands, and so they have developed the wet-hot-dog-bun hand clasp. It's a chiller. Some very formal Europeans often have a miserable handshake too. They only go as far as the knuckles and do a quick one-two as though they were shaking down a thermometer. Do grasp hands warmly, firmly, all the way in. I don't think there's anybody not to shake hands with at first meeting, including women. If you like to touch and pat people as I do, this is a way of getting at them legitimately.

Honey, Darling and Dear

If terms of endearment are natural to you, they're in so far as I'm concerned. Your fond salutes should be changed from month to month, however.

I have gone through lambchop, dreamboat, mushroom, cutiepie (a real low!) and Lady Catherine, Lady Jane, Lady Margaret or whatever the girl's name is this year. I could use a new supply. A very popular chap I know has a name for each girl—Bearcat, Crankcase, Flapjack and Birdbrain (said lovingly), but probably no girl should get quite that cutiepie with her co-workers.

YOUR PAST COMES BACK TO HAUNT YOU

Now that you have a fancier job, how much menial stuff should you continue to do?

If you've ever been a secretary, the temptation is strong to do it yourself. You figure every girl you give your typing to is thinking, "Who does Miss Uppity think she is? We knew her when."

It's not that you're too *good* to do your own typing, but if you type, valuable time and energy go down the drain that should be going into your new work. Chloroform your guilt feelings and turn the stuff over to the typist.

Don't let them stick you with taking notes in meetings either. Ask them to call in a secretary. Otherwise you'll be transcribing notes far into the afternoon while the other people are getting on with what the meeting was called about.

FOLLOW THE LEADER

How do you get co-workers to do what you want when they don't have to? Or even when they *do?*

Everybody doesn't subscribe to this "exaggerate the obstacles" method of getting work done for them, but it works for me. When you want something impossible, you make it sound worse than it is! "Johnny, this is a ghastly request. (Look as though you were about to faint with the hideousness of it all.) I don't know whether you'll be able to do it, but I'm hoping." Or, "What a miserable time to be bringing you this, Marguerite. I know how swamped you are." (You are almost putty-colored with compassion.)

As long as *they* know *you* know how ridiculous you're being, I think people often try harder for you.

Sometimes charm won't work, of course. Other employees sometimes push a new young tycooness around out of simple jealousy or resentment that you've "made it." You are *smart,* of course. Occasionally they do the work *their* way instead of how it's got to be done. This was certainly true for me as a young advertising copywriter. I would ask an art director for a layout showing plump doves circling around the classic head of a dreamy-looking creature *en négligée.* What I would get was a burlesque queen in a bikini surrounded by American flags.

"What happened?" I would wail.

"Your idea won't work," he would say.

The hell it wouldn't!

I gradually learned that what separates the girl successes from the marshmallows is the guts to fight for what you have to have. Letting a dissenter off the hook so he'll think you're a nice person doesn't make him think you're a nice person. He thinks you're a worm! Letting nut-skull helpers off the hook will certainly never get you the pay and the post that let you swish around sexily among the men.

You have to trust people who *know* what they're doing to *do* it, of course, without staying on their heels. I believe the biggest washout of a boss I ever had was one of the nine creative directors who couldn't, as they say, delegate authority. In his case, he couldn't let copywriters write copy. I'd go into his office with a television story board I'd struggled with nine days. He would lay it down on his desk and say, "Thanks, that's swell. Hey, what do you think about the idea of a guy getting out of a seaplane with a four-day growth of beard. His wife meets him, they kiss. She gets pretty badly scratched. She pulls out a razor. . . ."

What I thought was what *I* could do with a razor, but what I said was, "That's *marvelous!*"

Sometimes the underling's idea is just as good as your own but *different*—not the way you'd do it. That doesn't make it wrong. Let the people who were hired to do the work do their work, and you do yours.

GIVE EVERYBODY CREDIT

At a ladies' luncheon I attended at Temple Israel—second biggest temple in the second biggest U.S. city—the chairman of the day introduced ten committee women who talked at the mike half a minute each. Then she introduced twenty other women who had done something which entitled them to be stood up and clapped at. Then she read off twenty other women's names. Whoever was left must have been a real shirker! Actually the introductions only took a few minutes, and the chairman had managed to leave a lovely glow around the room.

If you're in a position to thank out loud, make it a long list, and I mean down to complimenting whoever got the conference room ashtrays emptied so snappily. Maybe you think it's going overboard to acknowledge so many. I say you can't *go* overboard mentioning names.

THE GIRL DOWN BELOW

It came as an enormous shock to me when the girl who had been my assistant while I worked as executive secretary to Mr. Belding (the ad agency boss) was instantly made his secretary when I moved on to write copy. Little Charlotte . . . dear little Charlotte . . . who had run errands for me on her lunch hours and even sewed up sagging hems for me while I hid in the closet.

What a fathead I was . . . assuming someone as smart as this girl would just go on and on delightedly doing these chores for some other executive secretary to the end of her days.

I think it is a good rule to remember that most people who serve you like sheep dogs don't do it because you're so glorious and they're so impressed with you. It's their job and they do a good job of it. You might just as well give them credit and see about advancing them, because if you don't, somebody else will and maybe over your still-warm body!

THE FELLOWS WON'T LET
YOU IN THEIR CLUB

Who wants to play dominoes at their silly "for men only" luncheons anyway . . . or choke to death in their smoke-filled, segregated dining room? It's quite a new thing for men and women to be companions anyhow. For centuries they just piled into bed together but had few discussions. A little more time is needed to integrate completely (and naturally there will always be some things men and women won't do together, and women wouldn't want them to). Meantime, I'm sure you have a million projects for your lunch hours, the most important of which might be to grab a nap against a very big evening or big meeting.

YOU'RE NEUROTIC

Is your ego so shaky that when somebody says a co-worker did a sensational job you can feel the spikes being driven into your ribs? Do you feel other people's hate, jealousy, tenderness toward another in the room before "the other" feels it himself?

"Overly sensitive" people do succeed in business. (How many executives do *you* know who are on the couch?)

You can "feel too much" and still be a fabulous executive secretary because you sense exactly what a boss needs before he needs it. (This also makes you a great lover but, as I said, we have to wait a bit for that discussion.) Coupled with other skills, the sensitive person can go just about as high as she wishes. She knows what other people need to hear and receive—including the public who buys the stuff—and she gives it to them.

Nevertheless, if you're frequently inclined to feel out of the group, the party, the meeting (or even if you're in but somebody else is *more* in), my advice is to try psychiatry, but also to show a few personal guts while you're suffering. Instead of withdrawing into a bruised little ball, make yourself get back in the group, the party, the meeting. Yes, you have to be a little phony—pretend to be animated when you're actually not enjoying yourself too much. I'm convinced that's what "normal" people do. They get bored almost speechless *too* (which is what you are when you feel "out of it"), but they keep the smile on, the valves open. They stay in there plugging instead of granting themselves the luxury of cold, miserable withdrawal! You can force yourself to do the same!

THEY'RE NEUROTIC

There certainly are a load of *them* around. One of my nine creative-director bosses at the ad agency used to get absolutely hivey if anybody stayed at the office after he headed for the car pool at five-fifteen. It was a reflection on him to have anyone working when he wasn't. Some of us workers should probably have offered to go get in the car pool *for* him.

Another creative director used to come out from the East Coast to Los Angeles (where I spent most of my office years) to mold us Western clay into copywriters. He adored company, so we all had to be molded in a body. And you've heard of night people? This cat didn't get his eyes really propped open until four in the afternoon. By dinnertime he was getting livelier, and around midnight he did his very best molding. I can remember us morning people trying to get our clay to cooperate at two in the morning, but I know *mine* was clammy and unshapable.

Neurotic bosses and co-workers *are* a lot of bother, but I've found they usually do themselves in before they do *you* in.

MISCELLANEOUS WISDOM

Hobbies

Isn't that lovely that you weave rugs out of old nylon stockings . . . and how nice you can out-field every teen-age outfielder in your block? To each his own. It's my opinion, however, that people who live for the weekend and the hobby must be fairly miserable in their jobs and should see about a new one. In your early years of making good I think your *work* is the hobby.

A Title

Titles are very nice things, although they are frequently as phony as plastic pearls. I heard one the other day—Creative Projectionist. Now what on earth do you suppose a creative projectionist does to be creative unless maybe run the film backwards? Nevertheless, I can't sniff at anybody's title. Get one if you can. They look very nice on printed business cards.

Speaking of business cards, have those too. Badger the company to print some for you even if you have no title and have to pay for them yourself. Just use your name, the company's name, address and phone number. These come in very handy at cocktail parties.

Speech-Making

If you ever have to make a speech, first write the speech out completely. It doesn't have to be very fancily said, but write it all down. Then transfer the main points paragraph by paragraph to 3 x 5 cards. These are what you will actually use when you give the speech. Practice and practice your "extemporaneous" address until you can practically give it without the cards. It will come out a little differently each time. That's what makes it sparkly.

THE SWEET FEEL OF SUCCESS

When you start having a rather terrific success in your job, it's like little firecrackers going off inside you . . . pop, pop, pop. Sometimes it's a few days between pops, but the sensation is a bit like the sweet, glow-y feeling at the beginning of a love affair. The difference is this: the best part of the love affair may be the sweet, falling-in-love period after which things inevitably go downhill joywise. The sweet-success feeling of work usually comes at the *end* of a hard pull and keeps building.

Miss Geraldine Stutz, president of Henri Bendel and one of the most breathtaking girl-successes of our time (she really *is* successful) says: "It's like having good legs. It's that extra lovely something in your life. It's the joy of having every bit of you used."

Miss Kay Daly, vice-president of Revlon and mother of the famous "I Dreamed I Went Walking in My Maidenform Bra" campaign says: "If there's anything more fun than just being a *girl*, I'd say it's being a successful-in-*business* girl. That way, you can have your cake and eat it, too—and the frosting is on the top. There the money is nicer and the men you meet are more fun to know, because they are usually many-faceted in personality and interests (and a little more *neurotic* than, say, the milkman—which makes them more interesting, naturally!). Even though a girl has to work a lot harder at the top, the grind is not so grim if she can afford to show up in a Chanel suit for those early-Monday-morning meetings . . . or tuck her hair into a divine Daché hat if she hasn't time to get to the hairdresser. If you're a girl who prefers the cake (plus the frosting) to the crumbs, and you're not afflicted with acrophobia (the higher you go, the fewer friendly hands will be reaching down to help you!), the top-of-the-ladder is far and away the pleasantest place you can perch."

One lovely thing about having a success is that you lose your jealousy, and perhaps for the first time in your life you can truly rejoice in a friend's—any friend's—good fortune.

Everyone will take credit for you, of course. As Mussolini said, "Success has many fathers. Failure is an orphan." You can afford to let all the benefactors and factresses claim you. The incredible thing is that they will not have discovered a genius or somebody who is that much smarter or prettier or crazier-gifted than anybody else. They will simply have "benefacted" a *very* hard worker.

WHERE WILL IT ALL END?

Herbert Mayes, president of the McCall Corporation, says, "Nothing recedes like success!"

We don't want that happening to you, and it shouldn't happen if you stay cat-vigilant and keep doing all the things that made you successful—plus some new ones. There is one blight, however, that can run through an office like carbolic acid . . . temporarily. Let's discuss this affliction and how to fight it before traveling on to raises, firings, expense accounts and finally fun and sexy games in the office.

CHAPTER 6

JUNGLE WARFARE

O NCE UPON A TIME about a million years ago, the forest started getting quite dark around noontime. A damp, chill wind went streaking through the firs and spruces although it was a summer day.

"My word," a woolly rhinoceros said to his wife as he squiggled his three toes in the mud. "They certainly are rushing the season."

"You can say that again," said his wife. "My snout is absolutely a-twitch with cold."

A giant beaver stopped building his mud and tree-trunk dam to murmur, "The union is going to have to do something about this light if it expects me to put in my usual fourteen-hour day." A great quiver went through his fat, flat tail.

A saber-toothed tiger nestled closer to her cubs. "I wish your father would get back here," she said. "Something's up."

At the sea coast, other creatures were being affected by strange developments. "Ethel," a Devonian shark said to his girl friend, "did you ever see a tide as low as this? It's all I can do to keep myself wet."

"I know," she replied. "I keep hitting my head on the sand every time I dive."

The great-great-great-great-great-great-grandfather of what later became a porpoise surfaced beside its mother to ask, "Mummy, mummy, where did the sun go?" "Hush," said its mother, "hush," although she knew very well something awfully funny was going on.

Just like the innocent creatures confronted with the first harbingers of the Ice Age, many a forlorn little office creature has been heard to ask as recently as yesterday, "Mummy, where did the *sun* go? Why is it so *cold* in here?"

Mummy may not have the answer, but *I'd* be willing to guess that the sun is being blocked, and the chill is being caused, by a virulent case of office politics!

DEFINITION, PLEASE

I define office politics—which exist in nearly all offices at least to some degree—as the struggle of people to hang onto their jobs, get better ones, get more power and money and occasionally drive a fellow worker out of his job and out of his mind.

My husband puts its more succinctly. "Office politics," he says, "is the art of loving a bunch of bastards."

A smart girl I know says that office politics is simply people being people—afraid, anxious, petty, jealous.

I think our definitions are all true ones, but the last definition is the truest. Any time you have a bunch of bast—I mean people— thrown together in any situation, you're going to have factions, frictions and squabbles. Kids fight in kindergarten, mothers fight at PTA meetings, girls fight with beaux, landlords fight with tenants; and sometimes they all fight dirty. You have lots of *people* in offices.

LET'S MOVE IN CLOSER

Office politics ranges from the petty stuff—girls being pussycats, girls *and* boys getting in a bit of apple-polishing, a boss favoring your rival—to major stuff, such as the power play, the proxy fight and the stockholder suit.

Office politics are like white corpuscles. A certain number of "corps" are necessary in the blood to fight disease. A certain amount of politics are necessary to keep the workers in an office from being too torpid, contented and noncompetitive to get anything done. When there are too many white corpuscles, you get leukemia. With too many politics, you get bedlam!

Politics get much more virulent, of course, when a company is in trouble. If the cars aren't selling or the stores aren't reordering, management starts looking around for somebody to blame. They even look at each other, and usually they form teams. A board chairman, executive vice-president and sales manager will hold hands for strength while the president, treasurer and export manager decide to go steady—temporarily. You know about politics making strange bedmates and all that.

Although some politics will probably always be necessary, and a company crisis may make politics multiply and divide, I'm convinced that the men and women who go beyond the norm and play them virtually as a way of life are sick. Politicians generally choose to play politics instead of being good at their jobs. They're not to be confused with the gruffs, the grumps and the grouches, of course. While these people are anti-everything you bring up and have fifteen reasons why it won't work, after they've gruffed, grumped and grouched a bit, they usually go along with what has to be done. We're talking about the real saboteurs. Here are three examples, all true but slightly camouflaged to protect the author.

THE GREAT ORGANIZER: The head of an electronics firm has reorganized the office twice since he took over six months ago and is headed for a third reorganization. One hundred and sixty-eight people have either been shifted, fired or scared hell out of since he arrived. Nobody can find the cafeteria without a road map because it's been relocated four times, along with every conference room, wall partition and stick of furniture in the place. The Great Organizer has charts to interpret his charts, books of procedure to show girls how to do what they have been doing competently for ten years and graphs to record every curve but the receptionist's. He doesn't discuss problems with his staff, he shows slide films. Interoffice memos litter the air like confetti. Sales are way off compared to last year, and his high-powered research team has almost completed its report on why this is *good*. In other words: *Office politician in high gear.*

THE GREAT BUTTER BALL: The advertising manager of a large company oversees the spending of a five-million-dollar advertising budget. He doesn't know any more about advertising than a salamander, but instead of ever having bothered to learn, he spends his entire day buttering. He butters his boss for one hour in the morning and another in the afternoon as they drive to and from work together. During prime time, he butters another top executive who's above him and whom he has managed to interest in his own hobby of deep-sea fishing. This makes the painful discussion of advertising practically unnecessary. The remaining hours of the day are allocated to keeping anybody in the office who *knows* anything, including what a frightened stoop *he* is, from spending too much time with his bosses or his client. *Office politician in orbit.*

THE GREAT ARBITER: The producer of a comedy television show hires eight writers a week. The guy can't write a line himself and doesn't even know what's funny, but the assistant producer takes care of such messy details as putting the show together. The producer is then free to spend his entire week pitting the four comedy-writing teams against each other so that he can step in just before script time and "bring order out of chaos." *Office politician supérieur.*

"Temporary insanity" may cause politics to run rife in an organization. For example, all hell broke loose in a public utilities company a few years back when the president fell in love with a no-talent actress and started buying TV spectaculars for her to star in. The ratings were nil. Profits fell. The stock dipped. Much whispering developed behind closed doors (closed doors are an absolutely necessary component of office politics), and the board of directors started hanging executives by their heels to see if any love letters fell out of *their* pockets. Secretaries were fluoroscoped. The chief finally resigned to go into independent television production, where he could lose money (his own) to his heart's content. *Office politician with wings clipped.*

All these things affect *you* when you work whether you're a principal or a minor player. Ladies can play office politics *too*, of course, although we usually aren't awfully good at it. We don't have the iced viscera *necessary*. Also, women hardly ever get responsible jobs without having talent and working hard, so there isn't so much reason for us to play. You more often find girls coping *with* rather than instigating office politics. Of course a biddy-bookkeeper in charge of all the girls may seem to concentrate her every energy erg spreading fright, fear and anxiety among her flock instead of running the department. She's an *office politician third class*.

COLLUSION AND CONFUSION

One of the most tragic outgrowths of office politics is that a very insecure or confused boss will surround himself with idiots while perfectly capable people are either fired or left unused. I know the head of a bottling company who hired an unfrocked Greek priest to replace a perfectly competent sales manager who made him feel uneasy (about his own job). "Think how he'll be able to commune," he told his startled salesmen.

One of my copy chiefs had a favorite favorite, an ex-football star who gave some signs of having had his head stepped on. "Pete is a tower of strength," my boss was fond of saying. What old Pete really was was a tower of blubber; but he was also the biggest yesman who ever lived.

Sometimes office politics create a situation in which competent people can't get their jobs done. In the second advertising agency I worked for, we three girl copywriters, considered as good as any in the business, were out of favor and almost totally misused or unused for over a year. The most creative of the three was finally fired outright. She went over to another ad agency, started working on $3,000,000 worth of business and is the darling of the place. The second girl, sick of the frustration, finally took a job in a giant agency in another city where she was made a copy chief herself. As for little me, one of my few assignments was writing a Max Factor column of advice to teen-agers for *Seventeen* Magazine. After I finished each column, five to seven men would rewrite, and eventually the assignment was taken away from me altogether. *Quelle* ego blow! Since I had very little else to do, I just sat down and, on company time, wrote a book of advice to girls about make-up, grooming, and a few other little things like sex and so on. The title of the book was *Sex and the Single Girl,* and it earned over half a million dollars for its author. (I also recently started doing a column on the same subjects for more than a hundred newspapers.) Am I angry about office politics? Don't be silly!

There are bosses, of course, who know how to get the best out of people and keep office politics to a minimum. Usually these paragons of maturity are found in smaller offices and they succeed by practicing *laissez faire* with creative people.

OFF WITH THEIR HEADS

Why don't boards of directors hire only smart, reasonably-at-peace-with-the-world men and women to run companies in the first place? Why do they let in all those nuts?

One very intelligent career girl I know has this answer: "There aren't enough smart, reasonable, well-adjusted people to go around," Nona says. "In any company you usually find one or two brilliant men surrounded by twelve or fifteen average-to-outright-criminal types." (And of course we're *all* average or less some of the time!)

Another friend says, "When you discover the inner workings of *any* company, you just can't understand how they keep the place open, much less turn out a product and make a profit."

This bears out what the first girl said. If there were enough fabulous business leaders to go around, boards of directors would hire *only* that kind (provided the board members weren't marshy themselves).

Don't the creeps, the stoops, the virulent politicians, the weaklings and no-talents ever get fired? Certainly they do. Those who live by the sword, etc., etc. Consummate politicians usually have a lot of staying power, however. What else do they do all day but plot how to survive while the workers work? The politicians eventually do get bounced, of course. In twenty-one years of working I've never seen a real no-goodnik hang on forever. And once they're fired and you meet them on the street, you wonder how anybody *ever* took them so seriously! That's *then!* Unfortunately, before they are finally carried out, a great many nice men and women have usually been bludgeoned, fired and carried out (in emotional tatters) themselves.

How come I want you to work when work is like that? Darling, *life* is like that! There are some perfectly dreadful people in one's own country, one's own community, one's own church and sometimes in one's own family. Would you resign from the thrills of life to save yourself from the chills and spills? Some people even think office politics are sexy because of the intrigue and danger inherent —like sitting ringside at a particular gory fight. (I think these people ought to read a little in the Kama Sutra every night to dope out some new thrills.) At any rate, office politics don't begin to dim the other joys of working. Besides, you're all in the mess together! In a family squabble or doomed love affair you may suffer quite alone. During a siege of office politics, a thrilling spirit of camaraderie develops like that which Londoners knew during the Blitz.

ESCAPE ARTIST

Why can't you, by being a dear, sweet, good little girl and wearing dirt-repellent miracle fabrics, just lie down and let office politics wash over you?

It's almost impossible! Though you should be safe as a secretary, for instance, your boss may be on the ten-most-unwanted list. If you're having an *affair* with a man who's headed for the firing squad, I suggest you stop whatever you're doing right now, get a big white hanky, cut two holes for eyes, tie it around your head and go to the mirror. You'll want to know how you're going to look as you both go down together.

If you're virtually your own boss in a company, you're too far up the ladder to stay neutral. When an involved executive friend drops by your office or opens up the whole mucky political subject at lunch, are you going to say, "Oh, dear! Oh, gracious! Oh, *please,* Mr. Gripsholm . . . you mustn't *tell* me these terrible things. Couldn't we talk about ice hockey?"

You're in an office. To remain utterly aloof, even if you *could,* would get you so hated by *both* sides that you'd finally have to leave the company out of sheer loneliness (and sooner than the people who took sides). To abstain from voting is like not backing a U.S. presidential candidate because neither candidate is perfect. Anyway, abstinence won't save your job.

THE ENEMY WITHIN

Personal enemies are another facet of office politics. Going around in a potato sack and trying not to cause another living soul any trouble will still get you hated by somebody. You may remind someone of how far he could have got if he'd played it steam engine as you have. A little turnip who spends most of her time backcombing her hair will feel outraged because you have the job she feels she deserved. And if your position calls for making decisions, the decisions are going to rub somebody the wrong way. And then there are the plain old everyday haters, for whom hostility is as necessary as food. You can't escape.

Though lying low doesn't allow you to dodge office politics and avoid making enemies, "playing" politics isn't the answer either! A friend recounts her experiences *trying* to play.

"There I was," she said, "finally past the secretarial barrier with a job in public relations. This particular office was a hotbed of political intrigue, and I determined to play the game. I immediately made friends with my boss's secretary. She would give me the scoop on the guy. As my friend, she would also put my calls through when others waited. My memos would be placed on top. She would tell him what a charmer I was and tip *me* off about pitfalls to avoid while others fell on their faces.

"All my plotting would have worked but for one thing. Mr. Tully was straight out of *Tobacco Road*. He was a vital-parts scratching, nice-girl-deprecating slob. He not only wanted the Kleenex brought to him—he wanted it *held* for him. And all the time he was busy holding Kleenex for *his* boss—an oily and insecure nothing. On the one hand, I was willing to do almost anything to make good and not be returned to the secretarial pool. On the other hand, I'd walk into his office and be told, 'Okay, baby, let's strip to the waist and get to work.' (He didn't mean it about stripping to the waist. He just wanted to put me on the defensive, which he did.)

"I tried hard to play the game—whole-heartedly at first, then half-heartedly, then quarter-heartedly, then no-heartedly. As the man liked me less and less, my work got worse and worse. I simply couldn't do anything right. I finally left before he fired me."

I think the point of this is that with a nice guy you don't *need* to play politics. You can just be yourself. With a creep, it's almost impossible to play and win.

All right then, what *do* you do . . . just stand there and wait to get your head handed to you?

It is my sincere hope that Vance Packard or Spyros Skouras or somebody will write a book someday and tell us exactly how to out-live our enemies at work and, furthermore, how to get them to stand still while the honey is drizzled over them and we get out the ants.

I've heard that a psychologist in Beverly Hills has come up with a plan for office in-fighting which he calls "stalking." You lay a trap for your enemy and wait for him to fall in. I'm dying to hear more about it. Every time I've ever laid a trap for my enemy, the wrong "enemy" wound up with the trap door clanking shut behind her. I can still hear the clank.

I know during troubled times you're supposed to play it smart, be seen only with the "in" people, avoid the untouchables and all that. It's all such a lot of bother though—snubbing your best friend in the hall, especially if he or she is your roommate.

I remember when Buddy Adler, the handsome boss of Twentieth Century-Fox Studios, died. The new studio head had not yet been selected. In fact, it was the morning of the funeral. My husband gave me a blow by blow on the phone. There was the maddest scramble to get into the "right cars" to go to Forest Lawn, but no-body was absolutely certain which the right cars were. God forbid you should be caught riding out with anybody who'd been impor-tant in the Adler regime. Heaven bless if you got into a Chrysler 300 with the leaders of the new. But who *were* they? Now, three years later, nearly everybody in that funeral cortege is out of the company. Shows you how much good handpicking the right chums can do.

It would be cowardly, however, not to suggest *some* course of action when office politics are rampant, so here are some little exercises. The first are mental. You are to memorize the following five "Don't Worry If's" and four "Don't Be Surprised's."

1. *Don't worry if* your boss shows rank favoritism for somebody in the organization who is a cluck. It's probably chemistry. A cluck's H_2SO_4 may titillate him wildly while your $CaCO_3$ leaves him cold. It may be just the other way around with the next boss. Play the waiting game.

2. *Don't worry if* you were the fair-haired darling for five years and now find yourself on the s - - - list. Your successor won't be *the* young *élégante* forever, either.

3. *Don't worry if* management went to the ends of the earth to get you into the shop and is now treating you like slightly moldy bread. Poor insecure management is probably figuring it this way: If she works for us, how could she be any good? (They may have something there!) Other managements are waiting to be dazzled. One may be eyeing you wistfully right now.

4. *Don't worry if* a genuine phony male or female is impressing the hell out of everybody temporarily and you seem to be the only clear thinker in the place. The flashy phony will fizzle eventually; if not, there is always a market for clear thinkers elsewhere.

5. *Don't worry if* nobody has gotten around to telling you you're doing well for six or eight months. In a New York cosmetics house famous for high salaries and terrible morale, a management member says, "Hell, why would you need to pass around compliments? If you're still here, you know you're good."

Now for the "Don't Be Surprised's."

1. *Don't be surprised if,* when things are at their absolute nadir, a dear "friend" cheers you up by saying he's heard you're going to be sacked. For some reason he thinks he's helping, but of course this is the kind of blabbermouthing nobody *needs*.

2. *Don't be surprised if,* after there's no question in *anybody's* mind you're leaving, they don't get around to *telling* you. "Phasing Out" is more popular—make the person so miserable he leaves without severance pay.

3. *Don't be surprised if* you are quietly separated from the

people you have to work with to get the job done. One publicity girl I know was supposed to publicize a television show but was told she was never to attend it. She had to sneak in and skulk behind cameras and props.

4. *Don't be surprised if,* while all this is going on, you feel suicidal and as though you'll never be any good again. You need a benevolent atmosphere in which things are *possible* to do your best. A veteran insurance saleswoman told me that, after racking up the biggest sales in her department for seven years, politics set in and she was unable to make the simplest exploratory phone call without getting the shakes! A new job or change of office current will have you ticking like a clock again.

Now for a few action possibilities:

1. Redouble your efforts to do a good job during an office political siege. As little as you feel like it, slaving shows you are *not* going to be easy to unload. Khrushchev was quoted during the Cuban crisis, "Let your bayonet thrust. If it strikes fat, destroy. If it strikes steel, withdraw." Well, when *their* bayonet thrusts, it should strike steel.

2. Do extra-curricular work for charities and professional clubs. This will help convince you you're still good—and it might even convince *them* if you get enough publicity.

3. Try not to sulk or be a sorehead. Don't go into seclusion. Try to keep your lines of communication open to the enemy.

4. Continue to charm. Though a certain executive can't stand you, this is no reason for you not to continue to be cheerful and adorable. Palm the *real* you off on your analyst.

5. Don't gratuitously discuss your trying situation with associates. One or two confidantes will know how bad things are for you, but keep the number small.

6. Wear your most beautiful clothes. Get your hair done often. Smell glorious.

7. Don't get off the payroll! Leave at your convenience *if* you leave. Exiting to prove how smart you are only proves how smart *they* were to get you to do it.

8. Do keep a plan in mind about what you will do if you get bounced.

9. No matter how shaky your own situation, see people who are looking for jobs. You should do this throughout your office life anyway. It's one of the ways you pay back the people who were kind to *you*.

10. I know most people will disagree with me about this one, but here goes. If you do leave with pretty sound knowledge about what's wrong with the company and who's running it, write a personal and confidential letter to the president. Keep it unemotional and back up your statements with as much proof as possible. (We don't want you tied up in a sticky old libel suit.) You'll feel better getting it off your chest, and maybe you can save the company after you've left.

YOU'RE FIRED!

Suppose it's all to no avail and you're axed!

Getting fired is pretty awful! I remember it well . . . walking through the office with the typewriters all clickety-clacking as usual, everybody still folksy and friendly because they haven't *heard* yet . . . and the sick, thuddy feeling of being a failure. The worst thing is looking about at all the people who are *left* and realizing these cats are still wanted, beloved, while you alone have been singled out for Siberia.

Just remember that *nobody* is fireproof; and the bigger you are, the more combustible you become. There's also almost no exception to the rule that people who are fired from good jobs go on to bigger and better jobs. Broadcasting companies, department stores, automobile factories and pharmaceutical houses are always being run gorgeously by somebody's old castoffs. As for little you, whatever got you into the place you got fired from won't desert you in your need to shinny up another tree.

That's enough brave and philosophical talk. Let's answer a few immediate questions.

Q. Should I try to get them to change their mind and un-fire me?

A. No! It can be done occasionally, but then it's rather like gluing a severed arm back onto the body. Plump for more severance pay if you like or a longer period on salary to get relocated, but don't beg them to take you back.

Q. What can I do to get even with the bastards?

A. Get another job and have a brilliant success. There is *no* other way. Greek retribution will take care of your enemies, and they'll do themselves in without any help from you.

Q. If they offer me the choice of severance pay or staying on until I get another job, which is better?

A. It's usually better to stay put until you get another job. You can't be sure you'll have one in a tiny time. Remember Rule 7— always stay on a payroll if you can.

Q. Do I frankly tell people I was fired?

A. You do not frankly tell people anything of the kind! Though your tendency is to announce your injury like a wounded child ("Hey look, fellas, I bashed my finger in and have six stitches!"), this is not smart. The minute you tell a handsome stranger at a cocktail party you were canned, a veiled, hooded look comes into his eyes. Somebody out there doesn't want you. He isn't sure he does either. Be honest with close friends but evade or lie a little publicly. Nobody knows for *sure* what happened to you.

Q. How soon do I apply for unemployment insurance?

A. Run, do not walk, to the unemployment office the day after you're severed. You may need to force yourself—stand in line with those *indigents?* Listen, Cary Grant has stood in line with them and so has Fred Astaire. You have a right to unemployment benefits— you probably contributed to them, one way or another. Start looking for work, however, without delay.

Q. What about people who want to celebrate your departure with a bash or two?

A. Watch it! When twenty-five people were fired in one swoop from Foote, Cone & Belding, the first ad agency I worked for, there was such a round of galas you'd have thought an automotive tycoon's daughter was getting married. We simply couldn't do enough for the dear departing. There were breakfast do's and luncheon do's and sticking-pins-in-effigy do's and I don't know what all. The one man who refused to have anything to do with us mourners was the first one to get another job. There could have been a connection. Let friends see you off in style, but don't let them lionize you as a loser.

LINING UP A NEW PAD

Unless you're a top executive (in which case you have to pretend you aren't really *looking* for a job and nobody could have you without putting up a stiff fight), you have to make a job of getting a job. And you *do* let people know you're eager.

First thing you do is make a snappy one-page résumé. There are many forms it can take, but the one outlined here is pretty good.

RÉSUMÉ

(Name)	Ann Tompkins	Single
(Address)	382 Thrush Street	Age 33
	Chicago, Illinois	
(Phone)	DEarborn 4-7327	

(Last Job First)

EXPERIENCE

1962–63   FIRM NAME, Address
(Job description. Make it sound good. Enhance and embroider. "Ran errands" becomes "production assistant," etc.)

1960–62   FIRM NAME, Address
(Job description)

1952–1959   FIRM NAME, Address
(Job description)

EXTRA-CURRICULAR ACTIVITIES

Business organizations you belong to, what you do in them, awards won, philanthropic work, extensive travel—any "plus" that might impress a new employer

EDUCATION

1948–1952   College, Degree

1944–1948   High School
(If you didn't go to college, list night school courses and any current studies)

SKILLS (if you're a secretary)

Typing: 65 wpm   *HOBBIES* (if you're a semi-executive)

Shorthand: 120 wpm   Skiing
Sailing
Costume Designing

Now get a large supply of 8 x 10 or 5 x 7 black and white glossy pictures (of *you,* silly!). Caption each with your name, address and phone number. A photo and résumé go immediately to everyone you know who could be helpful. Leave a set at employment agencies. If you live in a big city, don't register at more than four. You'll run yourself ragged.

Four interviews a day are enough, too. It takes time to travel through a city and executives do take two-hour lunches. When you've been on an interview that interests you, follow it up with a thank-you note the same day. Don't bother with jobs that didn't appeal. As for the interview itself, try these:

1. Study the company where you're going to apply—products, clients, stock-market position, advertising campaign, history and anything that's been written about them.

2. Wear whatever is clean, reasonably businesslike (you can dress sexily when you *got* the job) and makes you look pretty. Hats seem to say you're taking the whole thing *too* big these days, but you be the judge. Beautiful hair . . . definitely.

3. Come on strong charm-wise. A picture of the dreariest-looking wife and kiddies ever photographed gets a warm, "Your family? You must be very proud of them," from you. Glow a little. Bring up anything happy you've ever heard about the firm.

4. Do you flirt? Only by hanging on every word the gentleman (or lady) utters and not interrupting. As a matter of fact, this *is* flirting if it's a man; it's just being attentive if it's a woman. Let them do most of the talking. Your résumé will have said almost everything necessary concerning your career, so you don't need to blabber away about *that.* Most interviewers love to grow expansive about their companies. Encourage them.

5. This is another place not to be too frank about having been fired. You can say you wanted to make a change because the job had a ceiling on it, or they were cutting back and wanted you to stay in a lesser capacity, or whatever makes sense. You can say you wanted to change fields if it fits in with this interview.

6. If a man seems to be sizing you up as a woman, but lovely! A married man usually likes attractive, approving females around him whom he may or may not think of as sex objects. (You'll never get

me to say this is wrong!) He may not be planning to bag you for his collection but only trying to ascertain your basic attitude toward men. One Little Miss Priss who thinks hemlock is preferable to sin, even when it isn't *her* sin, can spoil a man's pleasure in his work. An attractive girl textile executive says, "I'd rather have a man making a good healthy pass at me any time than have him cutting my work to ribbons. One is flattering. The other is venal."

7. Make them commit themselves *first* about money. When they say, "What salary would you expect?" you say, "I'd rather you tell me approximately what you had in *mind*." The reason to hedge is that if you say right out how much you expect, the figure may be lower than what they secretly were willing to pay. If the figure is higher than you hoped, weren't you smart to make them speak up? If their salary turns out to be too low, you can always say that wouldn't be enough.

As to what to settle for, grab the job if you want it badly and can manage to live on the pay. There's usually a going rate for any job category, and you can't do that much better elsewhere. If the company needs you as much as you need them, hold out for the highest salary you can without losing the job. If they need you *more* than you need them, oh joy! You can grab for everything the situation will allow.

There's one catch to demanding and getting an outrageous salary! If it's completely out of line with what other people are getting for doing about the same work, you haven't heard the last of it! Every time the company has to cut expenses, you're the one they'll draw a bead on. If the amount is major, executives who know your salary may resent you from your first hour because your paycheck is too close to their own. Even if nobody's hostile, management asks itself regularly, is she worth it? Was she really such a bargain? (Remember that companies tend to undervalue what they own.) I wouldn't for a moment tell you not to gouge when you're in a good gouging situation. It's too often the other way around. Just don't expect people not to be trying to reverse your money coup.

One final word about job-hunting. While you're in limbo, you will be very sensitive about how your friends act. Perfectly understandable. There's no doubt your being jobless embarrasses some of them.

(*They're* embarrassed?) These spooks you have to forgive. For the most part, however, I don't think pals actively avoid you as much as they just don't think about you—one way or the other—all day, even though you *think* they do. One buck-up lunch and a call when they hear of something may be about all you can expect. (Didn't you play it the same way when you were an "in?") Job-hunting is a lonely, do-it-yourself proposition. You just have to chug chug through it like the little train going up the mountain. I'm sure you'll arrive at your destination soon. Now let's all go on to a happy place called Lunchland.

CHAPTER 7

LUNCHLAND I:
LUNCH WITH THE GIRLS

O NE OF THE LOVELY things that can happen to a girl in an
office every day is lunch. Lunchtime is *fraught* with possibilities!
There's all that lovely eating . . . *vitella con riso* in little al fresco
Italian restaurants, winter steak-sandwich lunches in chop houses
all dark and tweedy and huggy-bear, French *haute cuisine* the
marvelous week before Christmas when everything's sparkly and
champagne-y.

Aside from all the good *eating* during lunch, you could also be
asked to get married, to go merry-go-round riding, to accompany a
housing developer on a trip to see what develops or to help somebody
steal documents out of the front office. Lunchtime can also be a quiet
time of meditation . . . while you knit up messy ravels from the night
before.

Lunches with men are surely some of the best experiences of a
girl's work life. Those lunches *alone* could be the reason any woman
should want to hold a job. We'll get to the boy-girl lunches in a
moment. First let's talk about girl lunches.

My idea of an absolutely nothing way to spend a lunch hour with girl-pals from your office is in a mediocre, noisy, stale-smelling, second-rate restaurant. True, there are some great inexpensive restaurants but they probably aren't handy to your office, so you wind up in the hash-house where you still can't get out with a tab of less than four dollars, the management isn't very friendly and some of the things you get to eat wouldn't have passed muster in the galley of the *Bounty*.

On certain fiendish days you and your girl friends *need* to be soothed by icy martinis, of course, and waited on hand and foot for morale purposes. In that case go to the restaurant, but make it a *good* one while you're at it—for man-reasons as well as morale reasons. And take one—not five—dashing girl friends with you. You may find the foyer so crowded you'll get to cluck-clucking with strange dreamboats about the service. You may get seated in an alcove next to some of them or one may drop his overcoat on you in passing. *Anything* can happen, but not with five other girls.

Unless you have a definite, special lunch date or unless fellows and girls are going together and it's to be party-like, I think it's much smarter to bring your lunch from home than to go to a *dismal* eating place practically *ever*. Home-lunch can be delicious glamor-girl fodder instead of junk. You can enjoy deep-down quiet visiting with your friends and save enough money to spend Christmas in Jamaica.

Do I hear even a peep of approval? Of course not! The only things I hear probably are deep, nasty growls of contempt! It seems to me girls who ought to be bringing their lunches most bring them least. A brown paper bag is supposed to be degrading—like the scarlet "A" on Hester's sweater.

I think this is just plain silly! Many people who could afford twenty dollars a day at the poshest establishment bring their lunch regularly because the food is better and the office atmosphere more relaxing. George Cukor, the elegant director of *My Fair Lady*, totes a beautiful little picnic hamper to work every day in the back of his Rolls Royce and dines elegantly on cold pheasant, *foie gras* and Dom Perignon 1951. (At least I've been told this by people who know him.)

Rather than out and out bring lunch from home, some girls prefer making forays to the catering truck—figure it saves their image. How misguided can you be? Catering-truck stuff says *far* worse things about you than the brown paper bag fare I have in mind (which people will be hovering in your office just to watch you unpack). Besides, the chuckwagon food is often wretched eating and expensive. As one fastidious Detroit secretary (after my own heart) says, "I'd rather eat dog biscuits than any of Kiss-Me-Katerer's (her company's catering truck) mealy hamburgers, cold-cream pies or hot dogs on wet cotton buns." (She's right about the dog biscuits. They're formulated for nutrition and aren't a bit bad.)

"Kiss-Me has hard-boiled eggs," she concedes, "but they're twelve cents apiece, $1.44 a dozen, and I, for one, am not going to pay those prices, nor thirty-five cents for their twenty-five-cent cartons of cottage cheese."

No, you may not have a hamburger and malt sent up from the drugstore either! The tab is ninety-nine cents plus tip, and with the exception of the teeny-tiny piece of hamburger, you're only putting expensive junk into you. For the same money, you can *bring* a lunch from home that's good for you and delicious. You can even do it for a quarter of the money. After lunch is consumed, there are a dozen uplifting things to do during the rest of your lunch hour. (We'll list them.)

It's true some companies don't have a very good place for girls to *eat*. In one company I worked for my desk blotters used to curl up like snails from having so many tomatoes and peaches peeled on top of them. They would reach the saturation point, curl up and die! Another sufferer told me she wasn't *supposed* to eat lunch at *her* desk because of working for a wheel, but because of working for a wheel she couldn't get *away* from it. Consequently, whenever she heard foosteps during lunch, she slammed everything into the bottom desk drawer, then tried to get the mayonnaise, lettuce, meat loaf and tomato back into sandwich form after the visitors left. (Cake icing she ate right off the side of the drawer with a spoon.)

Another friend told me about sticking some cottage cheese in the back of a drawer for later consumption and then forgetting about it. Ten days later the whole department was gamy, but nobody knew what it was—only that the smell got worse when Priscilla was at her desk (presumably opening her cottage-cheese drawer to get things out). Finally, when the whispers got so loud Priscilla couldn't ignore them, she went on a thorough search and found her cottage cheese busily making penicillin.

If your company has no decent place for you to lunch, I suggest you stroll to the park in nice weather or eat in the back of an automobile. Very cozy and private.

THE CONTENTS

What should you put in your brown paper bag?

You've heard about the man who opened his lunch box every day, inspected it and said, "Ugh! Peanut butter again!" After several days of this, one of his co-workers said, "Why don't you ask your wife to fix something else if you don't like peanut butter?"

"Oh, I'm not married," he said.

There's no *excuse* for you to be stuck with peanut butter or anything else dull because *you* are in control. You don't need to be confined to sandwiches either—those dull, starchy, glumpfy things.

This may not be the time to pound you about eating healthfully, but just allow me one little pound. Lunch boxes are the land of opportunity, nutrition-wise. You can't get nutritionists to agree on *everything*. There's a school that's anti-squash and string beans, would you believe it? Too starchy! Another is death on orange juice . . . too sugary. Yes, sugary! But one thing you can't get a single nutritionist not to endorse, no matter how contrary, is *protein*. The whole living lot of them say you need protein to make your hair shinier, your brains silkier, to increase your horsepower and, oh, a lot of things that have to do with your being sexier at the office. There is just no reason why many of the fifty-one grams of protein you need daily can't be got into you F.O.B. through your brown paper bag lunch. And deliciously.

Here are two Brown Paper Bag Plans, both high-protein and satisfying. The first consists of inexpensive and homey items, some of which you've probably been packing for years. The second was outlined by my fancy cooking friend, Margo Rieman, and is the last word in Continental cuisine. It's even glamorous! Not a solitary sandwich to either plan, of course.

BROWN PAPER BAG PLAN #1

AMERICAN BEAUTY LUNCHES

These lunches will give you a body beautiful, save enough money to afford you chinchilla and are easy, easy, easy to assemble. The things you "cook" could be made Sunday or Monday night and go into your lunch all week if you like them.

For desk drawer: Sharp paring knife
                            Package plastic spoons
                            Plastic icebox dish to toss a salad in
                            Can-opener

Lunch #1: A twenty-cent container of yogurt in your favorite flavor—vanilla, strawberry, orange, prune or pineapple. A handful of almonds. One soy-date muffin. This doesn't sound like much, but it's *plenty*. And you can learn to love yogurt. Here's the muffin recipe:

GLADYS LINDBERG'S
SOY-DATE MUFFINS

1 cup soy flour (sift before measuring)	½ teaspoon salt
	¾ cup fresh whole milk
½ cup whole wheat pastry flour (sift before measuring)	½ cup honey
	2 beaten eggs
½ cup powdered skim milk	½ cup soybean oil
4 teaspoons baking powder	½ cup chopped walnuts

½ cup chopped dates approx. 14)

Sift dry ingredients. Combine honey, eggs, oil and milk in another bowl. Add dates and nuts to dry ingredients. Make a well in dry ingredients and add liquid all at once. Stir until moistened. There will be lumps. Fill greased muffin pans two-thirds full. Bake in a 400 degree oven until crust is golden brown—about 20 to 25 minutes. Makes one-and-a-half-dozen muffins. Store them in a plastic bag in the refrigerator to keep forever!

Lunch #2: A half-pint carton of cottage cheese plus a small can of dietetic fruit—raspberries, loganberries, prunes, pineapple. (Or take fresh fruit if you prefer.) One date-soy muffin (we have lots of those from the recipe). One small package of salted or toasted peanuts.

Lunch #3: Chef Salad. Take crisp from the refrigerator and put in wax paper bags any of the following: (they'll stay fairly fresh.) Lettuce—head, romaine, Bibb, watercress—tomato, cucumber, celery, green pepper or cooked vegetables. Chop and toss at lunchtime with a little salad dressing brought in a capped dixie cup. Bring a few strips of salami for spiciness if you like.

Lunch #4: Mother Brown's Rich Dessert Tuna Salad. Bring in container and eat with two Triscuits, Euphrates Wafers, Rye-Krisp or other crackers. Have three or four potato chips for wickedness, if you like. (This recipe lasts through five lunches, so I always had it every day for a week.)

MOTHER BROWN'S RICH DESSERT TUNA SALAD

1 4 oz. can white-meat tuna
2 or 3 dollops low-calorie mayonnaise (or any other kind)
2 or 3 sweet gherkin pickles cut up
1 cold hard-boiled egg, chopped
1 stalk celery, chopped in little pieces
Half an apple, chopped in little pieces (leave skin on)
Few sprigs parsley, chopped
1 raw carrot, chopped
½ small box of raisins

Mix everything up. You can leave out all these ingredients except the tuna and mayonnaise and still have the salad.

Lunch #5: Slice of Gladys Lindberg's high-powered meat loaf. Fresh fruit soy-date muffin.

GLADYS LINDBERG'S HIGH-POWERED MEAT LOAF

(This will last all week and then some.)

2 chopped onions	½ cup soy flour
1 green pepper	½ cup powdered skim milk
2 pounds ground round	3 tablespoons catsup
1 pound ground heart	1½ tablespoons salt
3 eggs	¾ cup fresh milk

Pinch of thyme and basil

(If your market doesn't have soy flour, just leave the flour out; also powdered whole milk may be used if they haven't powdered skim milk.) Sauté onions and pepper lightly in a little oil. Add the rest of ingredients and mix well. Mold into a loaf in shallow pan and bake at 350 degrees for 50 minutes.

Splurge any time of day you please with one or two pieces of Protein Energy Candy. It's delicious!

PROTEIN ENERGY CANDY

1 can Eagle Brand sweetened con-
    densed milk
3 tablespoons soybean (or other)
    oil

2 tablespoons vanilla
1¼ cups regular powdered skim
    milk
4 drops black walnut flavor

½ to 1 cup chopped walnuts

Mix together condensed milk, oil, flavorings. Add powdered milk one-half cup at a time, mixing until smooth. Mixture will get so thick it will be difficult to mix. Keep adding as much powdered milk as possible. Add walnuts. Place on platter. Chill and cut in squares.

BROWN PAPER BAG PLAN #2

LUNCHES WITH CONTINENTAL INTRIGUE

This plan's mother, Margo Rieman, says the fare may seem a little sophisticated at first, but in many countries these things would be considered merely every-day. (If Jean Seberg or Brigitte Bardot brought lunches to work, I daresay they would be things like these.) Margo says also, "If your stomach lurches at the smell of cheap, greasy food and your soul rebels at the cost of it, I believe these menus will please you." I believe they'll *fracture* you and have everybody meowing around your lunch box like jealous cats at lunchtime.

For desk drawer: Knife, fork, spoon
                  Can-opener
                  Small salt and pepper shakers
                  Box of paper napkins
                  A small plate
                  A cup

For the lunch cupboard at home:
                  2 small thermos bottles
                  2 small plastic containers with lids

FOOD

(Cans or jars of the following:)

Shrimp
Sardines
Kippered snacks
Pimentos
Anchovies
Caponata (eggplant and vegetable
    mixture)

Anchovy paste
Garbanzo beans
Soups
Olives
Red caviar
Smoked salmon
Regular salmon

Marinated artichoke hearts

CRACKERS

Rye-Krisp
Euphrates Wafers
Rye wafers
Melba toast

Triscuits
Soda Crackers (search for the long narrow ones called Saratoga Flakes)

To buy when needed:

CHEESES AND BREADS

Camembert
Liederkranz
Bleu
Monterey Jack
Sharp American cheddar
Black Diamond cheddar (if you can find it)
Cream cheese

Cottage cheese with chives
Romano
Black pumpernickel—two kinds:
   fat round loaf
   thin heavy squares
Thin sliced rye
Sour Dough French

At the use-rate of one or two slices a day, these breads *could* become stale. What you do is find a heavy plastic zippered bag, big enough to hold at least two loaves. After the bread is opened, wrap the loaf in Saran Wrap, zip it into the bag and keep it in the refrigerator. It'll stay fresh. If you have a freezer—even better! Wrap your daily supply individually, take out as needed—it will be thawed by lunchtime, and never stale.

Since the cheeses could spoil too, wrap them very carefully in Saran Wrap to exclude all air, then fit them in plastic containers . . . the kind ice cream comes in. Each will hold two or three pieces of cheese because you don't buy large hunks of any one cheese at a time. You do want to have several kinds of cheese on hand at once.

If you want cheese to keep even longer, wrap it up in a clean cloth wrung out in vinegar and store it in the refrigerator. Re-dunk the cloth every so often.

Also to buy as needed:

Fresh fruit and vegetables, depending on what's in season and what's cheap.

Added starter for your lunches (in the best Continental tradition):

Buy one gallon of light red wine, one gallon of dry white wine. "Get good honest wines," Margo says. (I guess after you've tasted a few you get to know which the sneaky, dishonest ones are.) Decant these as needed. (That means pour them from the big original bottle into a smaller icebox bottle.)

Before you go to bed, pop into the refrigerator one thermos, lid off, to chill. In the morning it will be filled with whichever wine you think will be best with the lunch you've chosen. You also dope out the menu for the next day.

The wine situation:

You may work in an office where consumption of an alcoholic beverage is strictly forbidden, at least on the premises. (No telling how many Manhattans and Gibsons are brought into the office in *people* containers after lunch.) Rather than make any shock waves whatever by pouring wine from your thermos into a long-stemmed Baccarat glass, pour it instead into a china cup. This can serve as your coffee mug during the rest of the day.

Should any of your co-workers discover your fine, boozy secret and giggle it up, smile sweetly and say, "I like a glass of wine with my lunch. It is a *very* civilized custom."

A younger girl might explain, "We've always had wine with meals at home. Daddy knew how good for us it is."

Now let's mix and match some of your supplies into delectable little lunches:

Continental Lunch #1: A small can of shrimp, opened and drained at the office, a small plastic cup of cocktail sauce for dunking, a hard-boiled egg, half an avocado, a couple of Saratoga Flakes for crunch, a piece of bleu cheese to put on the crackers and white wine to drink. In effect, you're getting the ingredients of a very expensive shrimp salad at about one-tenth of what you'd pay for it in a restaurant and without all the fattening dressing that usually goes with it.

COCKTAIL SAUCE FOR SHRIMP

1 cup mayonnaise	2 tablespoons sour cream
1 dash tabasco	1 dash salt
¼ cup chili sauce	1 tablespoon gin

(The gin does something very special!)

Lunch #2: A can of Caponata (eggplant and vegetable mixture. Very tasty. Look for this in the Italian Foods section of your market.). A slice or two of thin, heavy black bread to spread it on, a goodly hunk of bland but robust Monterey Jack cheese, half a tomato sliced, sprinkled with basil leaves and put in a little plastic container. Fill the thermos with red wine. A pear or apple could follow if you really want to *stuff*.

Lunch #3: Black bread, a can of pimentos cut into sections and fitted into squares of the bread, topped with anchovies—two to a piece—and some of the anchovy oil drizzled on the bread as well. Add a container of marinated garbanzos (drain garbanzos from the tin, soak overnight in a dressing of 4 tablespoons olive oil, 1 tablespoon vinegar, salt, pepper,

1 clove crushed garlic, 1 cup minced parsley) and a piece of Liederkranz cheese spread on slices of an apple. Red wine again with this.

Lunch #4: The hors d'oeuvres binge. Take a supply of Melba toast and Triscuit, a block of cream cheese, a jar of red caviar, a tube of anchovy paste, a glass jar of marinated artichokes, a few slices of salami, some celery sticks, a little container of mixed olives. The cream cheese goes on the crackers, then either a dot of anchovy paste or a spoon of red caviar on top . . . the other things arranged nicely around the rest of the plate. This day, add two or three kinds of cheese to the brown bag and a pear. The wine will be white.

Lunch #5: Make vichyssoise from a can of frozen potato soup dumped into the blender with a can of milk added slowly as it runs. Throw in a handful of green onion tops, chopped, for extra flavor. Chill overnight. Pop this into a cold thermos. The rest of lunch might be a goodly piece of cold chicken carefully hidden away from last night's dinner (you *do* eat a sturdy little dinner, don't you?) and a triangle of Camembert to spread on a slice of sour dough French bread or Triscuit. The wine would be white.

Lunch #6: Minestrone is a wonderful soup for a cold day. Heat it (from a can) in a saucepan before you leave home. Put a big helping of freshly grated Romano cheese in the bottom of the thermos, pour the soup on top. The two will blend during the morning's wait. Mix half a can of tuna with a *little* mayonnaise, some chopped celery and green pepper and put it into a container to spread at lunch on sour dough bread. Eat in alternate bites with half a tomato. "Dessert" would be grapes and sharp cheddar cheese. The wine is red.

Financing

Continental brown-bagging is not the least expensive way to dine although it is much cheaper than restauranting. To acquire your basic shelf of goodies you could earmark ten dollars a week (the price of only three lunches out) and eat all your lunches *in* during the two or three weeks it takes to build up a cupboard variety. Or, if you prefer, build gradually. Every time you market, buy one or two tins of delicacies to stash away. Acquire the breads and cheeses last. When you're all stocked up, begin the adventure. There's no end to combinations!

For a change of pace, with any brown paper bag plan at all, you could also do trade-sies. Bring your little luncheon to the office— anything that's edible—and trade lunches with a co-worker. This introduces an element of surprise! The watch-phrase here is "do unto others." No palming off five-day-old fillet of sole on an innocent or you'll never get another reciprocal-trade lunch partner.

MORPHEUS, ANYONE?

After lunch is over, one of the nicest things in the world to do is nap. As a matter of fact, I don't see how any girl with a full date schedule can hope to be as perky on the job as she should be unless she naps occasionally. You may have to improvise a napping place. I managed to snooze like a tabby cat one whole year by unrolling a little strip of red carpet (this was no ordinary body, it was *mine*) out from under my desk and curling up on it. The floor was otherwise bare. I always preferred my own floor to "sleeping around" on borrowed couches. You never know when an owner is going to return unexpectedly and drive you out like a dumb animal. If you nap on the floor, you must remember to lock the door, and no fooling. Otherwise, you can get your head bashed in. Also it gives cousins from Stillwater and prospective clients touring the office a terrible start to open a door and discover a flaked-out girl on the floor.

Here's how to pop off to sleep under the most adverse conditions —no rug, no quiet, and precious little time. It's a yoga exercise I lifted from Desmond Dunne's *Yoga for Everyone* (A London Four Square Book).

1. Lie flat on your back with weight distributed evenly. No lumping everything to one side. Having assumed this position, *don't move*. Absolute stillness is the crux of the whole routine. When you first start, you think you'll go mad not being able to twitch around, but it's the enforced stillness that makes you finally crumple and relax.

2. Now here's the yoga. Stretch an arm, leg, foot or even your neck very hard. Make the muscles contract and study what is happening. "You'll be surprised how other muscles start contracting in sympathy" (quoting Dunne). "If you clench your fist strongly, you'll feel contractions all the way up your arm and down your shoulders and back." Oh, boy! Hold the stretch while you trace these sensations in detail, then let go. That's the end of step one.

3. Step two. Stretch hard again, but this time do it in slow motion. Build the stretch up slowly and "observe" everything going on in your body because of it. (What's going on is tension.) Again, hold the stretch, then let go in slow motion. Let go slowly, slowly, carrying the "let-go" process beyond the point where you are conscious of any physical sensation whatsoever. Continue "letting go" until you reach the stage where you are no longer trying to relax but have completely lost all feeling of alertness. (This is why it's best not to have your head near an unlocked door.)

When you start, Mr. Dunne advises you to concentrate on relaxing one part of the body at a time. Later, you begin to "let go" more generally until you stop thinking of specific areas. It's probably best to begin with the head, then pass down the body relaxing groups of muscles as you find them, easing the arms from the shoulders, the legs from the hips, and so on. When you've practically blanked out all tension and alertness right down to the toes, go back up to the eyebrows, eyelids and eyeballs and start over. Mr. Dunne thinks it's more restful if you don't pop off to sleep, but I never can stay awake with this routine.

Here are two other sleep inducers . . . on the floor or in bed when you get to one. To get your mind to stop racing, rhyme. Start with a base word like "inch." Then go down the alphabet and see how many words you can make—bench, cinch, clinch, dench (nothing—can't use it), drench, finch, flinch, French, gench (nothing), etc., etc. The base word that makes the most words wins and gets a prize!

The second go-to-sleep trick is to take a letter of the alphabet—say "K." Then you go down the alphabet starting with "A" and find a name that fits each set of initials. "AK" is Anna Karenina, "BK" is Ben Kalmenson of Warner Brothers (you can use personal friends, famous names, or fictional characters). "C" is Christine Keeler, "D" is Danny Kaye, and so on. Sleep tight!

OTHER POSSIBILITIES

If you don't feel like sleeping, here are some things to do after you eat lunch.

Visit a museum. Study a particular subject that interests you—the American buffalo, Egyptology, other museum prowlers.

Stake out a pottery plant that sells seconds and replenish your china. It's very hard to tell seconds (at a fraction the cost) from firsts.

Scour the thrift shops for a dining room table to saw the legs off of and make into a coffee table, or a chest to refinish, or a jet brooch for $2.75.

Play at the zoo. Take some lunch for the monkeys.

Play miniature golf.

Drink up knowledge at the public library.

Take a book to the park and park under a tree.

Duck-watch by a pond.

Play tennis.

Snoop at the second-hand or first-hand bookstore.

Stroll in a foreign part of town.

Go to a gymnasium.

Shop.

Find a carnival and ride the merry-go-round.

Swim in a friend's pool.

Be an art lover at a gallery.

Go to the movies. Take your lunch with you.

I can certainly recommend the movies. The running time of some is less than two hours. When the two girl copywriters and I were in the fungus-y green advertising office, we saw *Ruby Gentry* and *All About Eve* practically one entire day by taking turns calling in to say we'd be downstairs to deliver our respective batches of copy any minute. Nobody was going to come up to fungus-ville to check on us, and it never occurred to anyone we were actually calling from the R.K.O. Pantages next door.

You may think I assume you don't like your work when I recommend far-fetched, far-away things to do on your lunch hour. Not at all. I hope you *love* your work, and I assume that sometimes you don't do anything at lunch *but* work right straight through. Other days, however, I don't see why you can't scat for a change of pace.

CHAPTER 8

LUNCHLAND II: BOYS
AND GIRLS TOGETHER

NATURALLY nobody works in an office just to have Continental lunches with the girls, snooze it up on the office floor occasionally or sneak off to foreign films. What about the lunches girls have with boys?

They're the greatest! Think about it. Lunching with men is a chance to have dates in the *daytime* on the pretext of business . . . and to have a whack at men who might not think of asking you—or be *able* to ask you—to dinner. Looking at it realistically, business lunch dates with men are sex at high noon!

Lunch-date men range from just plain office pals (with whom you pay your own check) to clients and prospects with whom you lean forward and they lean back or you lean back and they lean forward (depending on who's selling and who's buying), to chaps with whom love is building, boiling or running out.

These are the plain and fancy things business lunch dates with men have going for them.

1. A man who might not have the nerve to ask you to dinner—or be certain he wanted to spend an entire evening with you—will check you out at lunch. So let him. You'll very likely make it to the next plateau.

2. One little girl can have lunch with *six* big men and keep them all to herself for two full hours. Just try taking that many to a cocktail party—if you could find them. They'd be sniped at and made off with within seconds.

3. A married girl can bewitch-away at a handsome gentleman over eggs benedict and Rob Roys without wagging a single tongue.

4. A married man who isn't allowed out after *dark* can go where the Bunnies are, where the Gaslight girls flicker and bring his own girl along for added zest.

5. Although you may already be a man's right hand and helper superior, you can get closer to him on a personal level at lunch (and cement your job, the friendship or whatever you want to cement). I remember fondly the day I outfitted my boss in woolies and a tent for a camping expedition (with the fellows, not with me). A friend of mine had the pleasure of outfitting *her* boss and his car for the Mexican road races and then going to Tijuana to watch them perform.

6. A girl may be taken to a posh and exciting restaurant she never gets to see on an evening date.

7. Regardless of the positions you and your companion occupy back at the office, at lunch a girl is a sexy equal. Democracy fairly gleams.

8. A boys-and-girls-together camaraderie, not often experienced after a girl leaves college, can prevail at lunch. At the Hollywood ad agency where I worked, everybody would pile out to Scandia on the Sunset Strip to celebrate after we'd sold a campaign to a client. At other lunches after we *didn't* sell anything we remarshaled our strength with Margaritas and chocolate cake at the Cock 'n' Bull. (Who needs an entrée when you're depressed?) One day the Swinging Faction of our agency and the S.F. of another agency took over the dining room, the bar, the Mariachi singers, the waiters and the hat-check girl in a restaurant in Olvera Street (Los Angeles' old Spanish section) and danced and sang and drank beer for five

hours. You can get away with that if you've put in several nineteen-hour days—which this group had—and are due for some unwinding.

The boys-and-girls lunch needn't have a cast of thousands. Two girl friends of mine kidnaped the head of their company one day, took him to the Beverly Hills Hotel, had a drink in the Polo Lounge and discussed whisking him upstairs to a room. "Girls, now girls, I won't go through with this," he said, but he didn't run away. The girls never planned to go through with it; they were simply flattering a sweet older man.

Perhaps you're going to say these things couldn't possibly go on in your office. Well they go on in *some* offices which make a profit and have low turnover and maybe your firm ought to shape *up!*

9. Unlike a night date, at lunch there's none of that embarrassment of here you are, here I am, you Tarzan, me Jane, what are we going to do about it? At lunch you have friendly, comfortable business things to discuss . . . first.

10. Lunch can be overpoweringly sexy. A date on the town will never have that high-tension current of excitement that zings through the business lunch between an attractive man and a responsive woman. On a date, body contact is all part of the game and you can talk about anything—so, of course, that takes some of the fun out of it. (When is anything ever as much fun when you're free to have it or do it?) At a business lunch any personal talk becomes precious out of all proportion to its content and the random body contacts are like being hit with a cow-prodder. Hands brush when cigarettes are lit, eyes meet over the rims of cocktail glasses, knees touch but are quickly withdrawn. It's all exciting . . . and puzzling. Was it an accident? Was it an invitation? Did he or didn't he do it on purpose?

MAKING IT HAPPEN

Lunch dates with men are not so formally arranged as night dates, so it's easier to make them happen. You can have almost as much to say about them as *he* does, which makes it nice.

While you're working on a project together, what could be more natural—and sensible—than to continue the discussion through lunch? It may be you who says, "Shall we go have a sandwich and come back in thirty minutes?" Once out of the building, you may be able to "expand" the sandwich to a cozy-bar lunch.

Even without the excuse of a shared work project, if you're on his level or close to it, there's nothing unfeminine about strolling by a man's office close to noon and saying, "Do you have a lunch date?" It won't even seem as though you'd picked *him*, but only that you're rounding up someone to have lunch with. *Everybody* does it. (Never mind that you've checked his calendar and found this was the only day with nothing marked.) If it turns out to be the time he'd saved to play handball and have a steam bath, he'll at least remember you asked him and next time *he* may ask *you*.

Remember, all this happens to girls who work hard enough to be a man's near-equal. If you're not, he may make you walk *back* from your lunch date separately.

Men clients are a cinch to cinch for lunch. Call them up and ask them. Publicity girls must plant items with columnists. Women who sell may invite prospects. Girls who research must get material. Often your company will pay for the lunch. If they won't, you can pretend to your guest that they did and pay yourself. The investment may be worth it.

If the man you want to lunch with isn't your client or legitimate "invitee" but is somebody your company does business with, you can still ask. One girl who worked for a New York publishing firm called up an attractive producer when she was in Hollywood on vacation and said she had some literary properties she thought he might be interested in. Lily wasn't actually in charge of selling movie rights, but she had seen her boss handle that sort of thing dozens of times. The introductory lunch was on her. All the other lunches—including some in the evening—were on him.

What if you aren't a junior executivess or an "equal" but still like to lunch with men? It's entirely possible you'll be asked anyway if it's a folksy company. Some firms, however, discourage "fraternization." You may have to be bolder—in a non-detectable ladylike way. One secretary I know uses this technique. She has her eye on a particular man and plops down in the reception room of their company just before he comes by to go to lunch. When he arrives at the elevator, she puts down the *New Yorker* she's been reading as though she'd just finished the article and saunters to the elevator. As they ride down together, Mary says, "Do you know any good new place to eat around here? I'm so bored with Maury's and the Spanish Omelette." He says, practically on cue, "Well, there's Mama's Castle—I thought I might run over there. Do you want to come?" Bull's-eye!

A man doesn't always make the right reply, of course. He may already have a date. He may actually not *want* to have lunch with you. The thing is, you have to make it possible for him to ask you. You mustn't scurry off like the white mouse or try to go through the floor when you're in the presence of a lunch "possible." You must act as though it would be quite all right with *you* if he asked you . . . give off "expectancy" rather than fright waves. A touch of insouciance (go look that up!) in your attitude when you're leaving the building with an attractive man will help. Hardly *anybody* likes to eat alone.

THANKS, WE'RE STAYING IN

One secretary I know who works in an office which doesn't allow girls to lunch with men beat the system this way. She always remained free to join her boss for his stay-in-the-office luncheons whenever his work load was too heavy to go out. First, she would offer to get something sent in for him. He always suggested she get a sandwich for herself, too, if she was staying. Gradually she moved into his office to have her hamburger with *him*. All that camaraderie finally allowed for the transition to bootleg *à deux* lunch-dating out of the office.

If you know your boss, or another deserving man in the office, well enough and know ahead of time he's going to be staying in, you might bring him a tempting little luncheon from home. (Aha! I've got you cooking again!) The luncheon I have in mind doesn't contain any Mother Brown's tuna salad or wheat-germ fortified meat loaf, however. It could run into a little money also, but we'll assume he is a very deserving—and attractive—man. Here's the menu:

Forget about the brown paper bag and acquire instead a portable styrene-foam refrigerator ($1.39 to $1.98 at a drug or department store).

Inside it, place the following from your kitchen cupboards:

Tray of ice cubes (put in tray and all)

Bottle of cold champagne

Two tall stemmed glasses (as elegant as possible)

Two paper plates

Two forks, one knife to spread with, and these goodies:

1. Liver *pâté*. (This comes in a little tin and could be transferred to a pretty container.)
2. A cube of cheese—Castello, Liederkranz, Roquefort.
3. Crackers to spread the *pâté* and cheese on.
4. Celery Victor (in a long icebox dish). Recipe: Boil celery hearts in consomme, drain and marinate in French dressing. Add salt, pepper, capers and pimento strips.
5. Jar of Babcock peaches. Get Babcock if at all possible for this special lunch. They're the Cadillac of the peach world.
6. A halved papaya and lime wedge or other status fruit, such as mango, cherimoya or figs. Wrap in Saran.
7. Two candy bars to be eaten around four o'clock.

Is there such a smart popular girl in the whole world of working girls or any other world as you?

OTHER MANEUVERS

Conference Call. Perhaps you are the fortunate only-girl at a business conference. If you're an "equal" and they break for lunch, naturally the men will take you with them. If you are the secretary taking notes when the lunch break comes, don't give up the ship, however. If you look nice and don't scuttle off too quickly, they may ask you to come along. Use your antennae. As a baby stenographer among men much older and stodgier, you probably wouldn't want to go and probably wouldn't have a good time if you went. In your twenties, however, you're likely to be poised enough to handle this group even if you're the only girl. Some of the loudest, most super-charged meeting-attenders in the world become absolute kittens when a girl is brought along to lunch. They even have the items on the menu read aloud in order to avoid putting on their spectacles.

Once at the luncheon I'd plan just to be pretty and sweet and happy and content but not scintillating. To scintillate isn't necessary. They'd rather have you be a girl than try to come on like Jacques Barzun.

Getting Proselytized. If anyone should call you from another company to ask if you're interested in a job, Lunchland is a wonderful place to talk things over. The situation is sexy in a symbolic way. They want you. They're sounding out your responsiveness to their desires. You're cool—like a girl listening to any other proposition—and you may be just a bit hard to get. This pursuing is almost sure to happen to a good girl who does her office homework regardless of whether she's pretty.

Chowder and Marching. Perhaps you'll be the buzz-bomb who gets a choice, hand-picked (don't ask the whole office, for heaven's sake) group started visiting a different foreign or unique restaurant once a month. Keep the plans under-organized and relaxed. No desirable man wants to be mixed up with a Brownie troop movement. Just say casually the day before to the lucky man for whom you've secretly dreamed up the whole excursion, "Don't forget, Fred, tomorrow we're all going to Ah Fong West." Fred will either go or he won't go. Tying threads around his fingers or locking him up won't help unless he's really interested. No matter what, you get "A" for trying.

Private Club. Three girls and a man I know have formed their own little luncheon society. One Monday a month, the girls take turns entertaining the luncheon group at home. (This is in New York where it's easy to cab about.) Gary, who is the pet, is married and isn't required to entertain. He usually brings the booze. Other men have tried to get into the society, but old Gary says he'll resign if membership is extended and they humor him. I've tapped one of the four members for her chowder and marching menu. Here it is:

Nettie's Heavenly Shrimp and
Crabmeat Casserole
Mixed Green Salad   Brown and Serve Rolls
with Butter
Frosty Lemon Pie
Coffee
Iced Champagne

Prepare the casserole the night before and pop it in the oven for half an hour the minute you and the group arrive. The lemon pie is made the night before also, and the greens are tossed and chilling in a cellophane bag waiting for dressing. Make the coffee and brown the rolls. Lunch is on! If you serve only champagne as a beverage, which is heavenly, you'll need at least half a bottle per person. Otherwise, serve regular cocktails and have champagne with dessert.

NETTIE'S HEAVENLY SHRIMP AND CRABMEAT CASSEROLE

3 cups cooked shrimp
1 can crab meat
2 cups diced celery—dollop of butter

Topping
½ cup grated mild cheese
½ cup corn flakes
dab of melted butter
1 teaspoon minced onion
½ teaspoon salt
1 teaspoon lemon juice
1 cup diced almonds
1 cup mayonnaise

Sauté the celery and onion in the dollop of butter in a frying pan. Cut each shrimp in half. Drain and squeeze the crabmeat well. Add these plus salt, lemon juice, almonds, and mayonnaise to skillet (fire turned off). Then put them all in a buttered casserole. Sprinkle the cheese and cornflakes, mixed with the melted buttter on top. Hide away, covered, in refrigerator to be cooked next noon. At lunchtime, pop it into a 450 degree oven for half an hour. Should be bubbling when served.

FROSTY LEMON PIE

3 egg yolks
⅛ teaspoon salt
½ cup sugar
¼ cup fresh lemon juice

½ teaspoon grated lemon rind
3 egg whites
1 cup cream, whipped
¾ cup crushed vanilla wafers

Beat yolks, salt and sugar in top of double boiler. Stir in lemon juice and grated rind; cook over hot water until mixture thickens and coats spoon. Remove from fire and chill. Beat egg whites until stiff and fold in whipped cream and cooked mixture. Line icebox tray with crushed wafers and pour mixture in. Top with remaining crumbs and freeze until firm. Serve in finger-length slices.

Saturday Maneuver. Having to come to the office to work on Saturday can have its rewards. When everybody's in pants and sports shirts, adventure-luncheons are easily organized. Some of the best I remember were in a small sukiyaki cubbyhole on the east side of Los Angeles. Company presidents and lesser lights bought armloads of roses from the flower vendors and gave them to the girls. There was much talk of getting on a plane and going right over to Waikiki. Something tells me the atmosphere would have been different on Serious Monday. Perhaps there wouldn't have been any luncheon.

That Certain Auto. One girl I know—in fact I know her rather well—found that having a jazzy new sports car got her more lunch dates than she knew what to do with. She would no sooner get shifted down four gears and bring Bismarck II (her spanking new 190 SL) to a complete halt on the company parking lot than swarms of young men would come over and suggest a lunchtime spin. Sometimes they would suggest the spin without Bismarck's mistress, but she always said no, wherever Bismarck went she went too, and that settled the matter.

I wasn't the only one who made hay with horsepower. A super-executive visiting his Los Angeles office suggested to one of the girls that he and she drive out to Disneyland one lunch hour. He wasn't really asking favors, but bestowing an honor. Any girl in the office would have swooned at the chance. Janice explained that Disneyland was a good twenty-four miles out the Santa Ana Freeway and most people spent at least a day there. "Oh . . . well, then," he said, "how about lunch anyway?" They lunched and went to Disneyland the following weekend. He confessed after many subsequent dates that he'd picked the girl with the most intriguing car—a glamorous Sting Ray—and had no idea things would turn out so romantically.

No, of course you don't drive Benzes and Sting Rays the instant you're out of business college, but they're another of the lovely sexy fringe benefits that can accrue to a girl who grinds away at her job.

ACROSS THE TABLE

Once you're seated side by side or across from him and sipping your first *apéritif,* what can help you enchant this dreamboat?

If he's an abstainer, you don't need necessarily not to have a drink. Do what pleases you. If he's a drinker and you're not, you can at least have sherry. Unless someone is an alcoholic and really mustn't drink, I can't imagine not toying with a glass of beer to put a companion at ease.

How do you look? If it's a sudden date, obviously you didn't wear your prettiest dress to work. (But then you always look chic, no?) The most exquisite make-up job you can manage—if you've had even twenty minutes warning—can help. We've already mentioned the transformation that a face can undergo.

What do you talk about? There's a master plan on flirting and charming a little later in the book, but let's talk for a moment about charm at lunch.

The man comes to your lunch date in a certain mood. Specific things have happened to him that morning. He made a sale, he's floating. They canceled the order, he's sinking. His boss ate him out, he's suicidal. They picked up his option—he's manic! He *never* comes to you just no way at all even if he only comes with his mouth full of novocaine straight from the dentist.

My friend Ruth, who didn't invent the system but is awfully good at it, says you must listen with all your pores open during those first few minutes to see if you can glean what shape he's in. He may not actually tell you what's happened to him the first instant, but you must be prepared to go along with his *mood.* Any wife can detect a husband-mood practically from the way he opens the door. She learns not to be happy if he's miserable and to break out the champagne if he closed a deal even if she's just picked herself up from falling down a flight of stairs.

If, after you sit around with your pores open, he refuses to tell you anything at *all* about his mood or himself, then you proceed with conversation as usual. Perhaps he'll open up later.

Ruth says, "Most girls are so desperate to please, so anxious to show how vivacious and smart and sexy they are, they press their own mood on top of a man like a flat iron and practically send him screaming from the luncheon."

If he *has* turned his mood on like a good boy—which may be simply that he needs you to talk and amuse him because he's feeling dumb and silent—he will gradually get his mood normalized and then you can turn on *your* mood. It's no fun having things completely one-sided, but *start* with him.

OTHER LUNCHLAND GAMBITS

A man may have brought you to lunch to pump—so let him pump away! I hope you have something interesting to tell him! Some of the most fascinating women in the world are the good gossips. . . not the mean, vicious ones, but well-informed ladies who serve up all the fascinating bits of news deliciously on toast.

You'll know what information you can share, of course, and you must be very careful. Men are often bigger blabbermouths than girls. You may find the state secret you confided only to *him* ricocheting off the walls of the men's room—and this could wind up hitting you where your *job* lives. One man I know was on his way *out* the day after he labeled the new head of his company "Daddy Warbucks" (whom he most certainly did resemble). A girl I know got into a lot of trouble by referring to *her* boss as "Baby Dumpling" (which he certainly was) and was saved only by Baby's being called back into the service the next month.

A man in trouble may ask you at lunchtime for interpretations and emanations. One executive I know started lunch-dating the boss's secretary because she was the pipeline to Little Caesar's plans and moods. He married the girl later—some people think to keep her away from other would-be snoopers, but I imagine he also loved her.

You may be asked for your ideas and creative thoughts over lunch. Come up with some even if they're terrible. Your no-carat suggestions will at least encourage your interrogator to think his own stuff isn't so bad.

Never underestimate what a smart secretary or stenographer can contribute in the way of ideas, however. One girl I know lunch-dated a How-to-Succeed-in-Business type who became so absolutely addicted to her brainstorms he married her. This would be a romantic, happy ending, except that Scheherazade is now stuck out in Scarsdale. She still feeds her boy ideas with which to wow his colleagues at work the next day, but there are no lovely men for a girl to have lunch with in *Scarsdale!*

Does anybody ever do anything really romantic at lunch? Well, yes, they've been *known* to. In New York there's a lovely medieval-castle kind of restaurant with a darling little moat and drawbridge, Elizabethan madrigals piped into every room and the whole place black as an eclipse in a basement. When your eyes get accustomed to the gloom in the main room, you notice a little alcove room in which couples are draped over each other like tents. They may not be hungry—I imagine they all have had sandwiches at their desks or something—but they do seem *happy*. So is the wine steward —he does a wild luncheon business.

That's just one example of something romantic people do at lunch. There are others. I might have been inclined to let you use your imagination about them if some rather special Lunchland material hadn't fallen into my hands. Next chapter please.

CHAPTER 9

LUNCHLAND III: THE MATINEE (A VERY SPECIAL REPORT)

W HEN IT WAS DECIDED ages ago that I would write this book, my husband, David Brown; my publisher, Bernard Geis; Mr. Geis's beautiful young executive, Letty Cottin, and I were discussing what would go in the book. Miss Cottin said she knew of some subject matter that really ought to be included. "What?" I asked without enthusiasm. If I hadn't thought of it myself, I figured it couldn't be any good.

"A friend of mine," Letty said, "is having an affair with a man in her office at lunchtime. They never see each other *any other time,* but they're faithful and it's been going on like that for two years."

Mr. Geis, David and I said the following things at the same time. Mr. Geis: "Good God, I hope it isn't this office!" David: "You don't *find* women like that anymore." Helen: "Letty, you're clean out of your mind. Nobody has an affair only at lunchtime."

"Only at lunchtime," Miss Cottin said firmly.

As things turned out, Letty was able to put me in touch with the young lady. I didn't get to meet her in person—she lives in another city—but she was persuaded to write a little essay on the subject of The Matinee. I'm convinced it's based on her true experience, and I'm putting down just what she wrote, in her very own words.

THE MATINEE:
TWELVE TO TWO-THIRTY

This institution of the two-hour "little affair" [writes my informant] is as old as anyone can remember and probably has as many names as there are languages. In the South it's called a "nooner." Where the two hours fall in the day is entirely dependent on the national mores of the people involved. "The Matinee" encompasses the hours from noon or thereabouts to two-thirty on the American clock, but in Rio it becomes the hours from five to seven, when ladies "visit their dressmakers," and the time in Paris when people meet for the *apéritif*. In both of these places, this type of affair, then, is rightfully called *cinq à sept*. In America, where working hours are generally regimented from nine to five and where a great number of women work, the lunch hour seems most convenient for the small affair.

There are two conditions which usually must exist in a Matinee relationship: First, one of you is married; second, your time together is entirely restricted to lunch hours. If you were both single, there would be no point in seeing each other only at this particular time.

A married women participating in a Matinee must take greater precautions than a single woman. Her apartment or house is not, as in the case of the single girl, hers alone. Hotel rooms can be both risky and unpleasant. Accidental pregnancy can cause greater disorder in her life. If Mrs. X plans a Matinee with Mr. Y in an apartment borrowed from Miss K, Miss K will probably have to be let in on the nature of the appointment. Very risky.

Why become involved in a Matinee relationship? Such a man is generally marvelous for your ego. He will tell you that you are glamorous, beautiful, understanding and terribly accomplished and convince you this is so. After all, he *believes* it with all his heart, even though he has no intention of getting a divorce to marry you.

Another advantage. If you have just ended *the* love affair, The

Matinee can be a healthy relaxer for physical frustrations. You can do yourself much greater harm by becoming involved too soon in another heartbreaking grand romance out of loneliness and physical need. And, of course, your ego is always in need of repair at the end of that big affair.

Since it is impossible for your married lover to make demands on you, you can have this relationship on your own terms. You can do the inviting when you feel "in need," since the arena is usually your apartment. Or he can suggest the dates if you prefer. And very important—you can start the arrangement or stop it when you want to.

The Matinee is not for deep emotional involvements. When you really fall in love, one hour or even ten hours a week will not be enough, especially when they fall in the middle of the day! The normal demands which people in love make on each other have no room in this relationship and will, if made, do nothing but ruin it and make whoever is being demanded of feel guilty. You and your Matinee partner may be very good friends and really enjoy sex together, but if you're looking for someone to fall in love with, you'd better give up The Matinee and begin thinking about a more expensive ticket for evening performances as well.

One thing this relationship insures is that you always see the nicest side of your partner. Don't allow this to affect other relationships, however, by using this man as a standard. You see only a part of the whole person.

What kind of man is right?

The ideal partner for this *petite affaire* is someone you know and like very much; someone you find physically attractive; and someone, above all, who is *happily married*. There is nothing worse than spending what you hoped would be a liberating two hours in the middle of the day listening to a complaining comparison of the "wonderful, sexy you" with his absolutely inept, sad-looking wife. If your partner had the lack of perception to choose such a woman in the first place, you begin to wonder if he is really up to your standards of taste. Is he, after all, the correct choice for your lunchtime liaison?

It is possible to have a "spiritual" Matinee relationship with a man who admires you greatly but doesn't really want an affair. With this man you are "the girl." You may find yourself hunting antiques, going to museums, ferreting out quaint restaurants on your lunch hour. What he would like to do with you—and doubtless does in his fantasies—is all beside the point. He doesn't do anything in reality, and you have a fine time on the expeditions while you give your admirer the pleasure of your company.

Where does the assignation take place? With little exception, in your apartment, and your apartment must be within twenty minutes' traveling distance at the most or you'll be traveling most of the time. Using your apartment as headquarters means a certain amount of work for you, but the privacy is worth it.

Possibly you have a job which allows you only an hour for lunch. This schedule makes The Matinee pretty difficult unless you live next door to the office. You might, if you have a nice boss and resort to this ruse infrequently enough, develop a chronic intestinal ailment and have to visit your doctor. Generally, bosses can be pretty nice about doctor's appointments.

STANDARD OPERATIONAL PROCEDURE

Now for the basic ground rules for The Matinee:

1. You must never be seen together outside of your office. This means you cannot leave your office *or* your apartment together.

2. You must be very careful not to make evident the fact that you were home during your lunch hour. For example, never wear another dress back to the office no matter how tempting it is to feel crisp and fresh for the afternoon or for a date later on.

3. Be careful of tell-tale signs. You must take great pains to check that he has no lipstick traces. And no shower traces, like damp locks of hair.

4. If you travel by cab, be sure no one hears the address you give the driver. Others from your office may be leaving the building for *their* Matinee appointments. Even though clandestine naughtiness, like misery, loves company, there's no reason to make your Matinee a public affair.

5. Never wear perfume. It could turn into a mess if his wife de-

tected a strange, erotic aroma wafting from behind the ears of her beloved that evening.

6. Never spend a lot of time around him if he works in your office. This is a cardinal rule which many gauche Matinee-ers break.

7. *Don't tell anyone.* You have a responsibility to guard his reputation. Whether or not he works in the same office, you must be very careful not to confide in the girl at the next desk or your best friend. After all, he *is* married.

8. If he works in your own establishment, be careful to be businesslike with him both in the office and on the phone. Don't be *too* distant, however. Those clucking biddies who are a part of every office will be the first ones to spot phony-coolness.

Never, never call your friend at home. If he hasn't come in on a day when you've decided to meet, or if you can't make the appointment yourself, you still must not enter his private life. Even if it means you will leave him waiting on a street corner or at the door of your empty apartment, don't call! Don't leave any notes for him on that door either. Your mother may choose just that afternoon to drop by!

THE PARTY'S OVER

How does it all end?

The biggest and best reason to stop a midday affair is to keep yourself or your friend from suffering. As soon as you find yourself thinking about him when you're not with him—or dreaming about the state of being Mrs. Matinee instead of his luncheon pal—you'd probably better admit your Matinee is turning into the Big Affair. Run for the train! You can be honest. You won't need to trump up any other excuse than that you're falling. He's a fair guy, and he'll understand.

Needless to say, if you sense that he is falling for you, that is just as good a reason to end the visits. If, on the contrary, you're just plain tired of your Matinee partner, tell him he is wonderful and supreme but that you feel you must stop. No explanations. Let him guess the reasons. He'll be sure to guess the ones that are puffiest to his ego!

MATINEE PERFORMANCE

We know how to *end* The Matinee. Here are notes on the performance itself.

Your apartment should be immaculate when you arrive home at noon; therefore the tidying must be done the night before. The bed should be freshly made that morning. Last-minute preparations while he is on his way to your apartment can only include:

1. Taking care of personal hygiene. Don't fiddle after he has arrived. If you use pills, so much the easier.

2. Mixing his favorite cocktail with his favorite brand of liquor. Since time is so limited, this should be ready to pour when he arrives.

3. Starting a fire in the fireplace.

4. Putting the finishing touches to lunch. The bulk of the menu should be prepared the day before. Food may be the least important factor of The Matinee, but if you're going to serve a course or two, they had better be tastier and more appealing than anything he usually gets in a restaurant. This only adds to his conviction that "you do so *many* things well!"

Following are some quickie menu suggestions, plus recipes.

MENU #1

FISHY FODDER FOR A LOVER

> Clam chowder
> Cheese
> Brown bread (very fresh)
> Green salad
> Coffee

Clam Chowder:
> 2 cans minced clams
> 3 or 4 slices of salt pork or bacon, cut into cubes
> 2 medium potatoes, peeled and diced
> 1 medium onion, peeled and chopped
> 2 cups light cream (may use half milk if broke)
> A pinch of thyme, salt, pepper and paprika

Fry salt pork or bacon in one pan. Cook potatoes in salted boiling water in another pan until soft. When salt pork is browned, remove it from pan to sauté the onion in the drippings. Drain potatoes, but save the liquid. (Cook potato liquid down a bit.) Combine bacon, onion, potatoes, slightly cooked down potato water, clams and clam liquor. Bring to a boil. Lower heat and simmer for ten minutes. Season to taste with salt and pepper.

Add cream slowly, stirring. Heat gently, just to the boiling point, but *don't boil,* or it might curdle. Stir in thyme, paprika and a dollop of butter.

MENU #2

HEARTY LUNCHEON FOR
A TIRED WARRIOR

Minute steak (small and quick)
Home-fried potatoes (boil potatoes the night before)
Fruit
Coffee

Home-Fried Potatoes:

> 3 large potatoes, boiled
> 1 large onion, sliced
> 3 tablespoons butter or margarine
> Salt, freshly ground black pepper

Slice onion into pan in which you have melted butter. Cook until opaque. Add sliced, boiled potatoes, salt and pepper and brown quickly over medium high flame. Add more butter if necessary.

You may also serve a chilled bottle of wine with any of these luncheons if you like—perhaps a rosé or a riesling.

MENU #3

MOTHER'S COOKING FOR
A DESERVING LAD

Cold fried chicken—or cold sliced chicken from a delicatessen or
    your own roasting
Oatmeal bread
Cucumber salad

Cucumber Salad:

> 2 large cucumbers
> 6 tablespoons vinegar
> 1 tablespoon sugar
> Freshly ground pepper
> 1 tablespoon chopped parsley

Peel cucumbers and slice very thin. Squeeze cucumber slices to get out excess moisture. Marinate with sugar and vinegar dressing for at least a half-hour in refrigerator. Add salt, pepper and parsley before serving.

THE ARRIVAL

The first few times you rendezvous, your greetings to each other *could* be strained. Neither of you is sure of just what the other expects . . . or what you expect yourself. *Put him at ease.* If a simple hello will best do that in your opinion, don't extend your face for a kiss. The first few times, anyway, you are probably best advised to greet your friend in street clothes. The less self-conscious you make the first minutes, the sooner the whole relationship will be on comfortable and easy footing. Weeks or months later you can graduate to wispy silks and robes if you think the situation calls for it, or that he would enjoy seeing you in them. He probably will— to him you represent the elegant, emancipated female which his wife is probably too busy and too familiar to be.

FADE OUT

That's the end of my researcher's essay. It just stops. Not one more word could I get her to commit to paper or conversation, even though she was aware that she hadn't given us the faintest *inkling* of what to do *after* we've said hello, in either our little navy blue Chanel or our Pucci hostess gown. I got the impression she felt that if we're too dumb to know what to do *next*, we're too dumb to do it. And she's right.

I'm grateful for everything I *did* find out, however, aren't you? I understand now why this *petite affaire* never happened to me. I couldn't give up wearing perfume for anybody . . . or be cordial to a guy who apparently *never* brings his own liquor. I don't want to sound like a prude at *this* late date, but the whole Matinee relationship leaves me a little cold—and not just because of all the inconvenience.

All right, now we're going to leave the "arena" and go back to the office, to see what people do around *there* for relaxation.

CHAPTER 10

THE OFFICE PARTY
(AND OTHER PLEASURES)

THE FIRST OPPORTUNITY for an office party comes at afternoon coffee-break time. It's Alice's birthday. On your lunch hour you whip out for the card, the cake, some candles and several yards of ribbon. Instead of having coffee and *nothing* at 3:30, you have coffee and Alice's cake . . . with a very happy Alice on your hands.

To invite her, string a length of pink or white ribbon from the cake (in another office) to the door or desk of the guest-of-honor. Then burst open her door or sneak up to her with ribbon in hand. Tell her to follow the ribbon which will, of course, lead her to the party.

It is unthinkable not to celebrate everybody's birthday in your department in *some* manner. At *least* have everybody sign a card. If somebody can draw a personalized one, so much the better. Pregnant girls are easy to draw. Also almost anyone can manage to profile the birthday man's head on a large sheet of art paper. Block it off in departments just like the phrenologist's diagram of a head. In each space you indicate the areas of his life: Women, Wine, Poker, Women, Race Track, Pro Football, Women, Data Processing, etc. Write "Happy Birthday, Larry" across the bottom.

What else can you do on a coffee break?

My husband's charming English secretary at Twentieth Century-Fox Studios turned the period into high tea. Pamela started by inviting Stephen Boyd, Christopher Isherwood and a couple of other English people on the lot over for a cup of good English tea and a cookie. Her first mother-country invitees responded so enthusiastically she soon branched out to foreigners. Anybody who really didn't go for tea was quietly slipped a cup of coffee. Pamela's tea parties got so popular that one guest, long departed from the lot, used to show up at tea time every day, explaining that he'd been driving past the studio and heard the kettle whistling.

To go the tea route for visitors, for the people in your own department or just for you and your boss, Pam says you need a set of good bone china—teapot, sugar bowl, creamer and cups—a tin of excellent tea, and "goodies." Goodies may be English currant buns, English Melting Moments, English sausage rolls, all from an English bakery, whipped cream cakes, pastries or tarts from the French bakery, or dainty English-style cucumber or watercress sandwiches on wafer-thin bread without crusts which you make at home. (If you'd planned just to pick up jelly doughnuts from downstairs, forget it. You aren't the tea type.)

Refreshments should be paid for by your boss if the treat is for him and visiting friends. If office home-folks are going to attend, they must be collected from also. You aren't really the Home Savings and Loan Company.

The bone china is best acquired, Pamela says, by giving a cup and saucer to each department member as his Christmas present, the teapot (filled with cookies) plus sugar bowl and creamer to your boss. This not only provides the office with an English tea service but also takes care of a large number of Christmas gifts. (Much better than bubble bath or pink stationery.) If tea is not yours or anybody else's cup *of*, give handsome coffee mugs instead. Here is Pam's recipe for a delicious tea-party treat from home.

HOME BAKED SCOTCH SHORTBREAD

3 cups sifted all-purpose flour
2 sticks butter
¼ cup sugar

Mix soft butter and sugar together. Add flour until you have a crumbly consistency. Press into an eight-inch square tin and bake at 300 degrees for an hour. Cut into squares.

THE HOSTESS WITH MOST OF THE MOSTEST

Suppose you aren't Perle Mesta and your office isn't the Court of St. James. You can just imagine what they'd say if *you* tried pulling off a stunt like high tea. True, you do have to be an executive secretary and a good one to have these privileges. If you're that, however, you're usually so valuable you can pull off just about anything you wish. Actually, charming your boss's associates redounds very much to his credit and he should be pleased. The guests, even important ones, can also become your devoted personal friends. Pamela, who collected some wonderful people through tea parties, says you must be genuinely interested in them and care about their happiness if they are to be collected. Also she believes the office itself has to be a somewhat sunny and informal one, which more and more offices are becoming.

I don't need to tell you how to go *out* for a coffee break or what to do. You already *know* that. As for other entertaining, a friend tells me of a festive coffee drink you can make which will turn practically *any* coffee break into a celebration. It can be made behind a locked door of the ladies' room if there are just too many great big sunflower eyes peering at you. Most bosses enjoy watching this brew prepared, however, after they get over the initial shock of seeing the pretty blue flames shoot up. It's more fun if you can prepare *two* cups at one time—one for you and one for him—but you may have to make it privately the first time and serve it as a surprise. This beverage is particularly welcome when conditions are rainy, snowy, sleety, foggy or muggy inside or outside the office.

CAFÉ ROYALE

For each person: 1 cup of very hot coffee in a china cup. (*Never* paper or plastic)
1 ounce brandy
1 to 2 cubes of sugar, depending on his taste
1 *deep* tablespoon

Put the spoon in the hot coffee for a moment to warm, then balance it over the rim of the cup. Put the cube of sugar into the spoon and pour in a little brandy, letting the sugar cube absorb it. Pour in more brandy until the cube is saturated and the spoon is full of brandy. Wait a moment or two for the brandy to warm in the steam, then set fire to it with a match. Beautiful blue flames result and will then burn out. Tip the contents of the spoon into the cup, stir and serve.

Depending on the size of your spoon, you may have to refill it with brandy in order to use up the ounce. Let it burn out each time as you did the first time.

Some wonderful chemical affinity takes place between brandy, coffee, sugar, boss and secretary. The brew isn't sweet, nor does it seem to provide the nervous jolt that just pouring a blast into a cup of coffee has. Gratitude is inevitable, in whatever form you wish it, to the person who serves up such a blessing!

SNACKS (WITH OR WITHOUT COFFEE)

Most offices contain locusts. They can be very attractive people. I was a Locust S.G. (Senior Grade) for many years. There must always be something around for locusts to eat, otherwise they feel insecure. Preferably locust-snacks are kept in somebody else's desk drawer on account of a locust's almost pathological snacking habits. After the fourteenth trip to a neighbor for more jelly beans, the neighbor will finally shut the drawer on the locust's hand, which may be the jolt he needs to kick the habit for a couple of hours.

If you continuously dip into a neighbor's supply of snacks (with his permission, of course), you must repay him with exactly the same amount, kind and quality of snacks. One darling skinny fellow I knew kept dry, toasted peanuts and almonds in his desk drawer plus fudge brownies which his mother baked and mailed to him from Bangor, Maine. He finally laid down the law to us locusts one day and said, "Okay, how about replacements?" You ought to have seen what he got back . . . Goliath-size stale pretzels, bruised apples, corn chips from long-past kids' parties, halves of tuna sandwiches from lunch, trick or treat Halloween candy from Halloweens past. It was a shocking display of not repaying in kind. We had to sweep out his office to find him the afternoon a group of locusts re-paid with five pounds of peanuts still in the shell, then decided to help him eat them up right then.

It's all right to bring leftovers from home for hungry office friends, but you must follow the Hobo Rule. During the Depression a hobo knocked at a housewife's door and asked for something to eat. She gave him an ancient piece of pie which he ate. He then said "That was perfect!" The housewife knew exactly what shape the pie was in and gave him the raised eyebrow. "If it were any worse," the hobo explained, "I couldn't have eaten it. If it were any better, you wouldn't have given it to me."

You simply *must* not bring anything to the office that isn't edible, because locusts are just as likely to plow into it and be half dead of stomach cramps before they stop eating. I get the shudders *still* thinking about the batch of shelled pecans I brought in for some fellow locusts. They were from a theater date the night before, and during the second act I'd found a glossy green worm nibbling away at one. Do you just *waste* $1.65 worth of nuts? (I'd put Greeny on the floor with his own pecan half and two others for good measure for act three.) On the other hand, who *knew* what somebody might have fed me in an innocent-looking deviled egg one day? I brought the nuts to the office. It was only one little worm.

The ethical thing to do, of course, is to bring only food that you would cheerfully have eaten if there hadn't been so much of it. Party hors d'oeuvres from the night before or half a pumpkin chiffon cake are fine. Locusts are the greatest little helpers in the world for people who are about to start on a diet. They'll follow you around and clean out every last naughty snack that a dieter is not supposed to have.

BELLE AND BOTTLE

Should you or shouldn't you keep a bottle in your desk drawer? Oh come on, you're a big girl! If you're a secretary, you should not. As a minor executive I think you can. When I reached that level I stowed a pint of vodka and Rose's lime juice for emergency gimlets. In the ad agencies where I worked there seemed to be about as much work from five to nine as there was from nine to five. (Many art directors are night people.) I wasn't much of a drinker, but it just seemed friendly to have a small private stock.

Naturally a lady doesn't hoist her bottle and guzzle away like one of the boys, but if one of the boys has run out of his own J & B, you produce *yours*. (Doesn't a mother run for the snake-bite remedy or mustard poultices when her boy is bitten or ailing?)

I assume nobody breaks out a bottle in the office before closing hours. Some managements feel that nobody should drink in the office *ever*, of course. How misguided! Salaried persons usually take as much pride in their work as management does—or more—and are not going to do anything to impair its quality. Cocktails in the office before or during an evening work-bout can be friendly and warming and can save running off to the bar and wasting time. Creative people do some of their best *work* after five, but they may not want to do it parched.

A friend of mine who had just joined a national magazine was working late one evening after tragedy had befallen the country. Her magazine had immediately junked its entire ready-to-ship issue and was starting over. After the five o'clock noiseless gong sounded to close the formal day, Sharon noticed people making runs on the coffee pot as though rationing might be coming back. She went over to have a steaming cup of coffee herself and found the pot wasn't even plugged in. Instead of steaming black coffee, there was cold dark Demerara Rum.

Did the staff get the issue out? Of course it did. Was it a gasser? Several million subscribers said that it was.

The children's hour, or cocktail hour as it is known in more sophisticated circles, may hold unusual blessings for a secretary. Some girls, for all their charm and efficiency, simply do not get taken to lunch as they should. Stuffy company policy and stuffy executive cowardice. The girls may, however, come into their just deserts after five. Bosses making journeys to the far reaches of Westport, North Hollywood and Shaker Heights like to be fortified. They need help.

Now a man who won't take his secretary to lunch probably also won't buy her a drink in a bar, but he may teach her to *make* one. One executive I know spent a month teaching his secretary the art of mixing a really dry martini. They sampled batch after batch in an empty office until finally (at the end of twenty patient working days) the martinis were bone dry. The man had married his previous secretary and wasn't going through that again, but he *does* brag that his little helper mixes the best dry martini outside the Princeton Club and often invites other men—sometimes single—to join him and his bartender-Friday for drinks.

If you're the bartender, mix the whatever-he-prefers with great style and see that he has pretty glasses to drink them in.

MORE CHILDREN'S HOUR DEVELOPMENTS

Obviously many people go off the premises for cocktails. I think it's safe to say that whatever tactics you used to get yourself asked to lunch will suffice to bring off a cocktail date. And whatever happens to you in Lunchland ought to happen double (and sooner) at cocktails. One girl I know was chatting with a man about seafood at Boston's Ritz-Carlton Bar and they got right on a plane and flew to Fisherman's Wharf in San Francisco. At the very least you may go on to dinner *somewhere*.

If it's *your* date—you asked *him* (for business reasons, of course) —quietly sign the check and thank your patron saint for this neat arrangement that lets girls ask boys without seeming pushy.

When a group from the office is drinking, the men pay for everybody from secretary classification (if they're females) on down the job scale, usually. A junior executivess sometimes gets paid for, sometimes picks up her own tab and occasionally buys a round for the group. Go on, you had it free for years!

Back in the office there are many occasions for revelry in addition to those occasioned by secretaries dispatching bosses to the hinterlands and workers working late. There is a powerful little institution known as the Office Party.

THE BASH OF THE YEAR

It's as crowded as Churchill Downs on Derby Day and so noisy you can't hear a cry for help. "I'm not going to the country tonight, Clarissa," a corporate vice-president whispers to the blonde receptionist he's just handed her fifth drink. "Perhaps we could have dinner at my hotel. . ."

The five-piece combo is playing "Begin the Beguine" and the all-brain, no hanky-panky (up to now) company comptroller has the steno-pool director clasped firmly around the fanny as he glides her about the room in a very intense waltz.

The assistant receptionist has kissed every man in the place and is going back for seconds.

Two wastebaskets are on fire. One couch is sagging under the weight of the head bookkeeper, who has passed out. The assistant bookkeeper has been restrained from throwing a bucket of water on him.

The usually shy shipping clerk has just cornered the production manager at the water cooler and told him, "Mr. Bates, there's something I've been meaning to say to you all year. You STINK!" The head librarian has sweetly told the research director to go do something that is anatomically impossible.

In the second-floor men's room, the office nymphomaniac has backed the financial vice-president into a lavatory and is running her hands through his sparsely distributed hair. "For God's *sake,* Evelyn," he gasps, "somebody's going to come in here." "Who cares?" says Evelyn, nibbling excitedly on his ear.

In the conference room behind locked doors, the chairman of the board is lying on a couch with his head in the lap of the teletype operator, who is dropping paperclips into his open mouth.

"Why don't you and me get on a plane and go to Mexico?" says the man who was repairing the coffee machine when the party started and who stayed to have *one* drink. He leans closer still to his drinking companion, the president's Vassar-graduated secretary. "Usted habla Español, baby?"

The four couples who have already left the party are ensconced, in order of their disappearance, at: his apartment, her apartment, his wife's *family's* boarded-up summer place, the Cozy Corners Motel. A typist being delivered to her father's doorstep in Hackensack is trying to persuade the old man that the gentleman who drove her home really isn't *responsible* for her present condition— she didn't have any lunch and got hold of some poisoned sherry at the party. Her father isn't listening, having gone to get a gun.

Back at the party three desk lamps have crashed to the floor, five vodka bottles have been thrown out the window, a typist is having hysterics, the chief of data controls is trying (with obvious pleasure) to help fish an ice cube out of the bosom of the relief switchboard operator. It's eight-thirty. The party started at four and will likely not be over until four comes around again.

DO YOU REMEMBER?

Does any of this sound like what goes on at your office party? I didn't think so! It is the big bash—probably the Christmas party —of twenty years ago. Some office parties still stack up that way, but far fewer than once upon a time. Everyone I know who watched the office party in the movie *The Apartment* found it interesting as a relic of ancient folklore.

But why get maudlin reminiscing? It's all pretty much G.W.T.W. And you and I both know what killed these Yule parties, which were supposed to be gruesome but were actually some of the swingingest parties ever given. Wives killed them. Wives and the local police department, who complained that husbands were driving home intoxicated. They were driving *home*, weren't they? Doesn't anybody ever give anybody *credit*?

If you should be the fortunate girl whose company still gives a traditional Christmas party, cherish those bosses. They are probably all widowers, grass widowers and individualists as rugged as Ghengis Khan. The rest of us will just have to concentrate on smaller in-between parties and on an occasional *different* kind of Big Deal.

There still are lovely official company parties, of course, but they're different—and duller. Many conscience-stricken companies have taken to asking *wives* (and husbands). At my last office party I decided to liven things up for David (my husband) by pointing out who was sleeping with whom. That was easy. They were the ones who were conspicuously avoiding each other and holding hands with somebody else. What a state for an office party to have got to!

THE IMPROMPTU PARTY

Whatever its faults or advantages, a big office bash can only happen once or twice a year at best . . . or worst. *Small* office parties—the warm, intimate, brotherly and sisterly *fun* kind—can spring up like fat white mushrooms in a damp forest just every few days. And they're not poison, either!

You surely must know all the standard excuses for impromptu parties—toasting the bride, somebody leaving the firm, vacations being gone on and returned from, or any other reason you can get away with, from the birth of new kittens to Bolivar's birthday.

When it's decided to have a party, the best procedure is for the committee (probably one girl) to collect from everybody in advance. A dollar a head is a standard fee. A rich boss may kick in more, but if he's been doing it for fifteen years, don't expect too much largesse. Regardless of whether Miss Goody Two-Shoes plans to have only ginger ale or water, if she's going to attend the party, she must be collected from like everybody else. (In some bars it costs *more* to drink ginger ale.) Buy as much liquor as your collection will allow. When this runs out, a fresh collection can be made from those still at the party who wish it to continue. If there's any liquor left over (fine chance!) have another party next week. If it's just a tiny scrap, the party organizer gets to take it home. (Let *your* conscience define "tiny scrap.")

A party, of course, can sprout because someone receives a gift of Jack Daniels from a supplier that day and decides to open it after work. From such innocent beginnings nineteen people have been known to wind up on the Staten Island Ferry strumming banjos until after midnight. (These parties are not *official* parties and are also small, so they don't start the newspapers, magazines, police department, W.C.T.U., etc., etc., clucking and trying to stamp them out.)

One of the best after-work parties I ever went to sprang up among some leftovers who weren't going out of town Labor Day weekend. As one after another of the Las Vegas group began slipping away Friday at noon, we pitiful remainers rallied and started our collection of two bucks a head. With twenty-four dollars we bought a case of California champagne (I think the liquor store must have felt sorry for us *too* and knocked down the price), which gave everyone a bottle apiece. The store iced it for us and we had a lovely, smug, leisurely summer afternoon bash with love and kinship hanging heavily in the air.

THE GUEST LIST

Whether your impromptu parties are department-wide or company-wide would depend on the size of the organization. A general office party at a large insurance company could tie up several thousand people. That would be out. A "department party" in a tiny personal-service firm would involve just one person. Better to merge. I do think snippy-dippy little "private" office parties from which you try to keep out certain uninviteds are ridiculous. Start with a small choice list if you like, but if an interloper comes by looking thirsty, welcome him.

People who deride these little office parties as being rather scruffy and funless are, in my opinion, simply ignoramuses. Either they never *attended* one, or they are wives who remember them too *well*, or they attended a party where wives somehow got *in*. There's no doubt that one wife stopping by to pick up her husband can cause a party to go downhill faster than somebody shouting "Mad Dog!" (Husbands picking up wives are less destructive. They know a good thing when they see it and can join in the fun without eliminating it.)

The reason informal office parties are good is strictly because nobody *is* married to each other. Take a husband to a regular party and if he doesn't have a good time, you worry. You married a misfit! If he has *too* good a time—girls are lined up three deep to dance the Mashed Potato with him—you worry worse. In offices everybody is on his own, with no loved ones around to cause anxiety.

Other good things about office parties are:

A single girl doesn't have to bring a date. They like her just for her.

Fun is the single motivation. No hostess is showing off her Quiche Lorraine, her new Louis XIV chest or *her* chest. No host named Roger is burning the *Filet de Boeuf Roger* and cursing a blue streak. Only the *people* matter.

There's no discrimination at an office party. Class lines are unheard of.

Since I've left the office to work at home I honestly get so homesick some days I could crawl right up the street to the Pan Am Building to see if anybody would let me into a party.

THE MAKINGS

If your office has as many as two impromptu parties a year, I think glasses should be bought. Liquor tastes terrible in paper cups. It may well be that office parties got their seamy reputation partly from people belting drinks to get to the bottom of the cup before the wet cardboard taste set in.

I'd suggest peanuts and only peanuts—in or out of their shells— for hors d'oeuvres. Nearly everybody likes them and they have *some* food value.

If you want to go in for punch—the liquor goes farther and punch can be delicious—here is a basic recipe. You'll need a *large* container. This could be a plastic wastebasket from the dime store.

SIMPLE PUNCH

3 or 4 bags of ice
3 or more bottles of vodka (an inexpensive brand will do)
A gallon of Gallo or other white wine
1 can concentrated fruit punch
Jar green or red marischino cherries to pretty it up.

This would serve as many as thirty-five guests. Actually it's a very flexible recipe. You could use one bottle of vodka, a little white wine, cherries and punch for a small group; two bottles of vodka, more white wine, more cherries and more punch for a medium-size group; three bottles of vodka with a gallon of white wine, lashings of cherries and plenty of punch for a large, thirsty group.

You can start at Stage One and see how the party develops. If it's swinging along, proceed to Stage Two. If it promises to become a real bash, pull out the stops and dump in the additional quantities that make it Stage Three. Watch out for Stage Four. Redoubtable ten-year employees have been known to take lovers' leaps out to the sidewalk when this punch got past the third stage.

EXTRACURRICULAR

As for outside parties, I think a group organizing to do anything *away* from the office, like ice skating or going in a body to see a Van Gogh exhibit, is just a little too orphans' day at the zoo. I could be *wrong*. If you're a born organizer, organize!

The company baseball team with the attendant cheering section and awards dinners is a good thing, I've heard. (I loathe baseball and have still achieved a normal, healthy adulthood.)

A golf tournament at the miniature golf course is delightful. Run it just like a real tournament, except that handicaps are drawn out of a hat and so are names of foursome members. There are prizes, of course. The trophies are children's toys or figurines made from modeling clay. A champion's banquet follows the tournament at a nearby Chinese restaurant or Nineteenth Hole Bar.

You might have your office turtles (the real ones) handicapped and entered into a race some Friday afternoon. At my office it was Maid Marion by two lengths, Ben Casey trailing a poor second,

Oscar Levant and Marjorie Morningstar refusing to leave the starting gate.

Impromptu, *sneak*-away affairs by a small group can be fun. If
three or four people have been working nights and weekends and
have an afternoon off coming to them, you could all go to the track
. . . or the ball game. (Naturally I won't go to the ball game *with*
you, but I'm sure there are lots of people who will.)

THE OFFICE PARTY AT HOME

Should you ever give parties in your home for loved ones from
the office? Certainly! It used to be considered *déclassé* to socialize
with office friends, but that was when it was considered *déclassé*
to *work*. Now everybody's friends work in *some* office, so it might as
well be yours!

These are some nonserious, low-overhead Thursday, Friday or
Saturday night parties to consider throwing for an office group:

National Inventors Day Party. Have this in July. Everybody
brings an invention he thinks needs inventing. At the party I went
to an electronics wizard brought a self-hypnotizing machine. It
made so much noise it practically defeated its own purpose. Somebody else made an ashtray with wall-to-wall carpeting for people
who like to grind butts out in rugs. One fashion plate stitched up a
sequined headband with a pocket for mad-money and two aspirins.
A beautifully constructed fly trap was submitted. It had a little
ladder which led up from a courtyard of white pebbles to a tiny
wicker platform above. The platform was roofed and just large
enough to hold one sugar cube and the fly. Then the ladder went
down on the other side but there was a broken rung from which the
unsuspecting fly plunged to his death on the rocks below. Alas!

October 21 is National Whale-Watching Day. Gather a group to
watch for whales from your balcony. Have several pairs of bin-
oculars handy and a foghorn to sound in case anything is observed.
Whether whales are sighted a-sounding or not, grog can be hoisted
and sea chanties sung and listened to.

Polaroid Party. Almost anybody can lay hands on a Polaroid
camera for the evening. If not, pair up the haves with the have-

nots. All photographing will be done in your apartment. It's nice to have a few reflectors and light bars around but they aren't vital. Categories of competition will be: Nature. Portraiture. Advertising. (This should net half a dozen of Tabu's fiery fiddler.) Industrial. Animal. Still Life. Everyone must agree to pose for others but the original instigator of the picture gets the award. You may uncover a new Cartier-Bresson!

Bossa Nova Fiesta. Everyone brings musical instruments and plays along with the Bossa Nova records. I've seen one fiesta bring out three guitars, an accordian, the usual bongos, a boombass, two or three kazoos, a six-fingered Japanese flute and child's trumpet. People who have no instrument to play can be given emptied wastebaskets to pound. Barefoot interpretive dancing should also be encouraged. *Warning:* Either pre-soften the neighbors or invite them.

There, that should give you a selection.

And now I think we've had enough partying for a while. It's time to get you out of that sozzled crowd and fly you around a bit. Yes, we are going to travel on business, which can be as much fun as any office party and sometimes even sexier.

CHAPTER 11

THE WIDE, WILD, WICKED WORLD

Never mind what else it is—exhausting, demanding, nerve-wracking, sleep-robbing—traveling on business is sexy. Only a girl who hasn't done any business traveling (or one who has done too much) could argue the point. Of course, all the weary traveler needs to do to get souped-up again is stay home for a while. She usually wants back in again—or rather *out* again.

Traveling on business gives you a much better chance to meet men than traveling for pleasure—or staying home. If you've exhausted the supply of men in your town, a business trip gives you a whack at a whole new batch. And instead of piling into the coach flight at midnight as you do on a vacation to save money and add a day to your trip, you may very well pile into a first-class daytime flight where all the well-manicured *men* are. What a sight—row after row of Brooks-Brothered, Rogers-Peeted creatures sitting there just like salamanders waiting to be pounced on. On many a first-class daytime flight you'll find you're the *only* girl. (Don't fret if your company has decided to save millions by traveling the travelers tourist this year. Some of the men's companies may have decided the same thing and they'll all be back in tourist with you.)

Whether you're on the plane getting there or already in the town, your female attractiveness is enhanced by your having a business mission. A girl with appointments to keep and places to go and who doesn't seem *needy* is *exciting*. Once in town with business to transact, you can operate, prowl, chat with and check out the men far better than when you're standing in a line at the museum with thirty other lonelies. If it happens that no men show up on your trip—and I never went on a business trip that turned out that way —you weren't in town looking for men *anyway*. Of course you weren't. You were there to introduce a new miracle fabric, recruit employees or put on a fashion show.

Some of the best travel is with men from your own company as an equal. It's simply being let out of school. With your own built-in pals you can wind up in all-night poker games, a hundred-meter race across the hotel swimming pool, or on a lovely twilight drive over the Arizona desert to buy booze across the border.

Business travel has other pluses for a working girl.

You get yanked out of yourself! First you have to get your clothes and your shape into shape. Then you have to talk and sound your best when you get there. Sometimes positively horrible challenges await you and you have to speak up and cope. On foreign ground—Dallas, Detroit, Denver, Danbury—very likely you'll feel inspired to do some daring things you wouldn't dream of doing at home. Anything that puts you at your dynamic best, no matter how much it scares you, is good.

Travel is great for "older" women. Nobody can treat you like a granny if you're hostessing a cocktail party in your hotel room.

Wherever you travel you're going to see some places you haven't seen before. Breathing Hard, Nebraska, may not be Paris, but it's different from *home*.

You're going to talk to some new people. Cabdrivers in New York and salesgirls in Atlanta are experiences all to themselves. You may need an interpreter, but they're worth meeting. No doubt about it, travel gooses up a girl's social life and gives her something to talk about when she gets home.

A company trip often gets you in sudden easy reach of a glamour spot. You live in Seattle. They've sent you to Miami. For just a few dollars of your own you can pop on over to Nassau.

A company trip is also a wonderful way to nest-egg a little money if you're willing to go it thriftily. One girl I know has introduced a Jaguar into her life that way. If you prefer to use the last penny of your travel-allotment to travel in elegant-lady style, nobody's knocking that either.

RESERVATIONS FOR TWO

So, how in the world do we get you traveled? As a secretary your sole travel adventures may be confined to fixing other people up with tickets. (My boss at the ad agency was an Admiral with American, an Ambassador with TWA and a member of United's Hundred Thousand Mile Club; for five years I practically never got off the phone, either confirming or canceling a reservation.)

Some executive secretaries get to travel *with* their bosses, of course. Since a man isn't usually allowed to claim his wife's trip as a business deduction but may claim his secretary's, I suppose it seems wasteful to him not to bring along somebody. How much a man really needs his secretary on a trip is doubtful, considering that there's always the hotel stenographer or one of the girls in the company he's visiting who can take letters.

Let's face it, if a girl gets taken at *all*, it may be for purposes other than work. In order to have the benefits of travel, it's understandable that some travel-hungry girls deliberately give the impression that what they won't do at home, they might do in Cincinnati. Right? Then all that remains is to work out an escape route in Cincinnati.

A friend of mine using the Cincinnati System practically got lumbered in her compartment before they were even close to Cincinnati (Detroit in her case). The excuse she'd trumped up for going on the trip was that she would help her boss work on an important speech as they traveled. She probably implied she would cooperate in other matters too. Here, in her own words, is what happened:

"Mr. O. and I were in his closed-door compartment, which measured roughly six feet by six feet. The train was still standing in the *station*, for God's sake, when he began to talk about anything *but* the speech. Then the minute the train started to move—as a matter of fact, the middle cars were still in the station—Mr. O. leapt from his seat, covered the one-step distance between us, grabbed my hand and pressed it to his body. On the *Sabbath* mind you!

"Where to go? Sideways? No room. Backwards? No room. Forward? *That* would have been a mistake. Straight up? I just wished I *could*. Naturally I'd been chased through apartments and offices before and gotten away handily, but space was definitely Mr. O.'s ally. I guess we wrestled side by side, or standing torso to torso, for about twenty minutes. However we moved we were Siamese twins. I finally gave him one mighty push that landed him back on *his* feet. I pulled the small table between us, leaned on it and said, 'Mr. O., the next time we take a trip, you are going to leave your seething passions in the suitcase until we get the work finished.'"

She says she escaped in Detroit after the speech was delivered, and I'm not one to use a lie-detector on a friend.

The Cincinnati System may get you out of the office with your boss, and hopefully you'll think of some means to escape your eventual fate—assuming you want to escape it—when you've set down in the distant city. Being asked to travel without a boss because the company needs *you* is the ideal situation, however. Then you can choose whom you want to love in travel, or if you want to love only the travel itself. Believe me, this traveling as a Somebody for a company and having neat little stacks of company money stashed in your neat little lizard bag is one of the silkiest fringe benefits. It's well worth working yourself out of the secretarial ranks to do.

I don't know when or how your first travel assignment will come. Sometimes it exists and you get chosen. Other times you have to help it along a bit. "Wouldn't it be smart to send little me off to cover that convention?" you say. Or, "I'm going to be in Chicago next week anyway visiting my sister. Would you like me just to run on up to Minneapolis to see what they're doing at the trade fair?"

I got out of town several times "owning" a borrowed Rolleiflex. The agency was doing before-and-after ads for a reducing equipment client and I volunteered to dart thither and hither to St. Louis, Georgetown or Bicycle, Montana, to take exploratory pictures. If the subject looked promising, a real photographer was assigned to the story. It was great fun—even in Bicycle, Montana.

I just hope you'll keep your eyes and ears open and your imagination working and that you'll keep plotting ways to get yourself included in this travel thing. Let me now give you travel tips for the time when you bring off this coup!

OFFICE PROCEDURE

Be pleased about the assignment but not *too* pleased . . . on the outside. If you take off like a moon rocket on the news that you've been assigned, the company may get the idea you're too giddy to represent them or that you expect to have entirely too much fun. Others will be jealous too and may try to go in your place next time.

You're delighted to have been given this responsibility, eager to be of help, but it's going to be hard work, not to *mention* the inconvenience of having to travel at this particular time.

Don't cheat on time—come back to the office the minute you get home. Don't take an extra half-day to get started. The travel itself is larceny enough.

If your company has any overseas dealings, keep your passport up to date. It can take several days to get it reinstated after expiration and you don't want to muff a sudden chance to go abroad.

LUGGAGE

Everybody's been brainwashed about having beautiful luggage to show off. The trouble is that last year's beautiful luggage is this year's beat-up bunch of boxes—it all gets banged around pretty badly regardless of its distinctive lineage. Even if the luggage isn't too mercilessly beaten, it's still last year's, and breathtaking new fashions in luggage come out almost oftener than breathtaking new fashions in clothes. I'd rather splurge on clothes. I've been using that common-as-grass black and red plaid stuff for years— carryall, hatbox, duffle bag, overnighter. It all matches but is ridiculously inexpensive and I never worry about what some careless baggage-loader might be doing to its precious skin. It's good, too, to be able to plunk yourself down on a trusty old make-up case to read for ten minutes while you're stuck at the field gate waiting to load. You'd think twice about bearing down on a case that cost forty-five dollars and was plush red velvet.

I think a pretty good plan is to retire one or two pieces of old luggage at a time and buy a glamorous new piece that blends in with your remainders. A friend tells me she started out with Mark Cross luggage fifteen years ago, now battered but distinctive. She recently added a mustard velour train-case to it and a fold-over garment bag complete with carefully defaced stickers, which she picked up from the Salvation Army Thrift Shop for two dollars.

Some girls like to carry a beautiful little brief case when they travel, possibly as a badge of success. These are chic all right, but I find I haven't enough arms to handle a brief case, a king-size purse, a couple of coats, a make-up case for feet-resting in flight and probably a book. You can always *tell* the man next to you that you're a success.

CLOTHES

There is the take-everything-you-own-and-hang-the-excess-baggage-charges, the somebody-might-ask-you-to-the-opera-and-you'd-need-a-ball-gown school of business traveler. There are also the three-knits-and-one-change-of-underwear girls who feel that if you can't show up at it in one of your knits, it isn't worth going to.

I'm in between. You have to leave *something* at home no matter how insecure you feel without it. Nevertheless, it's nonsense not to take a silken number to the clime they've assured you will be frigid and a couple of woolly numbers to the place they've guaranteed you will be steaming. I can't count the times the one garment I threw in at the last moment on the chance there might be a cold snap was the thing I huddled in for a week.

If your travels will take you to several cities with a brief stop in each, settle for one or two beautiful outfits that you wear continuously. Even if you're staying in one city for a week, it's better to be seen often in an expensive, utterly right costume than to change daily into marginal things. The plan seems to be basic with traveling gown-shop buyers who could stock up with trunks full of beautiful clothes.

Don't be too stingy, though. My well-business-traveled friend Ann says a girl shouldn't even take a crosstown bus without a minimal resort wardrobe. Bermuda is close to New York, Hawaii is close to San Francisco, and you never know when you'll get to toot down there. Play it according to the probabilities, however.

As for how you want to look in the city you're visiting, I think you want to blend in with the best-dressed people who live there—unless the whole crowd is hopelessly dull. Other "experts" don't agree. They say, "Just be *you* wherever you go and you'll be adorable." I think New York girls running around Los Angeles on the loveliest day of the year in their impossibly chic gray-flannel suits and stacked heels look a little like bankers who don't know how to come off it. Conversely, Los Angeles girls hitting New York in January in their beige silk shantung dresses and beige silk shantung shoes are like butterflies in the deep freeze. It's generally true that you can wear the same important city clothes in any large eastern, midwestern or northwestern city. You can wear the same lighter, gayer, less serious frocks in any southwestern or southeastern city. Sometimes you can wear some of each in the other clime.

A wig I couldn't live without, could you? At least you'll need a *hat* or two which covers up every speck of your hair for travel—in case you don't get shampooed for six days.

Wool travels marvelously. You never see a wrinkled coat on a lamb or billy goat, and wool is so breathing and alive. (I sound like a wool ad.) If there's a stray crease, hang the garment outside the shower with the hot water turned on full blast. Don't let anything fall in the tub.

A taffeta half-slip is a must for knits.

Drip-dries are not for me when it comes to business travel. (I think they never should have escaped from the *underwear* field, if you want my opinion.) You need a posher look than little-or-no-iron to come on like Somebody at your meeting, and you don't want to spend your entire time dabbling things out anyway. Unless it's Europe, I think stockings, lingerie and gloves are about the only things that should wind up in the basin.

It's all right to borrow clothes for a trip. Most girls are delighted to lend greatcoats, jewelry, hats. These items rarely wear out but just go out of style. Try not to lose whatever you've borrowed. The donor might actually prefer to claim the insurance, but you can't be sure.

Carry a travel iron. Do the pressing on the hotel floor on top of a towel. Even if you can charge all the cleaning and pressing to your hotel bill, you may not have time to wait for the garment's return.

Pack alone. With a best friend gabbing at you, you'll get to that picking-things-up, walking-them-across-the-room-and-putting-them-down-again-without-getting-them-into-a-*bag* stage sooner. You'll also be looking high and low for the shoes or hairbrush you're carrying in your arms.

Some travel-guiders recommend making lists of items to check off. You can forget to put things on a list as easily as you can forget to put them in your head. After you've traveled a bit, you rarely forget anything you meant to take. Certain items you keep ready to go all the time anyway—one or two plastic make-up kits which contain night creams, hand-lotion, facial cleanser, liquid detergent (all in plastic bottles), deodorant, manicuring equipment, wash cloth, safety pins (big ones, too, for hanging up skirts) needles and several colors of thread, tweezer, razor and blades, plus any cosmetics you can afford to keep duplicates of for travel. I like paper packets of bubble bath. Bath water just looks absolutely naked to me unless it's full of fragrant, sudsy bubbles as well as a girl. Whatever helps you feel luxurious while you roam should be included.

Weigh your luggage on the bathroom scale to know whether you're way over or way under (fat chance!) the luggage allowance. A nasty surprise at weighing-in time can cloud your trip.

CHECKING IN LUGGAGE

Trains are no problem. If they can get the luggage up into your space, you're allowed to carry it and at no extra cost. I know a girl who took a St. Bernard with her in a compartment. The conductor, viewing the beast on the station platform, said, "Lady, that animal ain't going no place with us—only pets that can be picked up and carried are allowed on the train." Madelyn's beau picked Tessie up in his arms—all hundred and fifty pounds of her—and got her up the steps before he had his coronary.

Planes are something else again. There's that pesky weight business. I've got plenty on my conscience and not the least is having put everything heavy for *years*—pressing iron, camera, walking shoes—into a make-up case and then hiding the make-up case behind a post. After checking in, I would saunter to the post, pick up the case and tote it onto the plane unweighed. Last year I ran into a little trouble. Some ticket checker with eyes in the side of her head let me get all checked in, then said sweetly, "And *now*, Mrs. Brown, would you like to get your make-up bag and weigh it in?" I got the bag, of course, mumbling that I weighed only a hundred and nine pounds and felt perhaps I was entitled to a few pounds since most travelers started at about one-sixty and went on up. Miss Beagle-eyes said that I and I alone could be responsible for the plane's flopping down in flight when I failed to declare luggage. Naturally I had to get a new system.

This is it: Whatever is heavy that you don't wish weighed in just put in a paper sack instead of into your luggage. I don't care *how* suspicious or disreputable a paper sack looks—even if it's big enough to contain a *mummy*—they never weigh it in. (You'd better make that *two* paper sacks, one inside the other, to keep the bottom from dropping out.)

You are also allowed to carry coats and dresses over your arm unweighed-in. If you're overweight a few pounds, according to the bathroom scale, grab some things out of your bag, preferably mentionables, and carry them in a plastic bag over your arm to the plane. What with the paper sacks containing bottles, cameras and shoes, a few garments over your arm, your regular purse and coat, you may have to be led on the plane like a blind llama—but you're *legitimate*. At least, I *think* you are.

The airline will encourage you to carry your wig box with you. Don't do it. It's too big to put under your seat, and once you get it on the plane, the *hostess* will tell you there's no space for it. The wig may wind up sitting in your seat while you stand all the way to Oklahoma City.

I never buy insurance before a flight. You're safer up there than in your own kitchen (you know that, don't you?), and insurance companies have simply made a good thing out of people being cowards about flying.

SEATING ARRANGEMENTS

If seat reservations are made as you check in, there certainly isn't much chance of picking out the likeliest, dearest man to sit next to. In first-class it doesn't matter too much anyway. The section is so small you can usually manage to get acquainted with anyone there who interests you.

In tourist, most people try for the window seats. This seems short-sighted to me. On the aisle seat you have a whack at the two people, men hopefully, seated next to you, also those in the same row across the aisle and the ones in the row ahead and the row behind. Surely one out of this crowd will be of interest. When you sit on the aisle, a man sauntering down to chat with the hostess can be waylaid. You can drop your magazine or splatter your coffee in his approach pattern so that at least he'll have to slow *down*. Anyway, sitting on the aisle makes it so much easier to get up and move about without climbing over people. If you're stuck in the middle seat, possibly there'll be a man on either side. Cheer up!

I checked the last time I was on a Boeing 707 Super-Jet and found rows five, nine and eleven had more leg space in front of them. That was true of all six seats across—A, B, C, D, E, F. Maybe it was that plane only. Anyway, if you're going to go around worrying about leg room, you *could* miss out on some of the men.

If there are no reserved seats, you'll sit next to a man if you can. Of course you will! You didn't move heaven and earth to come on this trip only to be seated next to a female creature with sandwiches and children. Females, sandwiches and children are all lovely in their place, but that place isn't next to you in an airplane. For this reason I recommend *not* being the first one on the plane. Let the others get seated so *you,* like little Miss Muffet's spider, can pop down next to somebody promising instead of being a sitting duck for unwantables. If you happen to draw a clinker (it *could* be a man), you can read madly or feign sleep. And if somebody next to you reads madly or feigns sleep *forever* . . . well, you must have chosen the wrong perfume.

PLANE CLOTHES—BUT NOT TOO PLAIN

Let's talk about your travel costume. You want to look sexy and chic. You want to feel comfortable and relaxed. These two conditions *seem* mutually incompatible but they aren't. The comfort starts in leaving off your girdle. I don't care if you *sleep* in one, you can skip it for your plane ride. Comfort also comes in wearing clothes that are not fragile and in which you can squirm about.

Men passengers deserve a glamorous you. One girl I know thinks a suit proper for departures and arrivals but slips it off in the ladies' room of the plane to reveal underneath a scrumptious Pucci dress. My own travel costume is a black Italian silk Walter Bass suit, not new (because clothes take too much of a beating in travel) but good to begin with, so its stays smart. The blouse of the suit is sleeveless black Alex jersey with a low, draped cowl neck—utterly décolleté but again chic, because Mr. Bass wouldn't have it any other way. If I do say so myself, this little outfit seems to have an electrifying effect on men. The suit is severe and snooty—but off comes the jacket and there's that mad, mad blouse. A black lace bra, not too new (to insure comfort), completes the destruction.

I usually wear stockings and garter belt to the plane—along with those other things—and take them off once aboard if it's a long flight, putting them back on near my destination. Some girls like to wear little fold-up flat slippers while they travel.

To feel personally air-borne, I generally take off all my jewelry in flight and slip it in my purse—pearls, bracelets, even wristwatch.

If you do this sitting next to an attractive man, it has ever so faintly a strip-tease connotation. *Very* effective.

If you're chilly midway, don't send for your coat. A coat is uncomfortable and bulky. Huddle under an airplane blanket—they are usually blue and becoming. And imagine looking as though you were in bed. Travel really *does* have it!

It does pay to be quite beautifully made-up for travel. Nothing uncomfortable about *that,* because lipstick doesn't weigh much. Smell like heaven of course. Don't wear your wig. You can't lean back without worrying about its welfare.

PLANE TALK (ONLY TO MEN OF COURSE)

How do you get acquainted with the man next door? I assume you are now aloft, landing gear tucked under the plane, feet tucked under *you,* and you are reclining against the pillows you have stashed all around you. I always put one at the small of my back, one under my head and sometimes one under my feet. This is grabby. If everybody glommed onto three pillows, there wouldn't be enough to go around. Lots of people don't care for even one pillow, however, and there's hardly ever a shortage. If it's a night flight and you're dead for sleep, you can make yourself feel almost cloud-borne with all the pillows supporting you.

The man beside you? *Ah* yes! There's no real problem striking up a conversation with him. He's *there* and can't get away from you, at least during seat-belt times anyway. If you want him to get in touch with you first, however, I suggest reading a copy of *Sports Illustrated* from the moment you sit down. Don't think you're going to get the conversation away from trotting races and intercollegiate track meets for a good hour, however.

Taking out a cigarette but being unable to find a match is a sure conversation opener, although I must concede it's a bit primitive. If you don't smoke and he continues to keep his nose buried in a book or magazine, the thing to do is read along over his shoulder. He'll look up finally to see what in the name of heaven you're doing. If he doesn't look up and is reading, say *The Hat on the Bed,* it's easy to say, "Isn't it wonderful how John O'Hara just keeps turning out first-rate stories? Has he done it again?" If you can't make head or tail out of *what* he's reading you can say, after picking up a word or two, "Just what *are* cathode rays anyway?" Even if you don't understand a word of the explanation, the ice is broken and your conversation can drift to other things.

If he isn't reading but is staring into space and seems self-conscious and uneasy, I've found a simple, "What *are* you going to Pittsburgh for?" gets the introductions over with. You'd think a man might consider you pretty nosy for demanding an explanation of his actions, but usually everybody going *anywhere* is scared, excited, proud, happy or bored and wants to talk about it. Once he gets started, it may take some plain butting-in to get to tell why *you're* going to Pittsburgh.

Some girls feel that props make them more intriguing. I know one who favors a camera. She makes quite a thing of taking pictures up and down the aisle (which she never develops because naturally she doesn't use film). Small, high-powered field glasses are popular among other passengers. Another friend always carries a screwdriver in her purse and makes it a point to try to take something apart in flight—cigarette lighter, sunglasses or whatever. She says you don't really have to *do* anything with a screwdriver. Just the fact that you carry it is enough.

My friend Ann proclaims that, without any question, the best travel accessory in the world is embroidery. Men just go all to pieces over a girl who embroiders. She has been cross-stitching some beige linen luncheon napkins in flight for about a year. Cross-stitch, she says, doesn't require any great skill and is a guaranteed manmelter. Don't *knit,* she warns. Something about clacking knitting needles strikes fear in the heart of a man. Also he can't quite figure out whether what you're making is supposed to be Argyles or booties and he's embarrassed to ask. The fingers that wield the Tiffany thimble must be flawlessly manicured of course. And don't try making anything as big as a quilt on the theory that size is impressive. Few men want to be taken off the plane in a sea of lint.

I think every man deserves at least a trial run at conversation. I had completely written off the man next to me one night and was feigning deep sleep when he woke me up, the oaf. Rage lit up my beady little eyes. If the window had been open on his side, I'd have helped him *out*. This joker had on gum-sole shoes, blue and purple socks, a Scotch-plaid tie speared with his high school class pin, leather belt trimmed in turquoise and a patterned gray suit. (Yes, I'm the observant type.) I couldn't believe it either, except that I saw it. Well, once awake, I learned more about America's space program than I've ever been able to understand and assimilate since. He was a scientific genius and a marvelous man. You never *know*.

The stories you tell about yourself to your new-found friend should be more or less true. You're apt to run into him again and when you're *with* your father, who is not Count von Hohenzollern but a perfectly fine, though untitled, garage mechanic. A business assignment is fine to talk about because being a career girl immediately categorizes you as smart, respectable, hip, self-supporting and possibly susceptible to a dinner invitation. Speaking of eating, I must caution you right here about your table manners. A girl nest-egging her company travel funds sometimes skips several meals in a row. Regardless of the fact that this may be your first solid food of the week, a man seeing you wolf down a cupcake in one swallow gets nervous. *Chew slowly.*

If the man sitting next to you doesn't ask for a date (and you want him to), be sure you've managed to mention where you'll be staying and perhaps working. See if you can smoke him out too. An exchange of business cards is a good way.

Perhaps he has a rented car waiting for him at the airport and will ask to give you a lift into town. If it's daylight and you like him, why not? Hertz or Avis knows who he is. Anybody who has a car and driver I'd say is worth taking a chance on. Even if he's a gangster, he's probably so far up the ladder that he's harmless—in your case.

If you think giving your phone number to perfect—or imperfect —strangers and riding off to town with them is pretty reckless, I can only say I've talked to some lovely girls who could *kick* themselves for being suspicious, stand-offish and impossible to know on a trip. Having withered the man to a December maple leaf by refusing ever to be gotten in touch with again, they realized they'd probably lost a prince. One girl even asked me to say in my newspaper column that she'd made a mistake about a man on a flight from Ottawa to Toronto, and if the man were reading this to please get in touch through the column. How about *that?*

I don't say every man you meet in flight is worth knowing or even talking to, but I do know these can be a lovely, romantic two or three hours—little you suspended with a mysterious stranger in space, quite as close as buttercup sepals and nothing to do but visit. It certainly beats cocktail parties. (Though what doesn't?)

FEET ON THE GROUND

Once you get over the antique notion that all really beloved girls are met at airplanes, you'll travel better. Boarding school girls are. Full-fledged business women are not. It's heartless to drag your friends all those dozens of miles out to the airport. And what are you going to do with them if the man you've met should be someone you'd like to have drive you into town?

Now on to the baggage wait. It's easy to identify your own luggage as it comes down from the conveyor belt if you paste two or three inches of brightly colored freezer tape around the corners of each bag. The tape can be purchased at the hardware store. A foreign consul I know adds green crepe paper tassels to his luggage handles for identification, but they get rather messy when it rains.

Most luggage is ice cold when it comes off the plane. You have to resist the impulse to take it in your arms and warm it up. Or maybe that's just my idiosyncrasy. A lot of this book is, you know.

We can't just let this baggage-wait time go to waste, can we? Suppose there was a dreamboat on the plane you couldn't get *to* because he was way up front. Saunter around and come to rest near him. Muster the courage and say "Amazing how fast they get the baggage down nowadays, isn't it?" Or, "They seem to be taking forever," whichever is more appropriate. If you can think of something a bit more original, good for you!

If your baggage has been lost temporarily (hardly anybody's luggage is lost *forever*), this can be a blessing—it really can. During the initial crisis, three men will come over to tell you the same thing happened to them and offer advice.

Helplessness, though a bit incompatible with the kind of girl a company would send traveling, is a great travel "accessory." You can't get a fifty-dollar bill changed, the packages are too heavy and keep slipping out of your arms, you don't know west from south here in Wichita—or where to get a cab. The baggage-claim area isn't a bad place to douse a bit of this helplessness about. You may find yourself sharing a cab into town with a helper. Cab rides and limousine rides aren't as sexy as the plane or train ride—the suspended-in-space spell is broken—but they aren't *bad*.

THE GRAND HOTELS

It seems to me one of life's delicious little experiences is to be a reasonably young woman, say under eighty, fragrantly perfumed, smartly dressed, nicely heeled (with company funds), checking into the Ambassador East or the Beverly Wilshire or any other first-rate hotel in the world with company business to transact. If that isn't a sexy setup I am simply not a girl.

The hotels that rate four stars for women traveling on business are the old, more elegant hotels in a city. Next come the shiny, cold, modern new ones and, finally, motor hotels. I'd stay in a motor hotel only if it's headquarters for the convention or sales meeting you're attending. And has a pool.

Even old hotels often have two kinds of rooms now—standard "bedrooms" or the studio room with beds that slide under overhangs and look like couches. If you're going to entertain, the studio room is better. Sitting on a twin bed sipping your martini while he sits in the room's one chair is just a trifle too suggestive for openers.

Write ahead for reservations and get a confirmation back in writing. One friend tells me she always orders a three-fifty or five-dollar arrangement of white flowers for her room at the time she reserves it. This generally assures fruit from the manager, and, she says, adds an extra flourish to the service. You also have a fresh white flower to wear every day.

If it's too late to write before you leave home, wire—and ask for a confirming wire collect. If it's too late to wire, telephone—even if from the airport before you leave home or after you arrive. Never, never walk into a hotel cold.

The reason you need to have a confirmation in writing in your hand is that if you don't have it, you may find yourself out on the street with no room at the inn. If the hotel sees its own letter, someone will usually hustle around and find you a room.

If you know you are arriving after midnight, be sure to "guarantee" the room. This means they check you in the night before and you pay for the full night's lodging although you may not show up until four A.M. Scrupulously cancel reservations you don't use.

If the hotel has guaranteed one kind or price room and tries to palm off another, be firm. An eggshell-willed girl is popular and enchanting in many of life's situations—but not in a hotel. If they can push you around and intimidate you, they seem to like you *less* all the time you're being put out by their mistakes *more*. I arrived at a ritzy New York hotel one frosty morning maddened for sleep and ready to pile into bed in my guaranteed room. It was six-thirty A.M. and I'd traveled all night. The room wasn't ready, they said, but would be in about an hour. I set up a howl to be heard above the lions in Central Park across the street. "We'll put you in another room temporarily," they said. "And move you later in the day." More howling. I wanted to go to sleep *that* minute I said, to sleep for eight hours straight and not be shuffled about later in the day.

The only space they had available was a dear little suite. There they put me and there I stayed for the whole trip—at the cost of my reserved room. Their mistake for not having my room ready when I'd guaranteed it. They had to *pay*.

Ordinarily I wouldn't be as sharp as that with *anybody*, but I've found hotels are pretty cool customers and you have to cool-customer them right back.

If you're susceptible to noise, ask for a room away from the elevator and ask for it while you're right at the desk. Elevators clank up and down all night and people are always laughing it up and saying farewell outside them. A friend of mine brings along a little kit to disconnect the noisy air conditioners in hotels and on trains—but I suppose you can be *too* fussy.

LIVING GRANDLY AT THE GRAND HOTEL

However haughty you were with the front desk, you can forget it with the rest of the staff—switchboard girls, elevator boys, bellboys, maid. At least that's my code, schizophrenic as it sounds!

A housekeeper can be your best friend. She will rustle you extra coat hangers, a needle and thread, a second blanket, an ironing board. She'll set you adrift in towels, stitch you up if you're ripping, provide a heating pad if you're dying. Obviously you can't be a very good friend to somebody you're going to steal blind, so you have to decide early in the game that you aren't going to take her towels.

If you don't wish to be wakened early, hang the DO NOT DISTURB sign on the doorknob before you go to bed. It works. Otherwise the maids will be doing what is called "just checking" but which sounds like just breaking in (with four hammers) at dawn. (They have a certain number of rooms to make up every day and have to start *somewhere*.)

Occasionally you get into a hotel that is so noisy you think they are trying to drive you out of your skull. I remember one like that in Venice. It sounded as though all the armor in all the museums in sunny Italy was being hurled down the elevator shaft—at six in the morning. They were cleaning the rust from the pipes that week.

Sometimes they are building a wing onto the hotel—or building a skyscraper across the street. There's nothing much you can do about these acts of architecture, but acts of television or revelry next door you can call down and complain about.

Switchboard girls are usually nice, except in certain big city hotels where they're wretched and mean. It doesn't do a bit of good to get haughty, however, because then the service dries up completely—and so does your message flow. When they get you a wrong number, better say "*We* got a wrong number," not "*You* seem to have goofed; I said Plaza *five*." If you pick up the phone and get nothing but blank silence for fifteen minutes, I think "Was that operator delivered of her baby all right?" is preferable to pure, mouth-foaming, uncontrollable if justifiable rage.

I love the life in a hotel . . . the right to be babied . . . the right to complain . . . the right to privacy . . . the right to men you don't have the right to at home. Believe it or not, we're almost up to them. Just two other tiny departments first.

TOWEL-TAKING WAYS

Hotel managements say they don't worry unduly about towels. It's those bedspreads, blankets, rugs, lamps, dishes, ice buckets, radios, light bulbs and wastebaskets that give them bad moments. Even dignified businessmen who chairman the city's biggest charity drives have been known to pop one of those thirsty terry hotel bathrobes into their luggage before leaving town.

I must confess I took towels for years—never more than one per hotel and never from a room that cost less than ten dollars, to be sure. (Even thieves have their principles.) Nevertheless, this added up to quite a few towels. And what do I have to show for it today? A motley collection of scraps of terry that are ravelly and threadbare (towels are seldom new when you get them) with somebody else's name across the bottom.

It's not worth the black blob on your conscience. I've found that when you quit stealing towels you enjoy your visit more. You can be real friends with the maid, stop holding your breath when the bellboy touches the clasp on your bag, and look the cashier straight in the eye when you check out. You can also unpack in the presence of family and friends.

If you must take a little *something* (sometimes a thief can't just quit cold but has to taper off), there's soap, stationery, shoe-polish rags and Kleenex. Those the hotel doesn't miss very much.

TIPPING TIPS

While we're on the subject of who owes what to whom, there's the scratchy problem of tipping. It's hard to know what to give, because nobody will *tell* you. I've been trying to find out for *years*.

In one hotel I just came right out and asked one of the maids what she'd consider a proper tip for cleaning the room. Before my eyes she began to look very peculiar and started backing out of the room, muttering, "I'm sure I wouldn't know, ma'am . . . I mean it's whatever a body feels like giving . . . imagine *asking* . . ." Pretty soon I was alone with her mop, bucket and ammonia.

I also telephoned the public relations department of a famous hotel to ask if they'd put me in touch with someone who could give definitive information about tipping. I could hear the evasion waves jumping right through the phone before the girl even *answered* me. "I really don't know if we could supply that information," she said. "I'll have to call you back."

Good thing I didn't turn down any dinner invitations waiting for the call.

Deciding to try the tippers instead of the tipped, I next conducted a small private poll among three well-traveled businessmen and five women who also travel on business. I came up with eight different recommendations. After multiplying by nineteen, dividing by five and having four martinis, these are *my* tipping recommendations for the business woman who is somewhat less affluent than Helena Rubinstein but somewhat *more* than the Girl Scout mistress taking the girls off to the National Jamboree.

Porters at air or train terminal—twenty-five cents per bag. If you have five bags, two of which are very light (like a wig box), you might get away with a dollar for the whole bunch. If you have only one bag and it's hefty, fifty cents would be more appropriate than twenty-five.

Terminal bus that takes you into town—No tip for the driver even though he stows your luggage away and gets it out.

Taxis—Twenty-five cents for every dollar spent if you have no luggage. Add an extra quarter or so if you're luggaged and the driver helps.

Doorman at hotel—Twenty-five cents if he takes one bag into the lobby, fifty cents if he takes two, one dollar if you have a lot of things.

Bellboy (taking luggage to or from room)—Twenty-five cents a bag for several bags. Possibly you can get away with one dollar for five bags. Never give less than fifty cents even if he carries only one suitcase. If two boys and multiple pieces of luggage are involved, they would get from one fifty to two dollars between them.

Maids at hotel—Fifty cents per night for two or three nights' lodging. Three dollars for the week.

Deliveries from desk—Twenty-five cents for flowers, telegrams, letters. Fifty cents for heavier things.

Room service, food or beverage—Fifteen to thirty per cent of the check! (I don't like this any better than you do.)

Restaurants—Fifteen per cent of the check for waiter. One or two dollars for the captain in a fancy restaurant. One or two dollars for the *maître d'* if he seated you approximately where you wanted to be or honored your reservation promptly while others waited.

Doormen who get you cabs—Fifteen or twenty-five cents; more if it's snowing.

Yes, tipping is expensive and yes, the whole thing has probably gotten way out of hand—but bacon was once fifteen cents a pound. Are you going to pretend you can still buy it at that price? Tipping simply costs what it costs.

If you undertip or *don't* tip, it will come back to haunt you. I know. Remember, you aren't outwitting the hotel—you're outwitting the workers, most of whom are nice family people with mortgages and pets. Occasionally a famous *maître d'* is rumored to have been able to buy a mansion in the millionaires' section of town on customers' largess. More often he's scraping to pay for bridgework or somebody's college education just like the rest of us. I'm not even sure there's such a thing as *over*tipping if you can afford it, when you consider that you've made someone happy.

To make travel tipping less of a strain, I suggest carrying two or three dollars in change and several single dollar bills.

MAN HUNT

Meanwhile back at the libido, where are the *men?*

Hopefully you'll meet some in the course of the business day who will take an interest in you. Possibly you have an old beau or two stashed away in this particular city and you can call them up. Perhaps you're armed with telephone numbers of friends of friends. (Don't hesitate to badger and scramble for this intelligence if it promises men. I wouldn't fool around with anybody's sister's college roommate's *cousin* who's a lovely girl just like *you* are, however.)

The thing about traveling on business is that, with just the flimsiest excuse, a girl can call up men she used to work with, won a Charleston contest with or never laid eyes on, and nobody is embarrassed. "Doris wanted you to know her azalea finally dropped dead," is a perfectly acceptable message. See what develops. To an old beau you want to see you merely say, "I'd like to see you while I'm here." You don't have to be so subtle as at home.

It's quite all right to suggest to one of the friends of friends you don't know (a man) that he stop by your hotel for a drink. Anything below the third floor of the establishment is actually pretty businesslike. Natives often love having an excuse to drop by the city's best hotel. Sign the check like a good girl.

You may have dear old nonromantic friends to look up, too. Often it's better not to tell them you're coming until you see how the romantic situation is developing or not developing. Most people are happy to fit themselves into your schedule.

A little thing like your work could get in the way of your visiting *anybody*, however sexed. These are the misfortunes of war—and business. Don't forget that being successful is what *got* you traveled and you mustn't blow it all in a few ill-chosen nights on the town.

If you do have free time, one excellent plan for collecting, sorting and consolidating men in a travel-town is to give a small cocktail party in your hotel room. Have this right at the end of the first working day. Ask the people you're doing business with and any of the assorted old and new menfolk just mentioned. I guess you *could* let in a girl or two, *maybe*.

At the party you'll have a chance to get better acquainted with the work-people and to look over the strangers to see whether you want to invest an evening. The hotel will do the catering if you like. Food can be anything from simple canapés to a rather impressive nut-crusted cheeseball with crackers. They'll send a bartender and liquor and charge by the drink. Don't worry, they keep track.

If you want to keep the party to the absolute minimum cost, buy your own liquor from the store, also modest hors d'oeuvres. Order ice and glasses from the hotel. Perhaps you'll want them to send up a large pot of coffee, too. If one or two of the guests are clients, prospects, or the people you are doing business with, your firm should pick up the tab. Isn't it heaven?

HOTEL PLANS

Suppose you didn't meet anyone on the plane, your business has produced absolutely *nothing* promising, you didn't sit next to a dreamboat at the concert alone last night, and you don't know a soul in the city to look up. I'd be willing to let you be discouraged— except for one thing. There's always the hotel. Usually there are some very interesting and interested men there. I was present at one of these chance encounters which developed into marriage.

When I was traveling with Miss Universe, Sweden's Hillevi Rombin, on a Catalina Swimsuit promotion one year, I picked up a darling man in the elevator of the St. Francis in San Francisco. "Picked up" sounds so naughty. What he said was, "Didn't I see you check in earlier downstairs? You were wearing a navy blue suit." I said, "Yes, I'm sure that was I." He said, "Why don't we have a drink in the bar?" I said, "Marvelous, I'm expecting the girl I'm traveling with to be down in a few minutes. I'll just call up and tell her to join us."

I called up old Hillevi and said, "Hillevi, dear, I'm in the bar. Please don't hurry. We have all the time in the world." Hillevi, who could be slower than Dodger Stadium traffic when she was getting to a business appointment, was down the stairs in four minutes. Psychic or something. That was the last look my new acquaintance ever gave me. Hillevi and my date were married within the year. They now live in a hotel of their own in Florida.

Maybe the thing to do is not pick up a *hotel* man. I don't think *that's* the moral, however. The moral is not to travel with Miss Universe, unless you happen to be even *more* beautiful than she is. I still say there are good, sweet, susceptible men in hotels.

And now, here are some Hotel Plans to put into operation if you dare.

Plan 1. At lunch, cocktail, or dinner time, wander down to the banquet section. Having your own party to go to takes the heart-pounding scares out of the situation, but whatever you do or don't, walk into the room that seems to have the most men. Five of them will say, "Well, hello there!" One sensible one will probably add, "Yours is down the hall in the Sierra Room." You can say, "Oh, yes . . . please forgive me," then go on to your own party or back to the lobby. Later, when one of the men from the party sees you in the hotel, he'll be free to ask, "Did you ever get to the right room?" (No, but you certainly used the right plan.)

Plan 2. A dream walking lives two doors away on your floor. Wait until you know he is in his room, then put on your hat and coat, grab your purse, march right down to his room and ram your key in his door. He will come out irritated and sputtering "What's going on here?" Compare his room number with the key in your hand and say, "Oh, good heavens, how stupid of me." Then get ready to be asked if you've had dinner.

Plan 3. Sort through your phone messages. Pick one that clearly contains your name and room number. When the man is out, slip the message under his door. He's only two doors away, remember. Perhaps he won't return the message via the operator but will bring it over.

The bar is always there, but I'd rather present myself to the Salvation Army for a handout than pick up a man in a bar. It just isn't the way to start a great friendship. You're another needy character—not the smart, pretty career girl they sent to town to knock everybody dead.

When you start getting acquainted with strange men in hotels, no matter what sort of building you're in, you *could* get whacked over the head, of course. But this can happen to you in your own home *town* if you have no sense about whom to take up with.

A few weeks ago I was walking home on Madison Avenue and a man started walking beside me. "Like anything you saw?" he asked. I'd been looking at valentines in a card-shop window. "Yes, quite a few," I said. My friend continued to walk with me and we chatted until I said I really must say good-bye, that I was hurrying home to get dinner for a hungry husband.

He was extremely good-looking, well-dressed, tall, thirty-eightish, intelligent . . . and a nut. I'm sure of it. Him I think a girl could wind up strangled by if she played her cards right . . . or at least shaken down for some money. How do I know? Well, he was just "funny." Use your sixth sense. When in doubt, unload the man.

A few weeks prior to that I was getting into an elevator at the Park-Sheraton Hotel in Cleveland when a man stopped me and said, "Please let me buy you a drink." (By now it should be clear to you that your author is maybe the third or fourth most popular woman in the world.) "I can't," I said. I had the same hungry husband on my hands and *this* time he was upstairs. (I really am a good girl.)

My intuition tells me the "elevator man" was okay. How do I know *that?* I don't for sure, but by the time a woman is twenty-five years old, I think she has an intuitive feeling about who is A-okay or A-*not*-okay after she's chatted with a man for ten minutes. Many other tycoonesses, I'm sure, have found men in hotels who are good, safe and kind, traveling on business just as they are.

Naturally you stay out of a brand new friend's hotel room. Naturally you keep him out of yours. Certainly you learn a good deal about him over a drink before you commit yourself to anything further, even a second drink. The man should have a business card (although I don't rule out the possibility he might have lifted it off a still warm body). You get his by offering yours, or by asking where you might get in touch with him during the day, or simply by saying, "Could I have your card in case I need to call you?" Whatever business his card says he's in, he should know a great deal about it.

LITTLE GIRL IN THE GREAT BIG CITY

Suppose there *are* no men, and I mean *none*. You can't scare up anybody, and furthermore you haven't seen a thing you'd even care about *scaring*.

Being in a city you've never been in before is an experience regardless of how few people you know there. (After a few visits you probably *will* know some people.) I can remember being all alone in Philadelphia on a rainy Sunday morning and striking out to see Independence Hall, the Liberty Bell and Betsy Ross's house. Pretty exciting to a girl who'd never seen the historical East before. I mean that. A date with history can be just as fascinating as a date with a man. (Well, almost.) A feathery breeze caressing you as you splash about the pool of the Arizona Biltmore is still caressing even if you're alone. I personally think it's great to curl up in a strange bed—alone—with a sack of stale gumdrops (my *favorite*) and a Daphne du Maurier novel. If you were home you'd have to be changing shelf paper or something else sensible.

It may be you'll have the incredible luck to arrive in New York City during a World Series. If you're a baseball fan—and if the Yankees won the pennant—you'll love it. If you aren't a fan, you'll think everybody has gone off his rocker. To protect yourself from cabdrivers, I suggest this system:

Driver (As you get into cab): What's the score, lady?

You: I want to go to Lord and Taylor, please.

Driver: Yeah, but what's the score?

You (Innocently): Score?

Driver: Yeah, the score, the *score!*

You: Oh, you mean the store? It's Lord and Taylor, on Thirty-eighth and Fifth. You're a new driver, aren't you? Do you like New York?

Driver: I'm talking about the game, lady.

You: Oh, are we playing a game?

Driver (Very upset by now): The *ball* game, Lady!

You: I'm terribly sorry, I didn't understand. I didn't bring any balls with me . . .

Driver (Can't believe his ears): You mean you don't know about the *Ball Game?*

You (Sweet and apologetic): No, I'm sorry, I just wanted to go shopping.

At this point the driver will usually drive you to your destination like a greased rocket-ship. He may not even wait to be paid after he's dumped you out.

Another driver might have a radio with him. In this case he won't ask the questions, but you will need earplugs.

PROFIT AND LOSS

We haven't discussed yet whether you are going to make a profit on this trip. That depends on your desires . . . and whether or not your company has made profit-participation possible.

Some girls prefer to live it up on a trip. They enjoy "overtipping," ordering eight-dollar breakfasts and traveling about town by limousine. More power and God Bless.

Others prefer to live frugally and keep the change. The only trouble with the latter system is that companies sometimes make it awfully tough for you to get your hands on the dough. They'll cheerfully pay for plane tickets, hotel bills, car rental and a reasonable sum for tips, but they screech to a grinding halt over cash expenditures (for which you naturally haven't a receipt in the world). If your company is that perverse, there's nothing to do but live it up like a pasha. A girl doesn't want to miss out entirely on the economic benefits of travel. One girl I know got so disgusted when she couldn't even earmark ten dollars for the fox muff she had in mind that she had her hair done three times in one week in the hotel beauty salon.

One thing is certain. Until you get to be a rich-skin, you'll always live at least as well traveling as you do at home, and probably better. Even if you're frugal, certain travel benefits, such as maid service, room service, privacy, and somebody to take messages, can *not* be converted into cash (thank heaven). You've nothing to do but relax and enjoy them.

THE GET RICH SLOWLY NEST-EGG PLAN

Happily, some companies make it possible for you to nest-egg year in, year out. Not every girl can be induced to stay out on the road six months of the year, so a company rewards her with a little company-approved graft. You may only be out for a few days, but here's how to nest-egg, *if* you want to, with reasonable integrity. I've given up on this kind of graft myself, and not merely because I no longer need the money. I don't think it's worth it in the long

run. But as you will be able to judge from my expertise, an innocent I am *not!*

Most companies, except the Army, feel that an employee is entitled to live comfortably away from home. The basic plan is *not*
to live poshly but to say you did and then pocket the difference.
This is only possible by *not* running up a big hotel bill and by
making your outside expenses the big item (your own *alleged* outside expenses). Some girls run up the hotel bill and ask for large
outside expenses. They don't get sent out next time. You can't have
it both ways. You'll only get your sizeable, mostly mythical *outside*
expenses met if the hotel bill reads like an austerity plan.

Start by reserving a modest room . . . in a good hotel, however, or
you won't meet the right men in the elevator as you've been promised. Very important.

To "save" your company further money (which saving they will
never realize because it will accrue to you in added outside expenses
—surely I've got through by now), be sure to tell the desk if you're
checking out late. (Checkout time at the hotel is noon, your plane
doesn't leave until four. Tell the hotel you'll need the room until
two-thirty.) Usually they'll let you stay without charging you. Again,
the company's thoughtful little girl has saved the firm's paying a
night's lodging—and justified another expenditure for herself on the
outside.

You may like having a cocktail in your room. Drinks sent up from
the bar are expensive when you add room service and tips. Much
cheaper to buy a bottle and make your own. One girl I know brings
two or three miniature bottles of booze from the plane. If she's used
up her quota there, she wheedles other passengers out of theirs.
(One more get-acquainted ruse, and obviously only an alcoholic
would object.) Okay, you've "saved" the company a few more hotel
bucks.

Making phone calls away from the room can accrue savings—they
are usually fifteen or twenty cents apiece from your bedside. Perhaps
you can make them free in an office you're going to.

Along with keeping your hotel bill low, on a nest-egg trip you
might cheerfully have agreed to travel tourist instead of first-class.
Only do that if you're sure you can make it up in this other way.

We are *not* out to make the company richer—unless it's *your* company or you're a big stockholder.

Very well, now let's talk about those "outside expenses" you're going to run up.

Most companies assume you eat three meals a day—fat hefty ones—and give their approval. I suppose they think company bodies work harder well fed, but I've yet to see even a man eat at home the way he says he ate in Minneapolis.

Procedure: Even if you haven't eaten breakfast since you were six, your company will pay. (You'll need this money to get your tummy repaved someday.) Perhaps you can nibble some of the fruit a benevolent hotel management left in your room. If, in their minds, an eight-dollar room doesn't quite justify fruit, your scrambled eggs and coffee at a lunch counter down the street will be only about eighty-five cents. You will charge your company three-eighty-five for the breakfast you didn't eat at the hotel.

Lunch is cottage cheese. On the expense account you turn in it will read three-seventy-four. Dinner is something that a lovely man is going to take you to. It could be the lovely man *you're* supposed to take to dinner because he's a client. But oh no, he won't let you pay. On your expense account, dinner is listed as five-forty—or ten-eighty if you're presumed to have taken him. (It's a little dangerous saying you took somebody you didn't take, but I think you should know all the possibilities.) There, you've already nest-egged at least the price of a new pair of shoes, and you're working on the matching handbag.

Other minor savings will come in transportation. You take the airport limousine into town instead of the cab and save three dollars. The three dollars should be yours. (You'll list a mythical cab fare, of course.) If you walk about town or take the local bus, more savings, though again you write down that you were cabbing.

If you're planning to nest-feather further by undertipping, I'm against it. As for refusing help at all and doing it yourself, that's your prerogative if you're a big strong girl and have the nerve. I can still see the pretty Olympic diving star I traveled with on another Catalina promotion battling a Cornhusker Hotel bellboy to the floor to keep possession of her suitcase. "Does he think I'm a damned invalid or something?" she complained.

Push-them-yourself carts are becoming more prevalent in plane and train terminals. Why not use one? Naturally you charge the company (listed under tips) for the work you did yourself.

It's fine to have your travel wardrobe pressed and cleaned at the hotel. Some people I know bring everything they own and have it all freshly done up to take home. It seems to me excess baggage charges would eat up the profits. Anyway, that's going too far. Fair is fair.

Whatever plan you're on, it isn't easy to cash checks in a hotel unless you have one of their credit cards. If you travel often enough, it would be worth while getting one from Hilton, Sheraton and other major chains, or use a Diner's Club card. If you don't have a card, better start cashing your check a day before you need the money. An assistant manager will have to check on you, and he may be out of the hotel for a day.

Diner's Club, Carte Blanche, Air Travel and telephone credit cards are all good to have.

Whether you prefer the Get-Rich-Slow-Nest-Egg plan or the Live-It-Up-There's-No-Tomorrow travel plan, I *know* you're going to have a ball.

You've been a fine little traveler, my dear—drinking in the city, gathering up the men, raking in the money. And before we leave the tender subject of money to delve deeper into the world of Office Sex, let's look at some of the other possible fringe benefits you might be able to carry off.

As you can see from its title, the following chapter is a very *practical* one.

CHAPTER 12

HOW TO STEAL
A CHIPPENDALE BREAKFRONT

At one motion picture studio (my favorite poor, beleaguered example of how not to run a company), one of the executives used to send his teen-age children and a pack of playmates to the studio commissary for lunch on Saturday; then movies would be run for the moppets in Projection Room A. These outings involved roughly six employees on golden hours, but management never complained. That's the way the movie mogulled, and that's just one example of the pleasurable extras some companies allow top management.

I think a degree of trickery or misrepresentation or even outright thievery is "expected," which is almost to say "proper," on lower levels too. One girl I know was telephoned by the comptroller about an item on her expense account listed as "$43.84—marble-base Empire lamp for office." Employees were not allowed to buy furniture, but the comp said, "Look, honey, forty-three bucks for a fancy doo-dad lamp we aren't paying this week. Put it down as a couple of extra lunches and cocktail dates."

High-level or low-level, I sincerely believe that most companies are not stolen blind. They are stolen with their eyes wide open.

This is quite, quite horrible! If you don't overreach a little bit, you are probably a silly and a sucker—yet stealing is stealing. If you say that the lunch cost ten-seventy-five when it actually cost five-fifty you are lying, and lying is bad for you. When you operate like a South American dictator, it hurts inside, and that takes some of the fun out of it. Yes it does! Even the most outrageous grafters say they get this funny little twinge near the kidney every time they go too far. (It doesn't stop them. It just pains them.) The thing to do, I think, is work out a code of ethics you can *live* with. (Never mind what the company can live with. They can live with just about anything, I've decided. They're miserable paranoids about raises and indulgent sugar daddies about expenses.)

When you have arrived at a professional level which allows an expense account at all, I think most managements permit it to be stretchable. In other words, they *expect* you to pad a little. It's a ghastly state of affairs but a true one.

When certain executives seem to be getting away with murder— Christian Diors for the wives, trips to Jamaica for the mothers-in-law, chinchilla for the mistresses—I think the company is usually collaborating. Supplying super-luxuries may be a company's way of giving an executive more money without his having to pay taxes on it. (Don't bother to get in touch with *me*, Internal Revenue Service. *I'll* never tell *which* companies!)

I think people who profiteer most outrageously (without management sanction) are sick, of course, and expense account cheating is only one of the symptoms. The kindest thing you can say of them is that they're children . . . with an overweening need to be taken care of. Sometimes they fit the Robin Hood syndrome—lifting from the rich to help the poor. One chap I know smuggled his less-fortunate boy friend to Phoenix for a week as excess luggage and miscellaneous telegrams.

I can't impose my own expense account code on you, of course (I've got *enough* on my conscience); but I'm going to tell you what it *is*, because I believe this code is more or less subscribed to by many "reasonably honest" people.

As I've broken it down, and already mentioned in terms of travel, there are two ways to profit (we won't use that distressing word "cheat" again) on an expense account. One is to live it up and have the company pay. The other is to say you lived it up, have the company pay and pocket the money.

I used to favor the latter method. What could be smarter than steering a docile client into a health-food kitchen for marrow-bone sandwiches and putting in a tab for eighteen dollars at Le Chauveron. (Or skipping dinner entirely with the suggestion you both have a big bowl of corn flakes when you get to your respective homes, then putting in a bill.) Then I married somebody of a different fiscal faith, and *he* said, "Putting down a grassburger as a steak dinner is not only immoral, it is unthinkable! Whatever lavish meal you provide for a bona fide client is okay because your company is getting the benefit of the client's good will. But when you drag the client to a fourth-rate joint or don't feed him at *all* in order to pocket the money, you are sinking pretty deeply into the mire."

Very well, my revised expense account moral code (and switching over was no hardship really—the grassburgers were awfully grassy) is: Entertain whomever your company will let you entertain and as lavishly as they will allow, but do what you said you did and with the real person. To Le Pavillon (that's a verb) with someone not your client (or whatever makes him a legitimate business expense) is off-limits. As for exaggerating what you actually spent and pocketing the difference—though I often wonder how you can exaggerate a New York restaurant tab—that's okay if you only up the bill two or three dollars. No trying to work in a new beaded evening bag from just having had cocktails. (Isn't it handy how my moral code dovetails exactly with what you can get away with!)

Now, what about areas other than food—putting in for theater tickets when you actually saw a movie, charging for parking when you found a place on the street, collecting for a gift you kept yourself? I've done all those mangy things in my past, but I do think they're mangy. (Nothing is more sanctimonious than a reformed criminal.)

Though we know there is unbelievable cheating and stealing in companies, I think a "nice" girl knows where to draw the line. I believe it's possible for her to "profit" in only the mildest way to make life more gala without developing into a Ma Barker. A secretary I know puts it this way: "When I worked for (and she named a famous man) in his suite at the Waldorf Towers, our hotel bill was several thousand dollars a week. I never thought twice about ordering up an extra bottle of Scotch for my personal use when we were ordering a case of bourbon. I could just as well have had them send up a sixty-dollar bottle of Ma Griffe while I was at it because I okayed the bills, but I wouldn't have dreamed of it. That would have been *stealing!*"

In the actual making out of an expense account, I have just two suggestions: 1) Don't wait too long after the event or trip. You won't be able to remember what you did with the money, let alone make it sound convincing. 2) Make out everything in uneven numbers. Put down $5 for lunch, $10 for dinner and $2.50 for cab, and you're likely to get the whole thing back in your lap. Items listed in $4.87's, $11.02's and $2.76's will usually go unquestioned.

In taking a man to lunch, I suggest you not reach for the check with your limp little arm in his presence—unless you never had any intention of paying. Even if he's deserving, there's just hardly a man alive who feels comfortable while a lady hassles with money or even signs the check. Pick a restaurant in which to do your entertaining, tell the *maître d'* you will often have men guests but don't ever wish to pay at the table. Say you'll rendezvous at the cashier's just before luncheon is over, return later in the afternoon to pay or, better still, have them mail the bill, adding generous tips all around.

THE GREAT MAILROOM ROBBERY
AND OTHER THEFTS

Elizabeth McGibbons says in her book, *Manners in Business:* "Often the most lenient management has to say, 'no personal calls except in an emergency.' When this edict is put forth, it is usually because the youngest employees have been making dates on the phone, and the married women have been shopping, running their homes and often their children via the office phone."

Can you imagine? Making dates on the phone! And taking care of household business from the office! Must be some kind of kooks!

Listen, if Miss McGibbons really knows managements that have no-personal-phone-call edicts, I think in the interests of the work output she ought to print the list so we telephoners can give them a wide berth. It seems to me that making full use of the company telephone is the only way a girl can really concentrate on her job. If she has to run down to the drugstore to make or receive personal calls, she'll never get anything done!

The bills do run up, I'm sure. Since direct dialing has come in, I even feel a twinge of pity for the poor company. You see these pitiful little notes come around saying, "Will whoever placed the fourteen calls to Loganberry 7–3462 in Wilkes-Barre, Pennsylvania, please report to the accounting department at *once!*" You know very well they have about as much chance of getting a confession as trying to get a senator-elect to admit he stuffed the ballot box.

Before you excuse yourself to go make your nightly call to Calcutta, however, I will remind you that some companies are not above having a representative call up the Wilkes-Barre number and ask questions until they find out whose relatives live there. (For the cost of the calls they can even fly a representative *in* to Wilkes-Barre.) Other companies place a "monitor" on each phone, some sort of device that causes a deafening siren wail when you dial outside the local area. I think this is the best honor system. If your company hasn't cracked down yet and you want a little trellis of morality to climb by, I would say normal toll calls are okay, long distance is out!

Sending out personal deliveries by company messenger service should be reserved for emergencies. (The fish people are outside your apartment with eight live Maine lobsters, and you forgot to leave the key under the mat.)

What about company stamps on personal mail? This is probably academic in most cases, because you've no more chance of getting into the mailroom unattended than of slipping into Fort Knox with a basket. I do know one darling firm that tacks a sign on its mailroom door—"Stamps Are In—Plan Your Theft Early"—but to my knowledge they're unique. Maybe companies would be more lenient if it weren't for our tendency to take the entire yardstick when given an inch. (I'm beginning to sound like Miss McGibbons.) Haven't you noticed, though, when girls get to mail letters free, you rarely see a letter addressed to Maxwell, Kansas, Route 2, that isn't slathered with three or four airmails and a special delivery? How would you feel if they were *your* stamps?

I do have this slim advice about packages. If you have a personal package to mail that weighs at least eight pounds, bring about thirty-five cents in nickels, dimes and pennies to the mailroom. Say worriedly, "Chuck, dear, this is all the change I have; please bill me." Usually you won't get the bill.

What about out and out stealing? A recent article in the New York *World Telegram and Sun* said, "Management consultants estimate a fourteen-million-dollar daily loss by business through 'shrinkage and shortage' or internal loss of money and merchandise." Kind of scary, huh? I'm not surprised, though. I've seen everything lifted in my time from bookends to Muzak installations. Two friends managed to get a very expensive desk out of the Music Corporation of America's Beverly Hills offices in broad daylight a few years ago, and I mean the Brink's and British train robbery people could have taken notes.

I don't want to let any of us off the hook, but I think an employer's attitude can sometimes be a girl's ruination. The stingy president of a vitamin company drove one exemplary secretary I know right into a life of crime. In addition to his salary and profits, this joker had so many stock dividends flowing in that he never had to write a check. Whatever specific amount he needed—$11.34, $38.17, $6.09—he would just poke around in his desk drawer and come up with a dividend check for almost that exact amount. What he never poked around and came up with was his own cigarettes. He bummed from Miss Blue until she was sick to death of it and finally, in total disgust, she took home several pounds of amino acid.

I never thought I'd tell you *this*, but once a blabbermouth . . .

At the job I went to at double my previous salary, the day of reckoning came in two years. (Remember I said not to think that when you had made the deal of the century, you'd heard the last of it.) The office manager called me in one day and said, "Helen, love, we're going to have to cut your salary by a third. It doesn't have anything to do with your work (well, I should think *not!*), but what you make is really terribly out of line. We're in a bit of trouble on the West Coast, and we have to cut expenses. We know your husband can support you and all that."

"What if I don't agree to the cut?" I asked, fighting the tears and a very strong death wish for us both.

"I'm afraid it's take it or leave it," he said.

I thought it over overnight and decided to stay. There weren't that many good copywriting jobs in Los Angeles even at my reduced salary. It was true that David and I didn't need my income to live on. I even felt a twitch of sympathy for the company, so I continued to work hard and wasn't even terribly miffed with anybody. Then one day by accident (she accidentally left it on top of her desk; I accidentally waited for her to leave and snatched it up!) I saw another copywriter's salary check. She was making almost as much as my uncut salary. I knew this girl had always had an important friend at court, but I marched to the front office and demanded my original salary be restored. They said they couldn't manage just then but would keep working at it. I didn't stomp out—for the original reasons plus the fact that I was now writing a book and didn't want to start a new job at the same time —but I began to burn, slowly, quietly and around the clock.

One day I took home four boxes of carbon paper, five packages of yellow second sheets and ten stenographer's notebooks. When I got them in the house, David said, "What are you planning to do, open a stationery store?"

"No, I have a little work to do tonight," I explained.

The following week when I arrived home with a quart of type cleaner, four boxes of stencils and three hundred file folders, David marched me back to the garage for my trouble. "Look, dear," he said, "if you steal ten dollars worth of supplies every working day for the next two years, it won't make up for your salary cut. (You see, he'd figured it *out!*) Either be a good girl or leave the company."

I stayed and cut down to Lindy ballpoint pens and erasers. But I never forgave that place, although my salary was finally reinstated.

I'd just better say that as far as stealing is concerned, Tess Trueheart, you're on your own! I think if I had it to do over again, I wouldn't steal at all. My outright thefts in twenty-one years (excluding expense accounts, and we've *closed* that subject) probably didn't amount to more than fourteen dollars—mouse stuff to a real carpetbagger, ultimate corruption to a goodskin. Anyway, I wish this minute I could just write a check and get it off my conscience.

But enough of fringe benefits—honest, semi-honest or outright larcenous. It's now time to take out our curlers, put on our sexiest dress and find out what happens when lightning strikes in the office.

CHAPTER 13

THE OFFICE AFFAIR

W<small>E'VE COVERED</small> a lot of territory, I think you'll agree—getting ahead on the job, fighting jungle warfare, traveling on business in sexy style, stealing . . . What we haven't covered—or uncovered—yet are office affairs. (I know you thought we'd never get there!)

A lot of otherwise perfectly hip people, it seems to me, don't take the subject of office affairs very seriously. They think of office romance as mere purple puppy passion among some junior clerks and attribute carnal lust only to a few walrussy-faced tycoons who chase their secretaries around the desk.

Based on my own observations and experiences in nineteen different offices, I'm convinced that offices are sexier than Turkish harems, fraternity house weekends, Hollywood swimming parties, Cary Grant's smile or the Playboy center-fold, and more action takes place in them than in a nymphet's daydreams.

Office romance not serious? Dynasties are toppled, new beneficiaries named in wills, stock issues plunge, new corporation heads are elected—not to mention girls getting pregnant, sexually defunct men getting funct and married ladies who thought they had it made finding it's all unmade just because some man goes ape over some girl in some office!

We've got to keep in mind who's saying these things, of course. You know how one person will attend a party and say it was the greatest little party he ever went to while some other guy who attended the same party will say it was a thumping bore. Well this is my view of the party, and I do honestly believe these things to be true!

1. No office anywhere on earth is so puritanical, impeccable, elegant, sterile or incorruptible as not to contain the yeast for at least one affair, probably more. You can say it couldn't happen *here,* but just let one yeasty type into the place and first thing you know the bread starts rising!

2. Practically every man in an office has had, is having, or is capable of having an affair at some time in his life. No matter how fine his character, how much he loves his wife or how happy he is at home, under the right (or wrong, depending on your viewpoint) set of circumstances, any adult male is a candidate. The circumstances would, of course, include being acted upon by a certain person. If *she* never happened to him, maybe *it* never would either. (There are any number of "shes" around in a man's lifetime.)

3. Single girls are equally "good" candidates. In the life of almost every single girl in an office I think you will find a current affair, past affair or contemplated affair. Never overestimate the resistance of Miss Mousy Mousecrat typing away at her Smith-Corona. You think she'd thrash out like an octopus if a man tried anything funny! Of course she would if he walked right up to her desk and blurted out an indecent proposal. After weeks of wooing and flattery, however—people have *time* in offices, they both work there every day—she's apt to be in a more receptive mood.

With the exception of engaged girls, very young girls, deeply religious or frightened femmes of *any* age who have hermetically sealed themselves off from men (I know one who calls her sixty-eight-year-old mother every afternoon from work and says, "Is din-din on the table, dearest?"), I think most girls in offices *are* seeing or *will* see combat, if only with the man they ultimately marry.

4. Far from being minor, transient, pippypoo associations, romances and affairs starting through work can be some of the most cliff-hanging, satisfying, memorable episodes in any two persons' lives. Even when things end sadly, a participant rarely says (nor, I believe, even *thinks*) he would have given his right arm for the whole thing not to have happened. He—or she—fantasizes the rest of his or her life, remembering the best of it.

5. Most husbands, except utter nutburgers, don't cheat in the first few years of marriage. About 94 per cent do after that. This is the Gurley-Brown Survey, you must remember, not scientifically documented, but a product of personal research! (I was willing to turn all this information over to Kinsey, Pomeroy and Martin, but nobody asked for it.)

6. The girl a married man "succumbs" to is forty-nine times out of fifty—again by my "inside" information—a girl he has met through his work, although she may not work in his own office. She seldom comes to him from his country club, church group, social milieu or alumni organization. She is hardly ever his wife's best friend.

7. Married *women* who work and become involved in an affair often draw their partners from some place other than the office. And they don't get involved nearly so often.

8. The blame (or responsibility, depending on that viewpoint!) for affairs rests about equally with men and girls. Though men usually instigate the office affair, girls second the motion enthusiastically—while pretending with all their insincere little hearts they were talked into something! No girl, in my opinion, is ever the categorically "put upon," innocent victim of a predatory married or unmarried man. So there!

9. At least once in an important man's career he makes a decision affecting hundreds or even thousands of people—to say nothing of sales, earnings and profits—based purely on whether something is good for his romance. He moves the convention from Salt Lake City to San Francisco because *she* lives in San Francisco. He says, "We'll be open the day after Thanksgiving," because *she'll* be in the

office. And on a minor level, things are being done every minute not for the stated reasons but because somebody's romance makes them necessary. One man I know left his neatly typed speech on his girl friend's dresser in Cleveland and flew to New York without it. His office just had time to teletype the whole thing to him from their carbon copy. People wondered why Mr. M. read from yards and yards of scrollwork like a Roman senator.

Sex and the office!

10. Companies are not usually destroyed by sex. Except when kings or board chairmen abdicate for the women they love, most sex at the office concerns only the people it concerns. Other people may try to *make* it their business, but it isn't really.

An office affair doesn't necessarily undermine office morale either, except for the person who had his eye on one of the participants for himself or in cases where the head of the organization falls into the hands of a ruthless, power-mad girl barracuda. That's bad, of course, but usually they both get fired pretty soon and things settle down.

11. There is no more sex at the office now than there was twenty-five years ago. It's just come up from underground.

12. Some of the people who cluck-cluck the loudest about office affairs are ex-participants who played and knocked off—or didn't knock off, got their divorces and married each other—and are peculiarly hard-put, in their dotage, to remember that this sort of thing happens to perfectly nice, normal people.

SUBSIDIARY FINDINGS

Those are my personal primary conclusions about sex and the office. Now here are my secondary conclusions:

1. It's impossible to chart what kind of people will get involved with each other. Girls you know to be as wholesome as wheat germ and skim milk will walk willingly straight into the arms of a leech. The chandelier-swinging office "party girl" who plans to marry a millionaire can get hooked and stay hooked by the assistant bookkeeper. Chemistry!

2. Timing is everything in office affairs. It depends on who's

looking and who's there to be looked at. For the first twelve years of a man's marriage he'd be immune to Claudia Cardinale bringing in his breakfast coffee. In the thirteenth year he goes off his rocker for a file girl with a receding chin, crowded teeth and a twenty-four-inch measurement around each kneecap. When a married man has an affair, it's probably less likely that one special girl got to him and unhinged him than it is that he was ready to be happened to by almost *anybody pleasant.* His affair is a symptom of a troubled marriage rather than an irresistible urge to merge with a *particular* lovely new girl.

3. Office affairs are not the hurry-up, gobble-down, hit and run things people on the outside *think* they are. Only a Don Juan or maybe an occasional convention-goer would gobble. The grand passions that cause the stock-market dips and new marriages to form often develop after the two people have known each other for several years. (One friend of mine began her affair with an office crony after they had tried twenty-two tax cases together. Another saw her present husband rise from stockroom boy to display manager to president of the store to head of the chain before their liaison began. Very patient girl!)

4. Office affairs don't actually go on *in* offices—behind locked doors, on top of desks, in cloak rooms and that sort of thing—as the uninitiated seem to think. They are *rooted* at the office, but they blossom at tennis, in seaside villas when two people are on the same business trip, in penthouse apartments, in Buick Rivieras, or wherever lightning has room to strike. One man and woman I know (he's married to somebody else) have managed to rendezvous with each other in practically every major city on two continents since their affair began in 1951. That's how far things can branch out.

5. The office affair (except for that naughty Matinee thing I described), has more sustaining it than just plain sex. The people who think it consists of dirty little half-hour episodes—people sneaking off to a motel and that sort of thing—are fuzzy observers. Many an affair is grounded in friendship and mutual respect and has deep emotional and intellectual rapport going for it. That's why office affairs aren't so easy to bash in the head. Marriage may be

the only *legal* relationship, but it is far from the only meaningful one. So there, there, there *again!*

6. Participants in office affairs are not always dashing young executives and their beauty-contest-winning young assistants. A magazine publisher of fifty-six I know has been having an affair for fourteen years now with a woman who is mousy, motherly and about as chic as apple pandowdy. She is fifty-two, softly sensuous and very kind. Friends of this couple say he'd come apart at the seams without her. She makes it possible for him to get through the day.

7. Offices are yeasty because everybody is at his best—clothes, make-up, perfume, brains, jokes and energy! No girl ever sees a man in his scrappy pajamas and scrappy early-morning disposition, and he never sees her wired for sound in her curlers—not early in the game anyway. The hours spent together in offices are limited, therefore a little mystery can prevail indefinitely.

8. There are no friendships between virile men and womanly women anywhere, in my opinion, completely devoid of sexual overtones. (And that's *good!*) A man always wonders what a woman is like in bed, not necessarily with him but with *anybody.* She wonders the same thing about him. All this speculating among men and women in offices, even if nobody does anything, causes sexy waves.

Those are my major and minor conclusions about sex and the office—but wait, there's more! Case histories, too. (You can put down the cyanide. I've changed all the names and identification labels!)

WHY MEN DO IT

Nobody worries much about single men and single girls becoming involved with each other (except people who don't want *anybody* to have any fun in bed *anywhere*), but just everybody seems to worry about married men and single girl combinations. What *about* them?

The popular version of why married men "pounce" on girls at the office is that they are lecherous, spoiled, licentious, neurotic, treacherous, lascivious, selfish, undisciplined, lustful and immoral.

I think they do it because they *enjoy* it! Some men are all those adjectives, to be sure, but many are not. There *are* men who, if there isn't anything else around to chase, will chase and eat their own tails like the live lobsters do when they're shipped from Maine to California without enough ice. More often, however, I think married men become involved with girls at the office because men are human. Can any attractive man really go through life attracted to just one woman when waves and waves and waves of lovely girls continue to wash up against him every year at work? We keep pretending he can, but I don't think so.

Some men *do* stay faithful to their wives, but the reason doesn't have much to do with their desiring only that woman—in my opinion. Some men stay more faithful than others because they are not powerfully sexed. The factory was kind of shut down in childhood by too many parental *don'ts* and *mustn'ts* and *naughty-naughties,* so they married a girl who was also undersexed by the same influences and lived happily, unsexily ever after. I honestly think nobody has any idea how many husbands and wives simply don't go to bed with each at all and don't go to bed with anybody else either. The "undersexed" man can be shored *up,* however, if a patient, enthusiastic, possibly predatory woman happens to wiggle-waggle into his life. If she happens, she will usually be somebody he met through work.

Other men abstain from extra-marital sex because other things in life are more important to them and they have too much to risk. In my *opinion,* that's their reason. In the case of the high-placed government official, the desire for girls may just not rank with the fear that an enemy could "get something" on him. Every so often, however, one of these stable heads of dynasty or state does drop off the vine into the arms of the woman he loves, and hypocritical noises are heard from those who have yet to be found out.

Some married men do not get mixed up with other women because they prefer *boys.*

There are men, however, and I admit it, who never have anything to do with girls at the office because they are genuinely nutty about their wives. These obviously are well-adjusted—emotionally, sexually and every other way—men. Bless them! They too can be toppled! It can happen on a business trip with twenty lonely nights ahead, twenty lovely girls in the firm they're visiting, etc., etc. Yeast is no respecter of persons!

THE PHONY-BALONEY

A man who insists he never has a twinge of desire for another woman, never fantasizes about other women, and lusts only for his wife—after twenty years of marriage, mind you—is, in my opinion, a phony. Even the *young* husband who ostentatiously loves his wife but shuts out all other women from his friendship, kindness, affection and concern probably doesn't love *anybody* from the gut—*including* his bride. He's cold as Kelsey's. (That's a seaweed, dear, not another sex survey.) Either that or he isn't sure of her. A worried, tormented lover is usually faithful.

Aside from feeling a natural attraction toward many women in a lifetime, I think men also stray for other reasons. (I had some of this dope as far back as 1945, but the sociology department of Indiana University never sent for it.)

1. Husbands and wives get to living in different worlds. It's chauffeuring, soufflés and azalea club for her—back orders, production step-up, profit-and-loss for him. The girl at his elbow while the big merger is shaping up nicely may also get to be the girl at his elbow at cocktail time. (Husbands and wives who share business ventures together often stay more closely knit.)

2. A man may live so far away from his office he's too woofed to be a decent mate when he gets home—yet nobody, and especially his wife, will hear of selling Twelve Acres and moving to an apartment closer in. Earlier in the day at lunch or cocktails, before his charm and energy ran out, there were other girls around to be impressed by it.

The business trips that separate men from their wives are full of yeast, too, as we just mentioned . . . exotic atmosphere, expense account, freedom from spies and all that.

3. Husbands and wives get used to each other. She can finish his sentences. He can start *and* finish hers. They get bored with each

other in bed. As for becoming a sexy new her, as all the magazines promise she can, a zebra doesn't change stripes. Even a twenty-nine-year-old zebra—I mean wife—is still the same wife in new black lingerie. People are stunned when a man strays from a beautiful gracious lady to a creature with knobby elbows and no eyelashes at all, but you see, she's a different *zebra*.

If you think this is just one woman's opinion, here's what the eminent psychoanalyst and New York University professor Dr. Ernest van den Haag said in an article in *Harper's Magazine:* "Though by no means weaker, the marital bond is quite different from the bond of love. Yet, instead of acknowledging that love and marriage are different but equally genuine relationships, they (marriage counselors) depict love as a kind of dependable wheel horse that can be harnessed to the carriage of married life. For them, any other kind of love must be an 'immature' or 'neurotic' fantasy, something to be condemned as Hollywood-inspired and 'unrealistic' romanticism. It is as though a man opposed to horse racing—for good reasons perhaps—were to argue that race horses are not real, that all real horses are draft horses. . . . It is foolish to pretend that the passionate romantic longing doesn't exist or is 'neurotic,' i.e. shouldn't exist; it is as foolish to pretend that romantic love can be made part of a cozy domesticity. The truth is simple enough, though it can make life awfully complicated: there are two things—love and affection (or marital love). They do not usually pull together as a team."

Very well, while a man is deeply caught up in *one* of these loves at home—the affectionate kind—he is perhaps experiencing the other kind at the office . . . or at least daydreaming about it.

4. Men stray because they get cut off from sex in marriage. A friend tells me in the chic New York commuting town he lives in at least 75 per cent of his married cronies have been expelled from the conjugal bed. Nothing sudden, just a gradual shutting down of the shop. If he's anywhere *near* telling the truth (and apparently some of these men compare notes!), that town alone could be liberating as many as fifty or sixty deprived males into the havens of advertising, public relations and the law.

5. Wives get older and men prefer younger women. They find

the most convenient supply of fresh young beauties in offices—with new shipments every June when colleges let out.

6. A man strays if his marriage is really unhappy. I don't mean the kind we all have . . . fight, scrap, scream, kiss, make-up, fight, scrap, scream, and so forth, but I mean the man who's had it up to *there*. He meets a girl at the office who really seems to prefer him alive to dead, and the yeast starts rising!

THE PIE

I think you can sum up why some married men behave as they do this way:

A man is a pie. Part of the pie is his house, one portion is his wife, another portion his children, another his business and investments and then there's a golf or fishing or hobby portion and a sex portion.

People who don't know any better think that the only parts of the pie which really represent him are the wife and children and business part, and that the sex part isn't even a piece of the *pie* unless it's sliced at home. Well, anybody who knows anything about pies knows that every piece of the same pie is real whether it's eaten at home or away from home. For some men, for example, the *golf* and *fishing* part is the biggest piece of pie of all, and you can't say *they* aren't genuine pie, either. A girl having an affair with a man gets into trouble when *she* pretends the wife and house and family pieces of pie are smaller than they really are.

These are the reasons men get involved at the office. (Maybe Kinsey was too busy at the time, but I don't see why Pomeroy or *Martin* wouldn't have found all this enlightening.) Now what about the girls?

GIRLS' REASONS

With "everything to lose" why does a single girl fall for a married man with whom she works? Because a lot of single girls decide finally that the only thing they have to lose by falling for a married man is their *loneliness*, that's why! Any girl who's been single a few years, or single again after being married, knows how long it is between "live ones."

Two attractive friends of mine were discussing this man-shortage thing at my house the other night. "We got out a pencil and paper recently," Polly said, "and decided to chart the men in both our lives since graduating from high school. (One girl is twenty-eight, the other thirty-three.) Jean averaged one good eligible man about every three years and two months—somebody she could marry or fall in love with. Mine were slightly further between—one big possibility about every four years."

No, these girls were not losers. They were attractive women who liked men but found that big gaps between eligibles is just the way the ginger snaps.

In between eligible men there are, of course, the spooky-spooks and sub-men single girls do go out with but couldn't marry or have an affair with. Granted one girl's spooky-spook may be another girl's darling, if he's spooky to *you*, you can't help it. Meanwhile, back at the office, during your spook and sub-men dating era and before an "eligible" shows up, you keep running into adorable, whole, hale, hearty, smart, attentive *married* men who are supposed to be frightening, bad, naughty, revolting, scruffy-moraled, skiddy-scat taboo—but who can remember?

As for the built-in "safeguards" that used to keep girls from getting involved with *any* kind of man before marriage (and sometimes *after* marriage), a lot of them just don't exist any more. A young friend of mine who works for a woman's magazine (don't get nervous, *McCall's!*) says, "Modern girls are too informed and too comfortable with men to be as frightened of them as you'd have to be to stay completely physically clear of them. We've danced, fought, studied, played football and necked with them since we were teen-agers. How in the world are you going to be frightened?

"Girls know about diaphragms and how babies get here and all that too," she adds. "They also know their own anatomy and show off quite a lot of it in a bikini every summer. You just can't pretend

your own flesh is some strange foreign substance that doesn't belong to you the way girls did fifty years ago. We can't go back
to pretending we're untouchable and marble-coated."

When I recently visited Harry Richman, the veteran night-club
entertainer, he said, "When I first entered show business back in
the twenties, men-about-town and college boys used to flock to
the stage doors to take the chorines to dinner. Now they just take
out their own girl friends" (who apparently look as good as, dress
better than and know as much about men as chorines!).

Okay, then, girls in offices are not exactly untouchable. Would
girls in offices stay *more* cold-cream pure if men didn't tempt them?
My friend Charlotte, a wow of a pretty working girl, says, "I
don't believe for one moment that girls in offices are poor little
grasshoppers who are preyed on by those mean old praying man-
tises. A girl can say no. Just plain no."

A girl does say no all the time to door-to-door salesmen, the
service station guys who want to put new tires on her Chevy, dull
girl friends she doesn't want to have dinner with, parents she
doesn't want to move back home with. The word isn't unknown to
her. Just watch a girl get rid of a real creep who absolutely re-
volts her . . . it's swish, swash, wham-bam, right out the door
without any trouble. When a girl *doesn't* say no to a man, it's very
likely because she doesn't *want* to.

Girls who are bewildered and shocked by a man's physical
interest in them seem to me a little phony too. Girls happen to
have a powerful, built-in allure for men. It's *there* and God gave it
to us. To pretend to be outraged and petulant because a man
wants us "that way" is like having the Maltese Falcon buried upstairs in a dresser drawer and acting surprised because Sam Spade
and a bunch of hoodlums are milling around outside the door.

Whether a girl says yes or no to a man in the office, it's my
opinion she's not really *that* insulted by his desire for her. Unless
he is a real monster with one beady eye in the middle of his forehead or long green hair all over his back, I think she will remember
most propositions not unkindly. Somebody wanted her. Somebody
flipped.

MORE RESEARCH ON WHY GIRLS DO IT

Aside from the fact that office affairs come about because men feel needy and girls, while pretending to be fortresses, actually cruise around with their "available" lights turned on, what other specific reasons cause girls to get involved?

These:

1. A dynamic executive reminds a girl of her father—the one she lost or never had. If she works close to him, "his own dear little girl" finally gets *to* him and they become a thing.

2. A man has power and money—more aphrodisiac to some girls than the physical endowments of Mr. Universe. This particular girl has no wish (unless buried very deep) to be that powerful person herself, but she finds a certain thrill in thrilling a tycoon. The "dear friend" of an automotive tycoon—a girl I've known for many years—says, "To have this kind of man excited by you brings out the sexiest, most womanly, female equality in you. In bed *you* are the tycoon. Not that he is weak or unattractive or lacks potency, but that suddenly, simply because you're a woman whom he adores going to bed with, you become quite, quite power-laden. In his office, he is king. In your bed, *you* bestow favors, *you* are queenly and in command even if you are as highly sexed as he and need the love-making as much as he. It's delicious!"

3. Even if there's no affair, a poor girl may enjoy playing Cinderella by going out with a married man from the office who is out of her league socially, educationally, professionally or financially. One girl describes an Alice-in-Wonderland fortnight with a "foreign potentate" (she works for the government) like this: "He had his own private plane, his own private limousine and even his own private bagpipers to play concerts for us at dinner. He used to send the car around for me to go shopping at Ohrbach's or do whatever I needed to do on my lunch hour. Fair or unfair, it made my regular beaux seem a little hard up for things to do."

4. A barracuda girl may want professional power herself but not have the capacity for it—or her company won't hear of it. She takes on a lover who has the power she wants, gets inside him like a tapeworm (hope you don't mind mixed species) and starts

sapping. After she's sapped a while, he gets skinnier and skinnier, and the business doesn't look so robust either! Nobody can get the guy on the phone. His own lieutenants can't get in to see him, and heads start rolling from the bodies of anybody who threatens his girl adviser. Pretty soon his is one of the heads (management will stand just so much), and usually little Evita's rolls along with his. This is the kind of affair that can really damage a company, at least temporarily.

5. Sometimes an office affair provides a girl the opportunity of getting *out* of herself. You don't change leopard spots, of course, but you may discover some *new* spots you didn't know you *had* just by brushing your coat a bit.

"I'd always been such a nice girl," Evelyn recalls. (And of course this is a true story. With so many real ones to choose from, I don't need to make anything up.) "I'm kind of a Sunbonnet Sue, if you know what I mean—the one all the mothers trust to take their kids to the circus or ball game, and even wives don't worry if their husbands have dinner with me when the wives go to Portland to visit their sisters.

"Well, last year my company sent me to Detroit to do a drug survey, and the first day I was there I met the general manager of the drug chain. Usually I have to badger managers to let me talk to their clerks, but this man was extremely interested in the whole thing. He stayed while I asked all my questions, and I followed him back to his office still yakking away. I don't know what came over me that day or how I *knew*—I'm not one of those sexy broads who expects action—but it came to me—this man is *asking* to be led astray, and by *me*. I mean he was so sincere . . . so nice . . . so very attractive, but he didn't know he was. Or maybe it was just because I was away from home and found some new courage. Anyway, it was as though I heard Joan of Arc voices saying, 'If you don't do something about this man—or at least *try*—you'll regret it the rest of your life!

"'Look,' I said, 'I'll have all my surveying finished by this evening. If you'd like to look it over I could leave it somewhere for you.' (I wasn't up to asking anybody to dinner. Even this was pretty nervy for a Sunbonnet Sue.)

"He took the hint and said, 'Why don't you come back here about seven o'clock. We'll grab a bite ("grab a bite" is what a man says when he doesn't want dinner to sound like a big deal) and I'll look over the stuff.'

"Well, I finished the survey, went back to my hotel and put on the closest thing to a witching dress I own. It was just plain black crepe but had kind of a low neck. We had dinner—it wasn't just grabbing a bite, he took me to an elegant restaurant and we still talked about the drug business. But . . . I don't know . . . for practically the first time in my life I felt kind of 'lady of the evening.' I thought I might be having the same effect on him as Sadie Thompson had on that missionary. Where I got the courage I'll never know, but I said, 'Why don't we go back to my hotel for a drink?' and he said, 'Fine.'

"We never even stopped in the lobby. I had a key with me and we just got on the elevator without saying a word. I never did turn on the lights when we got to my room. The minute we were inside the door I put my arms around him and began talking as though I'd been doing this sort of thing all my life. I said I'd worn the closest thing to a wicked dress I owned because he was so attractive. I also said I'd worn the least possible amount of underwear because I wanted to be a slinky, sultry *minx*, which I'd never been before in my life but he inspired me. In other words, I *sort* of told the truth, so he'd know I knew I wasn't a sexpot but that it was he who brought this on, which of course he *did*.

"I wasn't a desperate old maid or anything. I'd had men before, but *they* had always made the advances. I just kept murmuring and purring this sexy stuff which I honestly felt toward this nice, middle-aged man. I was enjoying myself *utterly* because I was seducing *him* instead of getting mauled by some Adonis who was getting around to me simply because I was a girl—maybe number three thousand seven hundred and two on his list.

"I brought it off and it was wonderful."

To reprise then, a girl may get involved with men in the office because she's looking for a father, she loves a man's power and money—among other things; she loves *only* power and money; she wants to be Cinderella for a spell, or she is a leopardess who sees the opportunity to brush up her spots. She may also have a fling at the office to prove she isn't getting any older, to prove to herself and observers that she likes men (not girls), to sink into a man so he'll marry her and, well, just because she's a girl!

Married girls in offices have affairs, too, but I think they're more likely to stray for the same reasons men do.

THE GIRLS THEY LEAVE BEHIND

Married or single, doesn't a girl indulging in an office affair ever consider what she might be doing to a man's wife?

Remember about the pie. The girl friend only knows about the sexy portion that's with *her*. She hears very little about the family-man chunk. She knows there is a wife, of course, but the woman may be as indistinct as a smoke ring.

Technically the girl isn't damaging the wife if the wife never knows—and many and many a wife never knows.

A man who cheats flagrantly year in, year out usually doesn't stay married. One affair, however, doesn't necessarily make a divorce. By the time it happens, the marriage, paradoxical as this sounds, may be a pretty rock-founded institution which a man isn't about to dissolve and thereby disrupt his life. Too awkward. Too expensive.

"I used to think a man couldn't have anything to do with another woman without his wife being dashed to bits," a close friend told me. "It isn't true. I've found that a casual encounter with some bar-broad isn't the least bit important to me or my relationship with Tom. (Not his name, of course.) I did ask very early in our marriage that he never embarrass me by telling me about it."

Another married friend says, "You can't help but know when a husband cheats, and I've even giggled over the fact. Men think they're so smart at concealing these little peccadillos and then practically spell it out for you in bed! Any man has pretty standard bed patterns. Well, suddenly something new is introduced or suggested, and you know damned well he hasn't been reading any book on sex, so where did he get *that* idea? From some other dame, of course!"

Another reason a girl in an office doesn't balk at an affair or stop to worry about a man's wife is because of the great pleasure it affords her! Never underestimate the joy for a single woman—even one who wants to get married—of having a man around her house at an hour and in a room he wouldn't usually be in if she were only dating him. Some women just don't find that channeling their physical energy into basketball or nature-observing walks does the trick.

One girl I know stops short of having an affair—not until she's married, no siree—but has a trusty office friend who every few weeks squeezes the daylights out of her. Old Mike comes over to her apartment, they have a chicken sandwich, they tussle, she fights like a Zulu and nothing happens. But the physical struggle "gets a lot of it out of my system," she says. I haven't talked to this girl in months but I do keep tabs on the strangulations and ax murders in her city. Old Mike *could* lose his *temper.*

Some girls really have no reason to feel guilty on a wife's behalf. If the woman and her husband are not in conjugal harmony, the man's office friend may be supplying the one important commodity he doesn't enjoy at home. Ironically, while the girl plumps for him to get a divorce and marry her, the ingredient she supplies may be what's holding his marriage together.

Rightly or wrongly, some working girls think that if a man is attracted to them, they're entitled. Husband-luring is like landing a job in the Depression. There weren't enough jobs then. There aren't enough eligible men now.

Girls also rationalize that if a woman loses her husband she deserves to. The Jezebel may have something there. We all know husbands set adrift among models, starlets, and barracudas who do not start affairs. Are they more moral? Probably they are just happier at home.

One wife with a happy husband reveals this technique:

"He thinks I'm a nymphomaniac. Since the day we were married I have pretended to be out of my head about going to bed with Jack. Oh, I don't mean that I never actually *do* enjoy it. Perhaps one time out of six I have a good time myself. The rest of the nights I do an Academy Award performance, and this has been going on for thirteen years," she says. "Sometimes I'm so weary at the end of the day I think I would pay a hundred dollars to turn over and go to sleep (they have four children and no help), but he never knows. If I can lift my big toe off the bed, I respond. I'm such a 'sexpot' Jack is even a little bit afraid he doesn't supply me with *enough* sex, and I've never tried to talk him out of this!"

A girl may not feel too guilty about charming a married man, because if she works for him, she can't help observing what a spoiled, demanding creature his wife is. If a good secretary has to be away from the office two hours because her temporary filling fell out, she's a frazzle of anxiety for having inconvenienced her boss. Yet it isn't a bit unusual for her to answer the phone one morning and hear, "This is Mrs. Westerhaven, Miss Betz. Would you tell Mr. Westerhaven my car broke down over on Twelfth Street and they'll have to keep it overnight. I'm picking his car up at the lot and would you tell him to take the bus home?" That's what he does, too.

If Miss Betz should fall in love with Mr. Westerhaven, she may feel she has more real regard for him than his wife, although in all fairness, in about seven years it may be she who is taking the car from the lot and sending him home by bus. New wives get to behaving very much like old ones!

Despite everything, I think wives still have the best and biggest piece of the pie. (Listen, don't think this whole report isn't making *me* nervous *too*. I'm a wife, for heaven's sake!)

GETTING THE SHOW ON THE ROAD

All right, that's the why and how of sex and the office, but what are the actual machinations? Who does what to whom and when?

A man may do a simple thing like ask a girl to lunch. A girl may ask a man she works with to a party. It's like boy meets girl anywhere. You and a co-worker may work late several nights in a row and the last night out go off to hear Miles Davis. You may live near a dreamboat and have a car pool. Developments develop, that's all.

As for sinking into men who come into your office from the outside, the procedure varies. One secretary I know was told by her boss to map out a very extensive sightseeing and night club itinerary for a visiting general and his party. When the general got to town, there wasn't any party, just one youngish general. Her boss suggested Madelyn go on the tour herself with the visitor and . . . proceedings proceeded.

Another stenographer I know was sent by her firm to a visiting executive's hotel suite to pack up his belongings while he finished an important meeting. When he returned to the hotel she was to rush him to the airport in her car and get him on the six-fifteen jet for London without *fail*. He reached the hotel before she finished packing, took one look at her and announced, "I didn't make it back in time and missed my plane. People miss planes all the time. Where shall we have dinner?"

One boy and girl I know detested each other for two years. He absolutely made her flesh crawl. She, he said, was dense and untalented. He did everything in his power to get her fired. She got ill if he was in the same room. One Christmas a musical-comedy production was needed for a client's sales convention. She had been a singer and he wrote first-rate limericks, so their practical boss teamed them up.

For two days our boy wouldn't go near her. He locked his door. The third day she took a Miltown, telephoned him and said they'd really better have a conference. The fourth day they went home to her apartment to work because the office was so noisy they couldn't hear themselves think. The fifth day they moved to a rented house at the beach so they could really concentrate. The sixth day they were madly in love, and one year later (when his divorce became final) they were married.

Sex at the office!

Now the time has come to tell you three little bedtime stories. They all actually happened and they all started in offices. These three "heroines"—all of whom are personal friends or close acquaintances—came to my house and I tape-recorded while we talked. What you read here is right off the sound track—with only slight editing by me but with names, jobs, companies and cities changed to protect the guilty.

En garde!

CHAPTER 14

THREE LITTLE BEDTIME STORIES

1. THE LOVE AFFAIR

STEVE WAS co-owner and producer in the television packaging firm I worked for and came to Hollywood several times a year to do shows. (He's created three famous, long-lasting ones you'd recognize.) I produced "Tea Party," a daytime woman's show, and really liked my work. One afternoon he asked me for a date. We'd known each other six years by then and even that day he didn't ask for a real date. He just said, "Maybe you'd like to go to a movie with me Sunday." I said that sounded like fun. Why can't girls ever say anything except something sounds like fun?

Sunday came and I not only had a scratchy throat, I had the runny nose, watery eyes . . . the ague, the grippe or some damn thing. When Steve called to ask about picking me up, I said, "I'm going to die, or maybe I already have. But I sure didn't go to heaven. I can't breathe or see or anything, so I guess I can't go to the movies."

"I'm terribly sorry," he said. "Do you want me to bring you anything?"

"No," I said, "I've consumed roughly my own replacement in aspirin and I'm sure I have orange-juice blood by now."

"Booze?" he asked.

"I wouldn't dare," I said. "Then I'd be a sneezing *drunk.*"

"Well, listen," he said, "if you start to feel better later in the day, please give me a call."

"Okay," I said. I wasn't ever going to feel better.

We hung up. I thought about him tooting around Beverly Hills in his rented Thunderbird, going to church first, then delivering flowers to several Beverly Hills matrons who'd had him to dinner. That was his Sunday-morning ritual when he was on the Coast. Then I blew my nose and drank some more orange juice and wondered some more about how he'd got around to me. He was a popular man, nice-looking though not *good*-looking, because his skin was somewhat pock-marked and one eye was lower than the other just *slightly.* He must have got around to me because he'd run out of girls, I decided, although I couldn't remember ever hearing that he was a chaser. It seemed to me I would have heard in six years. Anyway I knew he was married—with a family in Westport, Connecticut. We'd had a number of friendly chats during our years in the same firm. If a man in your company is single, of course, you find out everything you can about him if you have to hire Pinkerton. If he's married, you don't go quite so all out. Perhaps Steve decided to ask me out because I *had* made some improvements since we first met. My psychoanalysis was all finished, I dressed and looked better at thirty-six than I had in my twenties, and I had a good female body.

I didn't call Steve back at his hotel for three hours, which was quite a long time when you consider that after the first half-hour I'd already figured this was a psychosomatic cold that I'd developed purely because I had a date with a married man and wanted a good excuse to break it. Having decided I was taking him *and* me *and* the cold far too seriously, I did call back, got him at the pool and said I was feeling better. He said great, would I like him to pick me up or maybe I'd like to come over and get some sun—perhaps it would be good for the cold. I said I'd drive over. The Bel Air Hotel was a good twenty miles from my apartment in Pasadena but

I liked to drive, and perhaps I had in the back of my head that with my own car I could leave exactly when I wanted to.

When I drove into the wooded parking lot in front of the Bel Air, he was waiting for me. I was snuggled into a woolly, pale blue dress which I adored and a coat the same color, and I felt nice—whether this was a cold or a psychosomatic defense.

We went inside to the bar so I could have a hot toddy by the fireplace—and no doubt perspire and really get pneumonia if this turned out to be a bona fide cold. Anyway, we started laughing and gossiping about his shows and my show and our associates, and we didn't stop doing that, among other things, for four long years. That's how it began.

We went to his bungalow presently to change into swimsuits—there were four big rooms so nobody was bumping into each other —and then we went to the pool. A number of people we both knew were there and we chatted and had a lovely time. The sun was good and hot, but then the afternoon cooled down as it does in California. First thing you know I had broken out in these damned hives. I never could take aspirin. And I had a chill.

We went back to his bungalow, and while I was still in my swimsuit I drank a bathroom tumbler full of brandy to stop shaking (and itching—hives are very itchy). While I was getting the stuff down and because it was gagging me, Stephen kissed me very gently on the forehead to tell me without saying so that he knew I really did have a cold, though we were both pretending I didn't; that he understood and that I shouldn't be hivey or embarrassed; that we were old friends and there was nothing to be nervous about. He was nice.

The love thing had already started by then, I guess. We didn't go to bed that night or the next or the next, but the build-up was fantastically exciting. I used to sit with my stop-watch trying to time "Tea Party," and my mind would be so many millions of miles away they couldn't possibly have had television sets wherever I'd got to. When we met in the evening, we'd go to some lovely place for dinner on the Strip or off the Strip, and we couldn't keep our hands off each other. I remember sitting in the parking lot at Romanoff's one night and necking . . . rubbing noses, kissing, hands on each other's faces, fingertips in each other's mouths. It was breathless and magic, but we had so much time and no one was rushing. We'd waited six years already.

We couldn't see each other for three nights. He was taping shows and I had no business being there, and I had recording sessions clear across town anyway. Then, Saturday morning, I brought enough clothes to his hotel in my car to outfit a girl for Bermuda, because I wanted to be gorgeously dressed for whatever we planned to do that weekend. As it happened I could have gotten by with a muumuu or nothing at all. We hardly got out of bed.

It was a found weekend. I was thirty-six, Steve was forty-seven, and it had never happened to either of us before like this. Well maybe it had happened to him (how do you ever really know?), but he seemed too proud of himself and too overjoyed for me not to think this love-making was something special. I know he was deeply moved.

Sometimes when he was completely exhausted I would seduce him again, and it wasn't difficult. Or I would be sleeping lightly beside him, and he would reach over and gather me in his arms and just hold me quietly for a long time. There was the lovely, languorous getting to know each other and each other's bodies, and the more we had of each other the needier we seemed to be. We had so much to give, and there was no embarrassment.

Sunday morning late we finally let the maid in to make up the room, but of course it didn't do any good. We were back in it the minute she left. Eight times, if you want a box score for the weekend, and I think we could have made it nine—but I had to be at an agent's office early Monday morning to interview actresses.

I believe in some people's minds there is still the thought that you must have either a wild, sexy, abandoned relationship or a traditional love affair—not both. Well, we had both. It doesn't happen often. Perhaps this was a loaded situation to begin with, more romantic than life really is. Steve was a "stranger" in hot and sunny Southern California—practically the sultry tropics for a man who works in New York—far from home where his real cares were. He had an almost unlimited expense account, so there was no end to glamorous dinners, Bel Air Hotel bungalow living to the hilt and champagne breakfasts. As for me, I was an angel from the moon all that time—cool, sexy, beautiful (as much as money and care could buy), kind, funny . . . I don't think he ever saw me at my worst. We went to marvelous parties because he knew lots of people who liked him and accepted me. I even gave a party or two myself. We went to church sometimes.

One morning when he finished his show we borrowed a beach house—a really palatial affair in Malibu that belonged to one of his movie-star friends—and swam nude all day, baked in the sun and made love. And always there was the gossip about the office and network executives and tales of our own two lives, which we went into in depth, and discussions about de-colonialization and the world market, or as much as I could discuss anyway. After lunch he gave me a rubdown with the Ballantine's Scotch from his flask, and then I smelled all boozy and we had to go swimming again. We were in love as much as two people can be, for a while, I'm sure.

The relationship lasted, incredibly—more or less like this—for four long years. It couldn't have continued so long except that he lived three thousand miles away from me, and we only saw each other four or five times a year. Also, I wasn't badgering him to get a divorce and marry me. It wouldn't have been right. He was married to a nice woman who loved him, though she may not have been very good in bed. He couldn't justify a divorce, and they had three children.

As for me, I was pretty hooked—but I was also a big girl, and I knew this sort of thing didn't always lead to marriage.

One afternoon we were lying in bed at the hotel when his phone rang—as it did eighty or ninety times a day—but I heard him tell the operator he'd take the call on the extension in the living room. He did, and when he came back to bed I said, "Will you light me a cigarette?"

"You don't smoke," he said.

"But I want a cigarette now," I said.

He lit one for me, and when it was going nicely I crushed it out against his knee.

"I don't like your being married," I said. "And I don't like your taking calls from Connecticut on my time."

The next time he was on the Coast, I made it a point to be in Chicago. Six months after that I met the man I married. I've never lighted another cigarette. Sometimes I wonder if my husband ever takes a call on the other extension in a hotel room for a reason I just might understand. I don't think so. I really keep him pretty busy.

2. THE KEPTIVE

I was twenty-three years old when Andrew A. Corwin, president and owner of Andrew A. Corwin, Ltd., investments—offices in New York, San Francisco, London, Rome, Paris, Madrid, Lisbon and Istanbul—interviewed me for a secretarial job. It was just ten days before my twenty-fourth birthday.

When he came in, I was already seated in his office, having gone through about twenty-nine screenings with thirty-eight people to get to him. The office was paneled in wood and was just plain rich . . . not ostentatious, but rich. The wood was real, the leather was real, the paintings were real. There was a Renoir hanging behind the desk.

I guess Mr. Corwin had just come in off the street. He still had his hat and muffler and overcoat on. He left the hat on after we began to talk, which I thought was odd, but later, when he took it off, I realized he was getting bald and was probably self-conscious about it. I remember thinking, how ridiculous . . . what difference would it make if you were bald and had all that money? Actually he was only forty-three, but that's like ninety if you're only twenty-three yourself.

He got me to doing most of the talking, which I only realized years later was rather unusual for anybody that important. He was interested in my family back in Nebraska. He asked about the jobs I'd had before and whether I enjoyed working. Then he asked whether I was engaged. I said no, and he didn't say anything stupid like "I should have thought a lovely girl like you would have been snapped up by now." He just said he had one or two more people to see and that someone would let me know about the job in a few days.

I wasn't surprised when the employment agency called me and

said I had the job. I was young, but I was a good secretary—shorthand one hundred and thirty words a minute, typing speed eighty. The last people I'd worked for had wanted me to stay, but I just had to make more money. Even though this was an investment firm, apparently I didn't have to know about finance.

On my twenty-fourth birthday, three days after I started working there, I said something about being almost a quarter of a century old that day. I've always been too talkative about birthdays. I think other people ought to share them. Mr. Corwin said, "Congratulations." Then he said, "Sit down, Paula, I want to talk to you."

He said, "I'd like to buy you a present for your birthday—maybe a wristwatch, or perhaps you'd like to order a Galanos dress." Then, before I had a chance to say anything, he went on, "I know, Paula, this is something you would not ordinarily accept, and I won't be dishonest with you. I would like you to be my girl. I hired you because I hoped you would be. I suppose I could have my choice of . . . secretaries. This job pays well (I'll say it did), and some people who know that I'm personally wealthy might take the job for other reasons. I don't tell you these things to brag. I'm just trying to be honest."

I sat very still and didn't say a word for a moment, but it wasn't because I was shocked. I knew somehow this was how it was going to be. It's even possible I told him about my birthday in order to give him an opening. (You never can be quite sure why you do these things.)

He went on. "Being my girl wouldn't be as sordid as you might think. As a matter of fact, I believe you would have a very good life. I don't promise you to get a divorce. In fact, the chances are very unlikely. I like Mrs. Corwin. She's a fine woman. She has never liked the . . . physical aspect of marriage. We've both tried and that's that. I won't sell too hard, but again I will tell you that I can more or less have my choice of girls. When someone is wealthy, these are . . . well . . . just the facts of life. Perversely, perhaps, I don't want those girls. I want you. I will see that by the time you leave you have a considerable amount of money. My last secretary, who just left to get married, had over five hundred shares of A.T. & T. in her own name. (I didn't realize what that amounted to at the time.) Of course, I'll give you the things you should have. We'll start with an apartment. Don't tell me now, Paula, but think about it."

I can't remember what I said, but I didn't say no. I'm afraid I wasn't insulted. I just opened my shorthand book and we went on with the dictation.

A week later we went to bed—in a hotel suite—and I began being kept. I wasn't out and *out* kept. I worked hard at the office and made a good salary, but you don't have an expensive apartment and charge five hundred dollars worth of dresses at a whack on a secretary's pay.

After I got the apartment we usually went there. It was a beautiful place, with a crystal chandelier and thick pale blue carpets and a very lavish fountain in the foyer. Once or twice we made love in Andrew's office—on the floor or on one of those creamy leather couches—and once in the board room with the doors locked and the lights on.

I told only one other person what I was doing, my girl friend. "I don't see why I can't take a year of my life and give it to someone who needs me and who will make me financially secure in return," I told Diana. Surprisingly enough, she agreed with me. I still went to parties when kids that I knew gave them, but of course I never took a date. Finally I stopped seeing very many people at all. It was just too complicated.

I'd like to say the arrangement with Andrew was gruesome. Actually, for quite a while, it was fun. Of all the fringe benefits, I think I liked shopping the best. Perhaps one afternoon a week I would leave the office at three—we were always busy—with Andrew's car and driver and go uptown to shop. I'd always struggled for hours before deciding whether I could or could not afford a six-ninety-five sweater, and usually I found I could not. But on these shopping sprees I could buy absolutely anything and everything I wanted, from fur-lined raincoats to Swedish crystal.

People to whom this sort of thing never happens are usually horrified by the idea. It just isn't that horrible if you like the man. It's sexy to try on lingerie knowing that someone you like very much is going to see you in it. Maybe it's even a little sexier knowing that somebody is going to pay for the lingerie. I remember one after-noon meeting Andrew at the door of my apartment in a black short chemise—all black lace and pure silk—and I wore high-heeled black satin mules. I'd just come home from a shopping spree. I'm sure he liked the fact that I was his quiet, sweet, efficient, demure little secretary at work and the rest of the time an adored and expensive courtesan.

He enjoyed making love to me but . . . well . . . I just didn't enjoy making love to him! I guess he was what you'd call "clinical." Just think of a passionate, uncomplicated Italian waterfront worker and then think of the exact opposite—that would be Andrew. He didn't know, of course. I'm sure he thought he was marvelous. Still, even though he was twenty years my senior, I used to enjoy giving him pleasure as though he were my child. At the height of love-making—you know, the climax—it was almost as though I were an observer. I was glad that he found me so pleasurable, and not getting swept up in it myself didn't worry me.

There wasn't a chance of marriage, of course, and I found myself getting more and more annoyed—petulant even—when Andrew and his wife swept off to the opera or charity balls or openings of art galleries. Finally I decided I had to do something to hurt him for *being* married, irrational as it was. I began to go out with other men from the office. That was the beginning of the end for me, and two of the men were let go. Andrew gave me six months' severance pay. He was very businesslike when we parted—obviously I wasn't the first girl in his life—and he saw to it that I got a job in another brokerage firm. I sometimes wonder what my husband would think if he knew how I paid for the psychoanalysis which made it possible for me really to fall in love with someone nice and marry him.

3. THE HYPNOTIST

What does an efficiency expert do? I still don't know, really. Anyway, whatever he does, *he* was one. He'd been "making things more efficient" at Wirtz and Feuthwanger, the shoe manufacturer I work for, for about a month—coming in every morning at nine-thirty with his brief case. Everybody treated him with some respect, although he looked hardly any older than I. Every day he'd ask to see certain papers or certain people, and finally he got around to me. We had a chat about whether I liked my job, if I thought I was overworked, if I had enough help during rush periods and so on. I wasn't going to tell him a blessed thing, but pretty soon I found myself yapping away about Muriel's being late four mornings out of five and my calculator being at least a hundred and fourteen years old and hard to work with, especially during inventory.

After that chat, when he came by my desk every day he'd say, "Good morning, Miss Lanebroom." "Lanebrawn," I would answer. I knew perfectly well he knew my name. One day he brought me a rose. His mother grew them, he said. It was a Helen Traubel. Fine.

Well, I never did like blond men, and though I was as eager as the next girl to meet somebody really good and get married (twenty-seven isn't getting any younger, and my current romance was a mess), he just never entered my head as a possibility. Not ever. He was *very* blond—pale eyebrows, pale hair, pale skin—and a little pudgy, and he wore turquoise socks which I found absolutely revolting.

I've decided since that a girl doesn't know *what* she likes, because after I got involved with him I started liking some pretty spooky things (which I'll tell you about), the *least* surprising of which was probably blond eyebrows.

The third week he was there he said, "Miss Lanebroom, would you like to have dinner with me tonight?" "Lane*brawn*," I said. "I really can't because I have a French class tonight." (All good single girls go to night school to get cultured as well as to meet men, as I'm sure you know.)

"Tell you what, Miss Lanebroom—Lane*brawn*—if you'll miss your French class this evening, I'll tell you a mnemonics system that will help you remember your vocabulary four times as easily all the rest of the semester. Is it a deal?"

"I suppose so," I said. A date is a date, and in spite of the turquoise socks I thought we might go someplace nice for dinner. (He did tell me the system, but I never had a chance to try it because I gave up the French shortly after that.)

That night I not only missed French class, I didn't get any dinner either, although I don't think he really planned it that way. He brought a fifth of gin, a bottle of vermouth and onions along with him, which was sensible if you wanted anything to drink around my apartment because I didn't have anything in stock except that fifth of Crème de Cacao Mr. Carruthers gave me for Christmas last year. What a present.

I can't make a really good martini—not enough practice, I guess, and I don't care really—but if I'm not mistaken, *his* martinis were practically undrinkable. They were *terrible.* I don't know how you could go that far wrong with perfectly good Gordon's gin and Noilly Prat vermouth. It must have been my ice, which sometimes has a cantaloupe taste. Anyway, we drank the martinis, terrible as they were, and I realized again what a good listener he was. All he said was, "How's your co-worker," and *again* I was telling him that Muriel had gone to lunch twice last week and never come back at *all.* He seemed to think everything I said was funny, though I'm hardly a raconteur.

After the third martini I was still doing *most* of the talking and hadn't even complained about not eating, which isn't like me. I usually insist on eating. I was feeling rather nice somehow . . . like a great All-American girl charmer and—I don't know—maybe just a touch superior to this boy. (We compared birthdays, and he was only six months older than I.) Tonight it wasn't turquoise socks. They were black and red plaid, speckled with blue dots. Honestly! He was a big square, too. He helped out in the rose garden at home —not that there's anything wrong with that—and he never skiied or went to parties or anything. I'd traveled a great deal more than he, and . . . well . . . he didn't know how to mix a martini. I doubt if he'd ever mixed one before. Let's say I was feeling a bit like the sophisticated lady entertaining a very impressed country bumpkin in her apartment . . . I was coming on like Gloria Vanderbilt, I thought.

Hah! I was somewhere in the middle of a sentence about the ski lift at Breckenridge when he kissed me. It wasn't a jerky kiss, or grabby or anything . . . it was almost as though he were shutting me up. But it was a good kiss, an expert kiss. *That* he knew how to do.

Then he began talking to me very quietly, and I'll never forget any of that conversation. He looked at me with those wild blue eyes and never let them leave my face.

"Miss Lanebrawn," he said, "I've made a bargain with your company. In return for my doing this very comprehensive survey and analysis for them, I am to have you as payment. They know you are very valuable, but they also know that what I'm doing for them may save them hundreds of thousands of dollars. Your company is in a little trouble right now, as you may know." (I knew.)

Despite the company trouble, I could just see my bosses, Mr. Wirtz and Mr. Feuthwanger, turning *any* female employee over to a management firm as payment for a survey! Mr. Wirtz had been trying to get the Playboy Club run out of Chicago ever since it opened, and Mr. Feuthwanger fired on the spot any employee caught dating another employee. I'd have considered leaving the company for that reason alone if I hadn't been so tied up with someone on the outside. (I'll tell you in a minute.) Yet it was fascinating listening to this guy weave this crazy story.

"I've been under a kind of spell since the first morning we talked," he said. "I knew you wouldn't be easy to own, but then I came up with this plan. Wirtz and Feuthwanger were dead set against it at first, but they realized their company was actually at stake and they couldn't very well refuse. We've agreed on it," he said.

"Don't *I* have anything to say about somebody getting me as payment?" I asked. "After all, it's me you're bargaining over."

"I'm afraid not," he said. "Your company's whole future may be resting on what I come up with in my work. Naturally I couldn't possibly accept any other payment now that I've met you."

Well he just went on and on, looking at me very steadily and talking away. It sounded nice. I liked it.

"When does the thing go into effect?" I asked.

"It's in effect now," he said. Then he laughed and broke the spell and went back to the kitchen to get another of those poisonous martinis. Ye gods! He may not ever have made any before, and I'm not even sure he had ever drunk any before but he was holding his liquor better than I was. He never did anything the least out of line the rest of the evening. He was quite full of respect and admiration, and to tell you the truth, I began to think perhaps I was some rare jewel without price . . . or at least that I was an Eastern princess who'd bewitched a visiting prince. (If it weren't for those *socks!*)

We went to lunch twice that week—once to a lovely garden restaurant and another time to the Cape Cod Room—and I *still* felt faintly superior because he wasn't at ease in those restaurants. Still, Wirtz and Feuthwanger really *were* treating him like the company savior, and all the time he was still spinning out this tale over lunch about my being his possession and that no one had ever consummated such a brilliant deal. He did it all with such charm, looking straight at me with those cuckoo blue eyes, and I had to keep saying to myself, "My God, Wirtz and Feuthwanger couldn't *really* have given me to this madman, could they?"

The following weekend I had a date with Roy, whom I haven't told you about. He's with the C.P.A. firm that audits our books and he'd been the love of my life—for the past two years anyway. That's how long we'd been having an affair. I suppose we'd broken off ninety-two times already, because he just didn't want to get married, but Sunday was the ninety-third . . . and this one took. I was sort of tired of the whole thing by then I guess, and besides, I was now a princess that some cuckoo nut had decided to forfeit his entire management consultant fees for!

The cuckoo nut—Lyle was his name, incidentally—and I began to see each other in earnest then. For all I know, he'd sensed there was somebody I really belonged to before, just as he sensed now there wasn't.

I worked hard at work. I thought I'd better, Mr. Feuthwanger's policy about dating being what it was. In two weeks I went to bed with Lyle for the first time, but instead of it being *he* who went right off his rocker with the princess, it was *I* who flipped . . . practically for the first time in my life.

With Roy I had spent the whole time trying to knock *him* out in bed. Really, I worked like a rat. He was so attractive to other women I thought I had to prove myself. He liked that. Well, nothing usually happened to me. With Lyle, who presumably cared much more for me than I did for him, I just sort of lay there and let things happen. I relaxed and let somebody love *me* for a change. I was knocked absolutely silly. He was so big and full of desire and so skilled (I don't know where he learned) and so full of wild and heavenly things to say.

I still hated the socks. His suits were too padded. He wasn't at ease socially. I couldn't take him places (or thought I couldn't), but who wanted to go anywhere? Then he began to lead me down a shivery path I've never yet got back from.

One evening in my apartment, when I was wearing green silk Capri pants and mules, with nothing on top, he said, "My Polaroid's down in the car. Why don't you run down to get it and I'll take some pictures of you?"

"*Me* run get it?" I said. "What's the matter with *you?*"

"I think you should go get it," he said. "Go on. Only take you a minute."

We were looking at each other very hard. I knew he didn't mean for me to put a blouse on, and I said, "All right. But what if someone is on the street?"

"It's late," he said. "There won't be anyone there. Here. Here are the keys."

He walked to the window while I flew out of the apartment as though I were possessed, raced to his car, unlocked it, got the camera out and was back in sixty seconds. I don't think anyone saw me.

"Good girl," he said. He didn't bother with the pictures. He just looked at me and started taking off the few clothes I *was* wearing. We made love.

A few days later we were riding in his convertible with the top down. His work was finished with Wirtz and Feuthwanger, and he was now at another company. The fantasy about my having been traded to him was finished too. It had had a good run, and we didn't try to revive it in conversation.

As he drove, he reached over and began unbuttoning the silk shirt I was wearing. He had long since persuaded me never to wear a bra. He got past the fourth button and then pushed the blouse gently away from my breasts on either side so they were quite exposed to all the electric lights and cars and everything.

"Beautiful," he said. "Absolutely beautiful."

I started to button my blouse up again but he stopped me. "Don't," he said, "we're going too fast for anyone to see you." So I didn't. And he reached over and caressed me every so often and cars *did* go by all that time.

I began to worry a little about myself. Men are supposed to be the only ones who sit around and fantasize all the time, but I was getting to be a worse employee than Muriel. At least she was *there* when she was there. I had already lost eight pounds, never seemed to be hungry, and when I met Lyle for dinner sometimes we got around to eating and sometimes we didn't. He usually picked out what I wore. One night he made a blouse for me entirely out of a large white chiffon scarf.

"I can't wear this," I said, though I secretly liked the way I looked in it. You could see my breasts through it, but not very clearly.

"Of course you can," he said. "Wear your jacket on top of it." I did, but during dinner I had to take the jacket off because we started playing "Chicken and Hawk." Whoever is "it" gets to tell the other person something to do, something silly. It can be anything. If the other person does it, he becomes "it" and gets to tell the first person what to do. You keep going until somebody refuses to do something, then that person becomes the chicken and the other person the hawk. The chicken then *really* has to do what the hawk says—though not right at the minute—and it's usually something big and often dangerous. Because those are the rules of the game, you mustn't start playing unless you agree to abide by them.

Of course I could have refused to play "Chicken and Hawk," but I figured I had as good a chance of coming out hawk as Lyle did. The first thing I was told to do in the restaurant when he was "it" was to take my jacket off briefly. A waiter saw me, and so did some people coming in. Then I was "it," and I told Lyle to go out to the parking lot and pretend to "steal" a car. He said he couldn't leave me, and that automatically made him the chicken and me the hawk. I let him off the hook, though, and never made him do the big dangerous thing. I later found out that if he had got to be hawk, he was going to take me to a friend's night club in Memphis and have them put me in the strip-tease show.

A few days later we all got two hours off to vote, and I saved my two hours for late in the afternoon with Lyle. When he arrived, he had his brief case with him as usual. I told him about not voting and how guilty I felt. "Yes, you've been a very naughty girl," he said, "and we're probably going to punish you."

"What did you have in mind?" I said, and I could feel the excitement start in my stomach or pelvis or wherever it starts when you get crazy.

"I'm going to have to beat you," he said. "Just a kind of symbolic beating, so you don't forget to vote next time. I won't hurt you."

Nothing he said anymore ever surprised me. I'd even stopped being surprised at not being surprised. He then opened his brief case and produced this handsome, small riding crop. I was horrified at the sight of it. And fascinated. And horrified. And fascinated.

Then he began to undress me. We went to my bedroom—he was still dressed—and I lay down on my bed and buried my head in the pillow. He struck me—not too hard, but it hurt. He started to strike me again, and I reached for his wrist. He was very quiet and very calm.

"It's too soon for you to know whether you like it or not," he said. "Let me bind your wrists and ankles so you can find out for sure. Get me something to use." So I got up and rummaged about in the dresser and found two silk scarves. He tied one around my ankles and the other around my wrists, and I lay on my face again and stuffed part of the pillow in my mouth so I wouldn't scream too loudly. He beat me—only across the buttocks—with perhaps ten more strokes, not terribly hard. It wasn't wildly painful, but it did hurt. Then he stopped and made love to me, and *that* was great.

The welts on my backside healed—after turning blue-black, then purple, then green, then yellow-chartreuse. I used to look at them fascinated. They were pretty exotic. Women like bruises, I think, maybe even non-cuckoo women. I've known two girls who came to the office with black eyes (I don't know what from), and I always got the feeling they were a little proud. Maybe bruises make a woman feel feminine and helpless.

We never did the beating thing again. I don't think Lyle enjoyed it particularly. I still sometimes take my blouse off when we're at a drive-in movie. And when we go to Las Vegas I wear terribly low-cut dresses at the dice tables, and Lyle pretends not to know me but watches other people looking at me.

We're going to be married this spring. He's all for it, though I get the feeling his mother isn't. Well, we won't go into that subject. I've only met her twice. I don't know what kind of marriage it's going to be, but I know I couldn't possibly live without him . . . efficiency, socks and all.

CHAPTER 15

GETTING INTO THE
ACT—AND OUT

So far this discussion has been philosophical and historical but how do you *personally* handle sex at the office . . . or the lack of it?

That depends on how you handle sex anywhere—or the lack of it, I should think—and *that* would be determined by your age, your background, your religious beliefs and your tolerance for the human race. Besides what your head thinks about sex, what your body thinks about it would also have some bearing on your responses to sexy overtures—or the lack of them—in or out of the office.

I haven't a scrap of reticence in advising you about your responses. But first, I have to ask how old you are.

CHILD WORKER

If you're the baby-worker at the office—under twenty—I think you have to bear in mind the difference between your age and everybody else's and not expect to get invited to do the things grownups do, much less enjoy them. When they *do* include you in, it can be lonelier and more depressing than when they *don't!*

A boss in one of my early jobs promised me a ride home one day, but said we first had to stop for a drink with some of his cronies. There we were, four drinkers and baby Helen, age eighteen, crammed in a booth. I just barely got down a Tom Collins, which I had heard was the mildest thing you could drink, when a new crony joined us, turned to me and asked, "What are you drinking?" I supposed he was just curious about what a lovely girl like me drank, so I said, "A Tom Collins." First thing you know I had another one of the wretched things in front of me. I was numb with self-consciousness and boredom in that group, and they would have been much happier if I'd been home playing with my dolls. An older girl might have enjoyed herself.

Okay. Don't rush fraternization with the grownups.

Eschewing office wolves when you're young—even if they are interested in you, which they may not be—makes even more sense than eschewing office drinking. Sometimes it's hard for you to determine whether somebody *is* wolfy or not. You *think* he is, but on the other hand you figure maybe you're just young and dumb and the way he's acting is the way men *act* in offices. Rule: Your natural instincts are usually sound.

In one of the ad agencies where I worked, an art director needed a picture of some pretty legs in a hurry, and one of the younger girls was rushed off to a photographer. (Sometimes photos are just for layout purposes, not for final ads, so they are whipped up with free office models.) The girl told me later that the leg photography took five minutes, but then the photographer told her he was supposed to do some head and shoulder shots. He somehow got her out of her shirt and into a bolt of velvet which he proceeded to drape and redrape endlessly around her pretty bosom. Could *any* photographer be *that* fussy about where the folds fell, she wondered, and what *was* all that fumbling? Still she didn't want to seem childish or critical or make anybody mad back at the agency. A few more pets and pats and she followed her intuition and bolted. An older girl would have spotted the phony much sooner.

Another young lady told me of going out to lunch with what seemed like a terribly nice typewriter salesman who often visited her firm. Thirty minutes and twenty miles later she found herself in a boarded-up beach house. Her date said he'd left some papers there and they'd just stop by and look.

Naughty, naughty, silly, silly men *do* pick on the wrong women sometimes. A grown-up girl might have enjoyed hunting for mythical papers in a beach house. This chap was a genuine creep to have snared a child. (Nothing happened. They tussled, she flew back to the car and demanded lunch.)

Second warning: If your instinct goes "sniff, sniff—peculiar, peculiar," trust your instinct, even when you're an older girl.

The same caution and sniff-sniff should prevail in getting employment when you're young. A wolfish interviewer isn't necessarily a reason to bolt if you're old enough to take care of yourself. Nancy told me of an initial chat with a tire tycoon who very smoothly caught her in a hammerlock and pressed his mouth to hers as she was getting up from her chair. She was broke and decided to take the job anyway. Her instincts said this lunatic acted that way with all girls and probably never followed through. She was right.

A young girl hasn't had enough experience in separating the cobras from the garter snakes, so she should avoid *all* snakes until she's older.

THE ABSTAINER

Some girls who are all grown up, filled out and not necessarily puritanical believe that all men in offices, no matter how nice or how important, up to and including a J. Paul Getty, are off-limits.

A very hip and man-loving friend of mine says, "An office romance? Never! So far as I'm concerned the men I work with are absolutely neuter. They might as well have 'eunuch' written across their Tattersall vests. I can flirt with them a bit, admire them and concern myself with their professional welfare, but they have the same appeal as my desk lamp. Bright, useful, ornamental—but turned off when I leave the office."

All I can say is that some girls won't visit Mexico for fear of getting hoof-and-mouth disease; and they'll just have to miss Mexico's exotic delights. The office abstainer never knows what might have been for *her*, either. As for you and me—who will hope to be south of the border often and who wouldn't pass up a dreamy, creamy man if we found him in *quarantine*—what men shall we accept from the office sampler?

Picking and choosing must be up to you. Does Merrill Lynch, Pierce, Fenner & Smith tell Walston & Company? You know who appeals to you better than I do. You know whether you think married men are poison ivy even for lunch. (If I were a married man I'd kind of resent this. If I'm good enough for somebody to have married, I ought to be good enough to go to lunch with.) Anyway the *selection* of the delicacies is up to you.

If by any chance there aren't any delicacies *around* the place, that's bad. You may have to change companies or even change fields.

If there are plenty of men in the office but they don't seem to be responding to *you,* perhaps they sense some unconscious criticism of themselves on your part. Many girls want the things men *give*— marriage, a playhouse and babies—without really liking *men.* I have a little friend who adores children but is secretly investigating the possibility of a virgin birth.

Some women of forty are still man-hating little girls too. They take great pride in their purity and choosiness, but their purity and choosiness have driven every last man away—as they intended. A grown woman should be womanly, warm and wooing, though with finesse. Prostitutes and call girls *do* get married (and for Pete's sake nobody is suggesting that you *be* one) while many child-women do not. Prostitutes are used to being with men, are comfortable with men and know how to make men happy. And they don't demand that all men have exactly the right credentials.

Some women in offices only go for SNAPUMS (Single Non-Alcoholic Paragons Upright Morally). The trouble is if you wait for SNAPUMS, even to *practice* on, you may be sitting there just waiting and waiting next to a whole pile of your unused wiles.

BASICS

Suppose you do like men, you are *not* a child-woman. Let's check off the basics and see if you've attended to them.

Basic 1. *Don't give away the whole plot.*

Easy friendliness is a wonderful thing. Do be easy to talk to. The girl whose male associates know everything about her, however, isn't particularly sexy. (Is a *World Almanac* sexy?) If you load more than one or two close friends up with too much personal information, it can be used against you at politics time anyway.

It would be silly to try to be mysterious with your mother, your intimate friends or even a husband. You *can* live in a little pocket of mystery for the men you work with, however. A man likes to speculate about you . . . to think you don't belong to *anybody* and therefore might be his . . . even if he's married!

A friend of mine saw one of the secretaries from his office in a restaurant one evening with a man. The next day at work she asked Tony how he liked the cuisine at the place but didn't say a word about the man she'd been with. Tony decided instantly it must have been her brother or her ballet teacher, definitely not a beau. Dreams unimpaired! You must remember that all office romances which were meant to be do not flower the first moment. Some have to be watered, fertilized and tended through two or more Decembers, and that means staying "romantic" in a man's eyes.

Basic 2. *Don't jangle his nerves.*

Men are appalled by harsh, nasal voices, seduced by soft, whispery ones. Try to clean up a bad voice if you have one. It isn't attractive always to be blabbing on the telephone with a girl friend when a man walks into your office, either. (Lock the door or telephone at lunch.) You're in a man's world, remember (and isn't it heaven?), not a sorority house.

Basic 3. *Insides of purses matter.*

Just pretend some man at the office is going to dump the contents of your purse right out on your desk today. Would he find you toting battle-fatigued Kleenex, eight shades of lipstick, and three shredding cigarettes? Why *are* you, incidentally?

Basic 4. Play the hankie game.

Leaving a lacy, white hankie with your initials and your fragrance in a man's office is foxy if not downright sexy. There's something old-fashioned and feminine about girls who carry hankies, and scent is the most evocative of all senses. That's another reason to let one special scent be yours. You can also leave scented hankies under a man's pillow or inside the pillowcase, but that's for later.

GO GO GO

All right, you've attended to the basics. You're enthusiastic about men. You also like yourself, dress yummily, smell delicious, are good at your job, seem eager to make friends and be approached by co-workers, have lots of white hankies—and *still* Ivan Denisovitch had a better social life in the Ukraine.

I think you're ready for a pep talk and some new ammunition. Pep talk first.

Perhaps you worry that men in offices always go straight for the beautiful sexpot. Naturally they go for her. What man wants his manhood impugned? But frequently they also go for some little nothingburger who looks to *you* like something even flu germs wouldn't care to hang around. Midge Dimsdale was that girl at a place where I worked. Midge didn't walk, she gangled. Her chest went *in* instead of out. She did have lovely skin and nice eyes, but that girl looked more like a boy. But the teeth-gnashing that went on over her! Half the men in the place were in love with Midge, and we girls were more depressed than if she'd been *pretty*. I finally asked one of the men exactly what she *had*.

"She looks at you with those eyes," he said, "and you get the feeling nobody ever listened to you before or cared what you said. She kind of drinks you in, then she acts as though what she drank had knocked her out and she'd gone straight to heaven."

It was a madly disappointing answer. Obviously Midge was a good listener. That's *part* of what she had. Aside from that I think she also had the Plain Girl Power, and this man just couldn't explain it. I've come to understand much more about it since then and used it many times. The Power comes to plain—or at least not-raving-beauty—girls who need men to like them so much they just sort of reach out like spring flowers and drink in the man's face and voice the way a blossom wolfs down the sunshine. This is how it works:

You want—you need—with every fiber of your being, to make a particular man like you. Perhaps you only have a lunch date in which to make good. Well, to start with, you never let your eyes leave his face. Inside you, you simply go on the make, in a very quiet, private, dedicated, personal, one-track-minded way. You pray and work right through lunch. You let your eagerness for him to like you and find you physically attractive filter through your charm. You accidentally touch his hand or brush his knee once or twice, as we mentioned in Lunchland. Being skittish and jumpy dissipates the Power. You've got to try to sit or stand still and seem to relax. (Hah!) But extreme primness and properness and only speaking when spoken to are out too. You've got to come on a little . . . say funny, happy things and discuss whatever he's discussing, but pay attention to his thought waves and talk waves as though you were a surfer trying not to fall off your board.

This kind of charm is actually more lethal than sexiness (not that you aren't sexy on the inside). The beautiful sexpot expects everything to come her way just because she's *there,* but the plain charmer reacts—and what man doesn't like to be reacted to? She impales a man, puts herself in his blood. This is what author Ernest John Knapton has to say about a famous charmer, anything but pretty, in his book, *Empress Josephine* (Harvard University Press): "Josephine . . . was mistress of the art of charm. Bonaparte was pale, thin, awkward—presenting anything but the image of a victorious general of the new Republic. His appearance, however, did not prevent him from being invited to call again. 'One day,' he long afterwards recalled, 'when I was sitting next to her at table, she began to pay me all manner of compliments on my military qualities. Her praise intoxicated me. From that moment I confined my conversation to her and never left her side. I was passionately in love with her, and our friends were aware of this long before I ever dared to say a word about it.'"

Your Plain Girl Power won't work on *every* man. Napoleon's brothers *hated* Josephine. A couple of men thought Midge Dimsdale was a bird. But how many men do you *need?* The PGP will certainly work on *several*. Fortunately, men at the office are *there* where you can get to them and work on them as many days as you need to.

Here's another Plain Girl technique. It's hitting just a bit below the belt, but when desperate measures are called for . . .

Over a coffee or cocktail date, or perhaps when you're alone in his office—you'll know the time—say to your beloved who doesn't know you're alive, "Dick, I've finally stamped out my crush. I've never told you this, but when you first came to work here I went completely out of my head. I can't remember in my whole life ever being so impressed with anybody or so taken with a man at first sight. You can ask Maryanne because I told her about it . . . I flipped utterly and completely. It seems insane now. We're such good friends and I know how crazy you are about Adeline (his girl friend, the bird). Somehow I just felt in the mood to tell you about this today."

Nothing, but nothing, is so unsettling and even inflammatory to a man as knowing a woman no *longer* wants him—especially when he never knew of her interest in the first place. He'll worry. He'll brood. And just let Adeline make a false move . . .

FLIRTING

It may just have occurred to you that Plain Girl Power is the same as flirting. How clever of you! I wrote everything I know about flirting, practically, in *Sex and the Single Girl* (deep-down gazing at him, lots of hair versus skimpy, etc.). I'll just add a few comments by another first-class flirt, my friend Ann. Ann says: "Flirting isn't swinging your hips or breathing heavily. It's being feminine to your quivering core and being totally aware of the man you're with. It's fun to love men and see fine and fabulous things in them. Tomorrow they may disappoint you because they are really very ordinary, but for a while they are golden people. And if they are golden people, you *want* to listen to them. You *want* to stand just four inches closer to them, to touch them *once* lovingly on the arm, to discover what they are saying in the depths of their eyes; you want to have them aware of the scent of you, the flicker of your manicure, the gloss of your satin-clean cheek, the quick tenderness of your sympathy, the elegantly ordered way your handbag looks inside, the way you respond to what they're telling you, the unique and treasured place you and they share in the universe *right this minute.*

"Whoever you are with is the only person who has any place in your thoughts . . . and the present, current pulsating situation is the first, last and only situation of its kind. It must be a built-in or unconsciously practiced ability to concentrate on The Big Present Moment."

Gee, I would think such a thing would help *any* girl get what she wanted out of office maneuvers.

As for being choosy about whom you flirt with, Ann says:

"I have—so help me—never gone out with a man—in fact, I've practically never known a man at work—who I didn't think was absolutely terrific in some way. Heaven knows, that special merit may not have been apparent to his own mother, and often I could not see it a week later, but at the time . . . So he was short, balding and sort of oily . . . well, he had an accent that sounded exactly like Yves Montand and he knew how to order wine, both attributes good enough for several evenings while I hung on to every seductive syllable and gazed in utter trancelike fascination over the rim of a wineglass. Or, he was two hundred and ten pounds of struck-dumb awkwardness in the office, but he taught me the most beautiful jackknife and full- and half-gainers you ever saw. If you have this attitude, the rest comes naturally. Your flattering, breathless murmurs have that ring of pure sincerity because you *do* mean them."

No, presumably you wouldn't flirt with office menfolk *all* the time, but a lot of this attitude of love and listening can prevail when you take dictation, chat with men in conferences, ride with them to meet the client, walk from office to office. Again, I would say, make every man you work with, from the mailroom boy up, just a little bit in love with you. You'll have a rich, full office life!

STALKING

Don't be afraid of a man's economic or social position. As I've said about a dozen times, stalking is easier if you are closer to a man's own professional level, but affairs cut across all class lines for an attractive girl.

In a fit of pique my friend Polly marched out of the steno pool into the president's office one day to say, "Mr. Halliburton, we girls have *had* it . . . we are getting as blind as owls with all that sunlight streaming in every afternoon. Now when *are* the draperies going up?" Mr. Halliburton said he'd look into the drapery situation right away but obviously wanted to look into Polly too. "Come in any time, Miss . . . Miss . . . Drury? Drury. The coffee pot's always boiling back here," he said. The minute the draperies are up, Polly's going right back to say thank you and have a cup of coffee. I wouldn't be surprised if something besides coffee began to boil soon around *that* office.

Besides watching for opportunities to fraternize with your own brass and other attractive co-workers, you will want to spot and stalk visitors too. Allison had her eye on a *New Yorker* cartoonist for three weeks before she pounced. "He'd been coming into the office regularly to see one of the editors," she said. "I knew their business was almost finished, so just before my time ran out I nabbed him at the elevator. I was so scared my teeth were chattering, but I said, 'Mr. Darrow (it wasn't Whitney Darrow but somebody just as famous, so I'm borrowing his name), I'm food editor of *Homemaker's* and I just can't resist telling you that I've loved your cartoons ever since I first spotted them. I think you are the finest cartoonist in the world, and I've always wanted to know how long you worked on that fantastic mural in the Peekskills.' "

Pretty smart girl. She established herself as an executivess so he wouldn't think he was talking to a stage-struck errand girl. She also asked him a question about his work so he would be drawn into conversation.

He was enormously pleased. They chatted. He didn't ask her for a date, but he may. At least she has established contact.

CARE AND HANDLING OF SPECIAL MEN

Small Man. Don't ever forget how rough it must be to be a little man. Think how impotent *you* feel when men rave about Playboy Bunny breasts and yours are built more like a real bunny's . . . or how infuriating it is that men think cutiepie petite little creatures are more feminine when you are female to the *depths* of your five-foot-nine Bob Waterfield frame. I'm not saying be nice to small men because it's philanthropy day . . . I'm saying you might come across something good. Do pick out an especially nice five-foot-five or under man and say to yourself, "Him heap big man *inside* . . . me bring him coffee, him open doors for me, carry heavy files for me, drag chairs across floor for me. Pretty soon him feel nine feet tall. Me have nice man in my life."

On your way, Minnie-ha-ha.

Neurotic. Compliment him for what he *isn't* . . . in a way. Pick a man who periodically turns into a raving, raging *beast* and tell him during a relatively calm period how much you admire his integrity. "You handle your staff so beautifully, Mr. Bates. I *have* seen you lose your temper, but we always know we'll be treated with complete fairness and compassion."

Tell any man he's so very "normal" and he'll love it . . . now that eccentrics are out and conformists are in.

Milquetoast. "It's so wonderful to know somebody who *thinks* around here. I always know that while everybody else is fighting and screaming, you're busy coming up with a solution."

Wit. If a man tells stories, whether he tells them well or terribly, badger him to tell you his latest. He is the *funny* man in your life. One of Bob Hope's gag writers called to tell me stories for years after he was married and I belonged to somebody else. He knew he broke me up and it pleased him.

We could go on and on, but you get the picture . . . tailor your compliment to the man.

RIDE, PLEASE

Asking for rides home from work is a good way to get things going. Offering rides is even better. Find out exactly what men live in your flight pattern and let it be known you're available in case of flat tires, dead batteries or other emergencies. If you drive a fair distance, fast friendships can form. If the man is married, you may not be interested in him romantically, but you *may* be invited to the next party he and his wife give. (She'll want to establish that you really do have pop eyes and wear braces as she's been told.)

One girl I know needed a ride to work after she dropped her car off at the garage. She knew a delightful office knight who drove to work that way. "Gee, Sandra," he said, "I'll remember if I can, but I'm usually so preoccupied when I go by that corner . . ." Occupied, schmoccupied! When Sandra saw his red Corvette hurtling down Glendale Boulevard, and she was sure there was no other traffic between her and it, she plopped herself down flat in the middle of the road and stayed there until he got to her corner! He had two blocks in which to stop, but let's face it, she was a brave girl . . . with a lumphead on her hands. She rides in the Corvette anytime she wants to now. And who knows where she'll go from there?

Parties outside your firm may be swinging places. I know one girl who has made an art of attending large business and professional cocktail parties and pretending to be part of the management group giving the party. She selects a likely man, finds out from spies that he isn't part of the host group and tells him she's been delegated to amuse him for the evening.

There's a system for you!

I know, I absolutely *know* that you can have acres of sexy fun at the office if you really care to.

Charming and flirting can, of course, lead to an affair. They don't *necessarily*. They may lead only to a busier, happier life more replete with beaux—or they may even get you married, if that's what you want. An affair, however, *could* result.

I don't suppose you need any rules to know how to conduct an office affair. They move right along like guppy schools and may flourish without complications for weeks or months or even years. Most affairs, however—even well-managed, office-based ones—often have wretchedly unhappy moments. So here are a few hints for survival.

THE BLOTCHY TIMES

Marriages have blotchy moments, too, of course, and are full of problems, but affairs are probably *more* full of problems because society doesn't approve of them. Society hasn't been able to stamp them out and probably never will, but it can and does make everybody feel awfully sticky.

Aside from feeling that what you're doing may not be exactly right, girls in an affair are often wretched because of the wretches they are mixed up with.

I used to think only a certain kind of girl went for wretches, for the exploiters. I don't think so any more. There *are* girls, to be sure, who never pick any other kind of man. Apparently they can't tolerate a man who really loves them and so they go around hippity-hop collecting one creep after another. Sacher-Masoch can roll over and expire *again* for all I care—I think there are very few dyed-in-the-wool, first-rate masochists. Why go ape over pain? I do think a girl can be *comfortable* in a situation that's bad. Again and again she picks the difficult man, because he's the kind she's dealt with in the past, and she doesn't have to learn any new rules.

Some girls pick "impossibles" to avoid getting married, I'm told. They carry on about how much they *want* to marry while grabbing off the one really *confirmed* bachelor in the territory, or the most solidly-married philanderer available.

Not all girls having trouble with men are aligned with "impossibles," of course. Some men just have plain old faults (if the faulty man happens to be married, the same faults are probably driving his nice, normal wife out of *her* skull too).

Although she may not make a practice of it, I don't happen to think *any* girl, no matter how "well-adjusted," is totally immune to being attracted to a nut at some time in her life. Maybe in her youth she only headed straight for baby SNAPUMS. At age thirty-two, however, she sails blithely spang into the arms of an impossible! I've seen it happen to my best friends. They had such nice men in their lives while they commiserated with me about some nut or other who was not cracking satisfactorily. Eight or ten years later I was married to a lovely "possible" (with whom I expect to spend the rest of my life) and some of my *friends* are now nut-cracking. I'm not smug. I just say that's the way the "impossibles" crumble.

Very well then, if you're temporarily involved with a monster and suffering like mad, I see no reason for you to think you're all that tragic, special and neurotic. You're really quite run of the mill!

THE D.J.'S AND THE M.M.'S

Two men in offices who undoubtedly give girls the most trouble are Don Juans and Married Men. I dealt with both species rather extensively in *Sex and the Single Girl* and will try not to repeat myself. (You have *read* that book, haven't you?) Just for identification purposes, however, let me say that the D.J. is generally characterized by being better than average looking, physically strong, tender, generous and smart. He also does the pursuing, which most girls love. (If you'd be a little more pursuing *yourself*—with some other kind of man, of course—you wouldn't be such a standing target for a D.J. maybe.)

The D.J. gives you the impression that you undo him as he has never been undone. "One night Van unbuttoned my blouse just two buttons," Gerry says, "and saw the mildest cleavage this side of an Indian brave. It was all I *had*, but it surely wasn't sensational. Nevertheless he gasped. He foamed. He had never seen anything quite so beautiful in his life. He was so profoundly moved he actually convinced me at that moment, beyond a shadow of a doubt, that no other girl in the world had cleavage like that."

To capsule a bit further, there are always other women in a Don Juan's life, and you sense it unless you have absolutely no female antennae. Nevertheless, if the panel chairman said, "Will Philip's real love please stand up," you'd get up . . . along with the rest of the mob.

After a D.J. experience or two you *can* get to recognize one. Janice says, "I dropped in to meet our new promotion manager the other day and caught my breath. 'He's one!' I said. The handshake, the straight, warm, steady gaze, the sexy waves coming off him . . . 'Could we have lunch one day?' he asked. 'Of course,' I said. You pretend he's moving in like mobile television equipment because you're so attractive, that he wouldn't do that with *any other girl*— but of course you're a ninny.

"We did have lunch and sure enough, we wound up in the back of a dark little cafe, arms around each other, declaring undying love by the end of lunch. If he'd thrown me over his shoulder like a sack of potatoes and carted me off, I wouldn't have cared. I got out in time, though. I refused the next lunch date to gain a little time. I'd just been through one D.J. experience and was battle-scarred. Sure enough, in only a few weeks I began to notice up and down the halls the broken bodies of girls he had got *to*."

I won't go into why Don Juans do it. I barely know why we're *attracted* to them. I do have several dabs of philosophy and advice for dealing with them, however, and here they are.

FRONT-LINE SERVICE WITH A DON JUAN

1. Don't compare yourself and your affair to a girl who doesn't have a difficult man on her hands. If you discuss it, she'll only tell you that all men are a bit eccentric . . . even her dear Jim is panting for a blue-eyed, blonde waitress in Schrafft's. Listen, you've got a different kind of man on your hands from dear Jim. Yours is *more* eccentric and the two fellows just aren't comparable. You might try to face up to the fact, however, that while your man is more trouble and won't fit into an acceptable mold, he may also be more fascinating and you can try to enjoy him while he lasts (or while *you* last).

2. Don't suppose you are less attractive a woman than your flaming Don Juan is a man simply because he has so many women after him. If you worked as hard as he does (and weren't in love with *him*), you could be quite a little scalp collector too.

3. You can save yourself a great deal of wear and tear if you stop pretending that he's true to you. You know very well you have a truth mechanism inside you which works as inexorably and flawlessly as an IBM machine. You feed it his version of what he did last night, it digests all these "facts" and pretty soon it shoots you back a card which says, "The son of a bitch is lying."

The smart thing to do, if you're up to it, is say, "All right, I'm not the only one, but I'm going to give those others a run for their money." Some very attractive and persistent women have, as far as outsiders are able to observe anyway, tamed and domesticated some flagrant girl-chasers.

4. If you've tried valiantly to tame and domesticate one and things aren't working out for you, don't blame yourself. While most life situations do respond to hard work, drive and determination,

most D.J. tie-ups do not. The more you put in, the more indifference you may get out.

5. Just because you may manage to get a Don Juan to some idyllic vacation hideaway out of the city and away from your competition, don't suppose you really have him. He will drive you mad writing postcards and buying mementos for the girls he left at home.

6. You may be confused about the turn things have taken. In the beginning he chased *you*. He had to slay ninety-two dragons (including your indifference) to get to you. Now he's acting as casual about you as Mr. Clean does about dirt.

Don't keep asking yourself what you're doing wrong. What you did wrong is done. You succumbed! Certain men can't bear a conquest. Anybody who likes them couldn't possibly be worth very much, they figure, because they don't like themselves much either. (That's junior-grade parlor psychiatry, but I just thought I'd throw it in.)

7. Trying to intrigue and torment this kind of man by turning down dates will bring only temporary satisfaction. He will be piqued. The moment you go back to him on a steady basis, however, you might as well not have bothered with your little war games. Their usefulness is as done with as last year's push-ups. Rather than acting hard-to-get, which is rough on a girl in love, you might just as well accept the parties, picnics and ball games— at least you get *them* out of him. When you take a stand—marry or else—you are going to have to do it by turning down more than a few dates. You'll probably have to disappear completely for a while —if not forever.

8. Don't be surprised if, without meaning to, you find you've broken off your affair prematurely and are sitting there with the bits and pieces around you. (You were only talking, one thing led to another and whammo . . . the fight of the century!) An unhappy love affair breeds this kind of fight. You'll probably be back together again in twenty-four hours. When the time comes to break up, you usually have to do it more deliberately or it won't work.

9. The pain induced by jealousy and insecurity over a man is much, much worse than anybody lets on, and the symptoms are rarely dealt with realistically. All anybody ever tells you is "don't be

jealous and insecure." The "don't be's" can only say it because they aren't dealing with the same kind of man you are.

Is there anything worse than the feeling you get when the IBM hands you the card that says he was unfaithful? Or it can be a breathtaking body blow when a girl friend innocently tells you he asked *her* for a drink. You are not alone! Others too have known the three-o'clock-in-the-mornings that are greenish-white with worry and loneliness, when the room is full of wet, cold, soft, floating amorphous things more frightening than nightmares.

Dawn's approach helps some. Having a job you must go to helps even more.

10. You can be this worried about *another* man later—how's that for consolation! Anyway, don't think this man is so terribly special and different for causing you such pain, or that you are particularly neurotic and "different" from your girl friends for letting him.

There, that's enough about pesky old D.J.'s!

THE ONE YOU LOVE BELONGS, ETC.

That brings us up to the married men at the office. One of them may bring you special and different problems in an affair, but the problems are so boring and commonplace we don't even need to describe them! I'm not altogether unsympathetic to strayed married men (for all the reasons delineated earlier, and considering the creatures they're expected to remain faithful *to*). Having been a single girl working in an office many years, however, I know the wracking problems of a single girl involved with such a man, no matter how deeply he cares for her.

In all fairness—I can run toward either goal post—it is more difficult for most married men to conduct an affair than a single girl ever realizes. She thinks he's just a little out of breath when he gets to her apartment. Actually he's been plotting and scheming, lying and conniving, dodging and running for four solid days to get there. Men sacrifice—money, time, energy and integrity. Never mind that nobody twisted their arms. You, a single working girl, have some advantages you never even think about. You never have to sneak. You never have to lie (which *most* men don't really enjoy). You never have to feel guilty about hurting someone dear to you. When it's over, you can suffer in public if you like. He can't tell *anyone,* now that he doesn't have *your* ear.

You both pay—with different tender—but *you* pay most. (I'm running for the other goal post now.) He has the practical responsibility of running the affair, the awkwardness of explaining at home. You, however, pay with your insides.

I don't want to talk you out of any liaison you may be involved in, but here are a few philosophical thoughts and twigs of advice for the girl who is involved with somebody else's husband.

1. If you're willing to go through a series of tortures and shocks that would try a fakir's nervous system, you may get him. One woman I know stuck it out for six years and finally, in exasperation, married another man who'd been in the wings. On receiving her telegram from Greenwich her real love telephoned and said, "Okay. You win. Don't consummate the marriage. I'll fly in and get it annulled." He did, got a divorce himself, and he and she have been happily married seventeen years now.

I think you know in your heart practically from the beginning whether you have a real chance of marrying him. If you do, you're on your own. I suggest morphine, yoga and a copy of *Jane's Fighting Ships* to see you through. If you *know* that marriage is completely out of the question, then you're an *idiot* not to keep other men in your life. Perhaps you can't break off with the man just yet, but you can have lots of other friends. They are the only things—plus your job—that can knit and purl you when you become utterly unraveled.

Janice (a real live girl with another name) goes a step further. "Never, no matter how much in love," she says, "be faithful to a married man you aren't married to." The other night Janice had her two current lovers and one ex—all with wives—for dinner. The men didn't know about each other. The wives didn't know about Janice. I watched her charm, feed and captivate everybody that evening, wives included. She would have done well at the court of Louis XIV.

2. When you feel you are giving more than you are getting by practically *anybody's* reckoning, you must take a stand. Many mar-

ried men are *grievously* thick-headed when it comes to understanding that what you want from a relationship may not be the same thing they want (brief and idyllic dalliance at *their* convenience).

Gretchen gave an *à deux* supper party for her lover recently— breast of pheasant under glass, braised endive, iced champagne, perfect crepes, fire in the fireplace and Gretchen herself in a costume that would have unloosed Tristram from Isolde. She didn't hear from her friend for two weeks, and when he *did* call he said, "Shall we have supper like that again?"

Gretchen explained the facts of life. She *adored* having dinner parties for him, but there would be no more until he showed that he could reciprocate with kindness, affection, loyalty and dinner plans of his own. He did.

When a married man behaves selfishly and you know he "isn't really *like* that," chances are he's become lodged in a gelatin of guilt, fright and remorse. (I've got to send this off to Betty Crocker!) That is understandable, but these are *his* problems, really, not yours. If he continues to see you, he must behave like a big boy, and you must get more out of it than on-again off-again affection. Otherwise, unload that man! (I promised I wouldn't say it, but it might be a good idea to unload him anyway.)

3. Don't fret that you are not the cool, practical beauty who can bring off these liaisons with more equanimity. Give a man a girl who enjoys sex for sex's sake, without guilt feelings or possessive qualities, and who doesn't care *what* he does between-times so long as he sees her every other Thursday, and she'll quickly become a puzzle to him and a problem to herself. In our society that girl would have to be considered a kook. Her being a completely "sensible" biological creature would be no more desirable to him or "good" for her than her being that mythical ideal girl—the nymphomaniac who owns a liquor store. At least that's how things stand with us twentieth century ladies right now.

4. When you are going to a psychiatrist during an affair, the man in your life is usually horrified, especially if he's married. He will gingerly say to you, "I'm sure you don't talk about *me* to that doctor, do you?" Don't hit him! Just say, "I'd really prefer not to talk about my analysis until I'm a little further along, if you don't mind."

Girls in love with a Don Juan or married man don't have *all* the problems, of course. Paula is going with a guy who is always telling her, "That's a good light for you" when they are *practically* sitting in the *dark*.

Jean is stuck with a nonlicensed magician who puts his arm around girls' waists at parties but so high up he can tell instantly whether they do or don't pad.

If your man, whoever he is, is a bit of a terror, and if the affair, as affairs will, is backing and filling and going *nowhere,* here are a few general words of condolence and advice:

1. The weaker your ego, the more devastating the love affair. Girls who have a pretty healthy opinion of themselves generally don't suffer so much.

If you're suffering badly but aren't ready to end it, off to the psychiatrist with you! Go on . . . shoo . . . scat!

2. Don't be alarmed if you are inconsistent in behavior . . . one day it's love and kisses, the next day you're looking for a blunt instrument. The less you are on equal footing with a man—he's a chaser, you're constant; he's married, you're single; he's famous, you're obscure—the less possibility there is that you can be eternally sweet to him. People who bring the same set of liabilities and assets to an affair—you're *both* single, both divorced with children, both married and have to be home before dark—naturally have greater understanding.

3. If a man doesn't want to marry you, of *course* you're in pain. This isn't a Chagall, a new Simca or a lease on a Swiss villa he's turning down—it's *you.*

If you've fought him down to the mat for several months running, I suggest you let him up off the mat for a breath of air. Granted most men have the pick-up of a tortoise when it comes to rushing off to get married, but the man *may* have a *reason.* You're too young for him. He thinks you wouldn't be faithful. He *knows* he wouldn't be faithful. He doesn't love you enough. (That's not a bad reason, dear.) He's contemplative and you're a swinger. He likes boys.

The man could be trying to save you a rather somber life.

4. Few affairs are severed with dignity. You usually wind up bawling and screeching as you promised yourself you *never* would

when the end came. It doesn't make a particle of difference whether you play it like Margaret Leighton. The important thing is to get across the idea that it's over . . . if you really mean it to be.

5. The more "desperately" in love you've been—the more insistent on marriage, the more clobbered, the more mauled—the more you have to stay away when you break up. A girl who has only toyed with a man might call him up from time to time just for old times' sake. *You* have to stay away completely.

6. A man is hurt at the end of an affair too. To the naked eye he may seem as unaffected as spring's first robin, but don't you believe it. Someone really close to him—a sister, a mother, a buddy—will tell you he's actually in shock. He may suffer even more than you because he's a man and not supposed to show it.

7. When an affair is over, it usually isn't possible to continue to work in the same office. It will be you who must get the new job, too. That's protocol. Maybe you were ready for one. I'm *sure* everything is for the best!

There hasn't been much talk in these pages about love. So what *about* love—the true, tender, trusting, everlasting, with-all-your-heart kind? I don't think I have to tell you about that! You'll know when it happens and you'll know what to do about it, and all the "false" feelings you've had before (which seemed real at the time) will look like a Christmas tree out in the trash can on the second of January. It could be, you know, that *he* will be somebody from the office—*his* office anyway.

CHAPTER 16

SOME GIRLS GET PAID FOR IT

So far we've been talking about the kind of sex that can happen to you in an office—some of it lovely and shimmery (flirtation and romance with dreamskins), some of it sad and regretful (when a dreamskin turns out to be a ratcreature and troubles are heaped on your shiny, shampooed head).

There's still another, totally different *kind* of sex connected with offices, however, that we haven't dealt with. In fact, it's an institution. You don't actually participate in it or have dealings with the institution, but some of the men in your office *may*. I assume that anything which concerns them *could* concern you.

There's another reason for you to know about this kind of sex and the institution which packages it. Being the sexy dreamboat you are, a boss may sometimes prod and poke you to go out with him or with clients and want you to be friendlier than you care to be. It's lovely to pick and choose the men you want, but being pressed into service is something else again. Well, a boss doesn't *need* to badger you, because there are these girls from the institution who are his for the selecting and who have no inhibitions whatever.

They're rather costly, but that's no reason for him to economize by trying to use *you*.

Listen, if you're having even a *scrap* of trouble with any man in the office expecting you to do things you don't feel like doing— for him or anybody else—I suggest you put this book under his nose, opened to this chapter, so that *he'll* know *you* know there's another way out.

THE WICKEDNESS OF IT ALL

If some people want to stop the world and get off when they hear about *amateur* sex at the office, they want to float right on out to Ursa Major and *homestead* when somebody tells them that call girls are a business institution. I remember when Edward R. Murrow did a television documentary on the subject a few years ago, he was screeched at by one industry leader after another. "You're not talking about *us*," they all howled. Maybe he wasn't talking about them *personally*, but I daresay he could have been talking about their industry and maybe their *company*. Apparently men at the top can be as innocent as lambs while dark-operator underlings traffic with the girls. (I worked in a company where an expediter made book in his office from ten to four daily. Management just figured he had to use the phone a lot.) Sometimes, however, men at the top are *not* so innocent . . . about the girls.

One man I interviewed on the subject—he had considerable insight, what with being a procurer—said, "I don't see how you can say any industry is totally free of involvement with call girls. I've fixed up guys in practically every line of work you can think of— electronics, finance, pharmaceuticals, food, government. They included the presidents of a soup company and a surgical company, not to mention a couple of science professors. Executives get the urge just like clerks. Only the prices change. There's really no more paid-for sex in Paris or New York than there is in Decatur or Dubuque, when you consider the difference in population."

Having told you this kind of sex does exist and explained why we're delving into it (the men in your office may be involved; under no circumstances are *you* to become involved yourself), I think you should know the information you're about to examine is authoritative. I went out into the field, notebook in hand, and interviewed the following experts:

Two "high-class" procurers (who only procure for important men in industry).

Five men who "date" call girls.

Four call girls (whom I paid their regular hourly rates while they sipped gimlets and I took notes).

An attorney whose office girls are "available" for clients.

A policeman.

These thirteen interviews may not add up to a report by Dr. Kinsey, but I do think they give a sampling. *The Call Girl*, by Dr. Harold Greenwald (Ballantine Books), makes good supplementary reading for anyone who wants to continue the course.

WHAT'S A CALL GIRL, MOMMY?

A call girl, darling, according to any definition mommy has ever heard, is a girl who can be hired to go to bed with a man. She gets the name "call girl" because most of her contacts are made by telephone. If a man wants to engage her for himself or a friend, he calls her answering service. Only the service and a few close friends have the girl's private number. The service may put the call through to her house and let her make a date with the caller, or it may be the kind of service that only takes messages—in which case she will call in regularly. Call girls are always calling their answering services to find out what's up. The four I interviewed—Norma, Anita, Barbara and Colleen—called their services about three times apiece during our separate interviews. I managed to get in lots of questions anyway.

There are, of course, girls other than call girls who get paid for love-making. Apart from mistresses, women who hate their husbands and girls who are sleeping their way to the top in business (dreadful!), these are:

Street walkers and B-girls who depend mostly on personal contact to make dates.

Girls who live in "houses." There aren't many of these any more except in lettuce-growing areas and very poor districts of a few towns and cities.

Party girls who take paid assignments only occasionally and work the rest of the time as starlets, models, salesgirls and secretaries. (It wouldn't hurt to keep an eye on girls in your office who have two new ostrich bags in one season and *never* bring their lunch.)

It may surprise you to know that the call girl—occasionally referred to as a "hustler" or "hooker"—is considered the aristocrat of her trade. She makes more money and is better looking, better dressed and better educated than most of the girls just mentioned. Some people, in describing her, even say she has more "class!"

How does she operate?

MODUS OPERANDI

A call girl usually has an apartment in which she entertains clients. Many of her assignments are also completed away from home. Since customers are often businessmen from out of town, hotels are a popular place to converge. The call girl doesn't mind trotting off to a hotel because she can more easily control the length of the visit when *she's* the one who called. (Apparently customers can overstay their welcome maddeningly in the girl's apartment.)

In addition to her business-address apartment, the professional often maintains another house or apartment as her actual residence. This is necessary if she lives with parents, husband or children (which many call girls do). It's also good to have two apartments, I was told, in case the girl is picked up by the police. After the arrest or questioning, she will not use the same business-apartment again but will get a new address.

Wherever she works, as soon as one assignment is completed (the very second it's over or even *before* it's over, if it's taking too long) the girl checks with her answering service to see if there are any interesting new developments. She calls back whoever has called, and if he wants to see her immediately, she may skip to this new assignment from the one she has just finished. In sprawling cities like Los Angeles, call girls have their own cars. Otherwise, taxis are used and added to the client's bill. The important thing is for a call girl to stay busy!

Morning business is usually light. One or two callers may drop by around noon. By mid-afternoon activity gets brisker and by evening, her schedule should be fairly full.

The four girls I talked with saw an average of five customers a day but occasionally fitted in as many as ten. All said they preferred a rapid turnover (spending not more than half an hour with each customer) to a long drawn-out assignment with one man. "Getting through cocktails, dinner, night club and finally to bed with one guy can be rough," said Colleen.

Anita agreed. "You have to be so damned charming and interested on a date," she said. "It wears you out!"

Because they're accustomed to dealing with civilian girls who are always yammering at them about being taken to dinner, some customers can't understand why the call girls wouldn't be delighted to dine with them *free*. "They forget," Norma said, "that we must be paid for our time regardless of what we're doing. If the dinner consisted of twenty-four-karat-gold shad roe, it wouldn't make up for the income lost from other paying customers while we're eating."

THE GOING RATE

To these aristocrats of the trade twenty dollars is rock-bottom minimum for a single act of love (and that only for an old buddy who is broke). The minimum usually is twenty-five dollars. For this amount, the girl will spend up to an hour with a man. She prefers to get the engagement over with much sooner, however, and usually succeeds. Of that hour, usually no more than ten to twenty minutes is spent in bed. If the man should want to dally there for the entire hour, Colleen said her fee would have to be doubled to fifty dollars. "Staying in bed all that time is too exhausting," she explained. "You aren't fresh for the next customer."

The girl who charges twenty-five dollars for a twenty-minute (more or less) hour would probably charge fifty dollars to go to cocktails, dinner and then to make love providing she is free by ten-thirty in the evening to book another appointment. She would charge the second man fifty dollars to go to a night club and then go home with him to bed. If her entire evening is taken up by one man, the fee would be a hundred dollars. Obviously these are not inflexible fees. If the man is *terribly* rich, the prices might go up a bit.

Certain girls are able to charge fifty or a hundred dollars per assignment regardless of the scanty amount of time involved. Whether a girl is a twenty-dollar girl or a hundred-dollar girl seems to depend on two things—how young she is and how beautiful. Experience does not necessarily pay off handsomely in this field. The girls are honest with themselves about their attributes and rarely have inflated egos. "No girl of thirty is going to have the unmitigated vanity to think she can charge as much as a seventeen-year-old," said Barbara (who looks twenty-one and is now thirty-three).

A call girl of thirty who has a beautiful face, great clothes, a handsome car, a stylish apartment and great charm may charge as much as fifty per assignment (one of the rapid-turnover kind) but she is still not considered the prize that an innocent flower is. However, innocent flowers from small towns are occasionally so green, the girls say, that they may not realize their worth in the open market and may get swindled. A friend or philanthropic customer usually explains to the flower what she has going for her —youth and inexperience—and she raises her prices.

Sadistic acts—which Barbara, Norma, Colleen and Anita loathed —call for double, triple and quadruple rates. If two girls are engaged by one man, each girl receives her individual fee.

THE PROFIT MARGIN

In a good week the average "successful" call girl makes from three to four hundred dollars, the girls said. She *can* make up to seven hundred if she hustles and has enough fifty- and hundred-dollar appointments. Anita (at twenty) claims she could probably rack up as much as one thousand a week if she were willing to work hard enough. "I'm a little lazy," she said.

A call girl has her busy seasons and also her slumps—just like the ice-cream industry. If a big convention is in town, she needs four hands to call her answering service often enough. During Thanksgiving, Easter week and the Christmas season men stay close to home and the call girl's life is uneventful. Colleen reported a "disastrous" January and February this year. Everybody went to Florida or California.

As you can imagine, a call girl spends a great deal of money on her clothes, her hair, her apartment, her car, hush money, bribes to the police to keep from being arrested, bigger bribes to get out when she *is* arrested, sizable fines if all else fails, medical bills, and tips and fees to the people who arrange dates. Some girls support husbands, children, mothers, fathers, pets and boy friends. The boy friend, contrary to popular opinion, is more of a pet than a business partner and generally does not procure for her. He is kept in every sense of the word. The better kept he is, the more respected his keeper is in her own circles. Norma and Anita were both "pirates," refusing to support a man. In case you're worried about how a call girl makes ends meet, it must be pointed out her income goes further than ours because she is unlikely to declare very much of it to the Internal Revenue Service.

SHE TALKS THINGS OVER

How are financial arrangements worked out with customers? If a man has been her date before, he knows her rate and pays at the end of the evening. On a first date he pays in advance. If a stranger calls her, he must be recommended by a friend and presumably a friend with whom she has had no financial or other kind of trouble. Preferably the friend will have been in touch with her first to say, "Hank So-and-So is going to call you."

On the phone with Hank, the girl will ask, "Did George tell you the arrangements?" Assured that he did, she usually meets her "blind date" at his hotel or a restaurant rather than having him pick her up at home. At this meeting she once again checks to be sure he understands about her fee. "What did George tell you the arrangements were?" she asks. If she is satisfied with the answer, the date proceeds.

Apparently a girl can't be too careful. The man who wants to see her could be a policeman in plain clothes. Occasionally a man will pay the girl's fee at the beginning of the evening, then beat her up and take back his money when the night is over. (There's nobody she can go to for redress of grievances, but of course the chap gets a mighty bad name among her friends.)

"If I don't like the way a guy acts while we're having a drink and getting acquainted," Barbara said, "I just walk out. I have a reputation for being independent, however, and people rarely fix me up with creeps."

What about the man she meets at a party or bar who doesn't *know* she's a call girl? Naturally he has to be told, so that she doesn't waste her time. The girl might say, "I'm afraid I'm going to have to leave soon. My child is with a baby-sitter and I have to pay her." Her friend would ask, "Gee, can't you just call home and tell the baby-sitter you'll be late?" "Well, you see, the sitter is rather expensive," the girl will explain. "It will probably come to about fifty dollars."

If the man chokes on his drink or crashes off across the room, the girl has been dealing with a loser (lost to her anyway). If he says gallantly, "I'll pay the sitter," she's got a winner—and nature, helped along by finance, can take its course.

There are other tactful and "innocent" ways a call girl lets a man know she has a price. She might say, "Oh dear, I've got such a pesky problem. My rent is due tomorrow morning and I haven't received my TV-residual check yet." Or, "Geraldine needs four new tires and I am absolutely flat-smashed *broke*." A telephone bill may be clouding the girl's evening. "Well how much could a little old telephone bill *be* anyway? Why don't I clean it up?" says her worried friend. This will just happen to be the month she made those five calls to Sydney, Australia, and the tab is a not unimpressive $112.74 including tax.

All my interviewees said men occasionally try to chisel. Some even have the audacity to request credit. Anita recalls an evening with two Saudi-Arabian princes who could speak English perfectly until the subject of her fee came up. They then resorted to their native tongue and she was unable to continue the negotiations.

Barbara told me about being one of several girls hired by a bankers' group to be hostesses at an afternoon cocktail party. Their job was to look beautiful and circulate among the guests for two hours. (Not *all* call-girl assignments center on anatomy.) At the end of the party, the head banker told the girls they would be expected to entertain the bankers during the rest of the evening for no increase in price. The girls said nothing doing. The banker refused to pay them for their hostessing chores. The girls hired an attorney who called the banker on their behalf.

"I don't know these girls," the banker said. "They are trollops!"

"They seem to know you," the attorney said, "and they are planning to take an ad explaining the particulars of their withheld fee."

They were probably bluffing, but the banker decided to pay.

WHY DOES SHE DO IT?

I am not the first person to ask a call girl, "How come a nice girl like you gets into this kind of racket?" Everybody under the sun has been asking her that for years, and about ten times out of ten the answer is that the girl *fell* or drifted into call-girling. Nobody goes to school to learn how.

All the call-girl histories detailed by Dr. Greenwald in his book, *The Call Girl,* indicate an unhappy childhood with little real love or understanding from parents. His girls were always running away from home, being abused by foster fathers, checking in and out of orphanages. My girls were too.

If I interpret Dr. Greenwald's findings correctly, only a girl with an unhappy childhood or unfortunate early conditioning would be likely to accept a *first* paid assignment, let alone tolerate the kind of life a call girl leads. The circumstances that drive a potential call girl into call-girling—no money, broken dreams, family to support—would simply drive another type of girl to find another answer.

One of the high-class procurers I interviewed doesn't agree. "Any kind of girl can get to be a pro," he says. "I don't think it has anything to do with hating her father or mother or not getting enough love. I've seen a girl come from the nicest family . . . the parents really loved the kid and spent time with her. Pow . . .

right down the drain! A lot of it is luck . . . who a girl gets mixed up with at a time when she's down."

My *other* procurer said, "A lot of girls who nearly faint dead at the thought of somebody's being a call girl never had the opportunity, you see. They weren't pretty enough—so nobody ever asked them. If they'd been real lookers and somebody kept offering them a hundred dollars to do what they're already doing *free*, who knows how long they'd have held out?"

It's a thought.

Whether you agree with Dr. Greenwald (and me) that a girl has to have a wretchedly low ego to take this kind of work, or whether you side with the procurers who say it could happen to any pretty girl in tough circumstances, it is apparent that being pretty makes a girl more *eligible* and, in some cases, more *susceptible* to the life. Doting parents and relatives may have given her the idea that exceptionally pretty girls don't have to *do* anything . . . people always take care of them. People very often *do* care for them, as a matter of fact, but they demand more in return than a smile from the fabulous face or a pat on the balding head.

Many pretty girls automatically head for a career in show business without bothering to train for anything else . . . or for show business either. They are only mediocre actresses, singers or dancers. When the fabulous career doesn't materialize, rather than dig in and be waitresses, stenographers or receptionists, they choose the better-paid, presumably less-grubby life of a call girl. Or they grub a bit first and then move on to call-girling. This has been known to happen to beauty-contest winners who get into the finals but don't win the top prizes. If they've landed in Hollywood, they can always get the interview with the talent agent, television or movie producer . . . for a while. Everybody loves to talk to pretty girls, but the jobs don't materialize. The disappointed may drift to call-girling.

Broken love affairs have catapulted some girls into the trade. The ingénue gives her all to a man who discards her like an old flashlight battery. Disillusioned, the girl says, "Look what happened when I loved and trusted a man! I couldn't be any worse off being a pro, and at least I'd make money."

Some girls have simply been going to bed with one chap or another for several years and finally figure they might as well get paid for it.

The housewife call girls who were recently apprehended on Long Island said they joined the club out of boredom and contempt for their husbands. Other girls *adore* their husbands and are supplementing the family income. The husband often knows what his wife is doing on his behalf and encourages her.

Many call girls are divorcees with young children. "It's a very satisfactory arrangement," Norma said. "You can be with your children all day but your evenings are free for work."

It probably can't be gainsaid that some girls get into call-girling because they are simply too dumb to stay out. They are ignorant children from backwoods places trying to cope with life in the big city. Some fast-talking predator gets hold of them and, as that procurer said, "It's pow . . . right down the drain!"

HOW THE CALL GIRL IS RECRUITED

Once a girl is psychologically disposed *toward* the profession (full of doubts about her own worth, greedy to get rich quick, disillusioned in love), she finds the machinations of becoming involved in the trade quite simple. A waitress may say to her employer, "Sarah Jane seems to be going out with this man and getting presents and money. Why can't I do the same thing?" Her employer may know just the man, and presto—Sarah Jane's friend is in business. If her employer doesn't know a man, he may repeat the girl's remark to some customers, pretending to be horrified but actually fishing. One of the customers may check back later and say, "About that girl who's interested in presents and money." The girl's new life is a-borning.

A disreputable-type landlord may procure. His tenant is behind in her rent. He tells her of a friend who'll be glad to take care of the back payments if she'll be nice to the guy. Not-too-bright girls who share apartments with other girls and haven't their share of the rent money are particularly vulnerable to schemes for getting it together. They don't want to let their roommates down.

A seedy landlady can have "madaming" aspirations. She bakes a cake and takes it to the charming girl living alone on the third floor. "I see a lot of men come to take you out, honey," she says. "I know one who'd probably just be crazy about you . . . he'd buy you things and give you money, too." If the girl agrees to see the gentleman and things go well for him, the landlady gets a commission from the girl.

Cuckoo-sounding want-ads are a lure. A company purports to be paying up to two hundred and seventy-five dollars a week for special sales representatives . . . "no experience needed!" Applicants are screened, the unlikely ones are brushed, and the attractive hopefuls who might do well in prostitution are told in heavily adorned terms what the setup is. The susceptible succumb. The organization presumably has clients who'll buy . . . all they need is the merchandise.

A friend of mine worked as secretary (until she found out what they were doing) to a man who was supposed to be rounding up chorines for a night club in Rio de Janeiro. His ads said the girls would receive one hundred and fifty dollars a week, round-trip boat transportation to Rio and a chance to meet multimillionaire South American socialites. (Who *wouldn't* be interested?) Just as with the girls who answered the special-representative ads, the doggy-answerers to this ad were discouraged from calling back (but they called anyway, Mary Jane said—the more doggy the oftener, and it was *heart-rending*). The creamy answerers were strung along about South America and finally taken to see the wizard. Now the wizard did *not* own the South American night club, although some people say he owns South America. He did and *does* own a controlling interest in two major American companies and is something of a legend—business-wise, personality-wise and girl-wise—in our time. (He is rarely interviewed because nobody can find him.) My friend's boss procured for him. Every afternoon the agent took one of the dance applicants, still under the impression she was about to leave for South America any day, to see the wizard. The girl and the agent would sit in the bar of a posh hotel discussing the subtle differences between a Miami and a Rio tan while the wizard, usually wearing tennis shoes, strolled through the bar to see whether or not he liked the girl. If she appealed to him, he joined the party. If she didn't, he stole away in his tennis shoes to await the next screening. (The agent was left to get off the hook about Rio or string the girl along for himself.) The girls whom the wizard selected never got to South America *either,* of course, but old gumsoles is so rich and legendary that many a girl was willing to abandon precious plans to have a whack at him. She became a call girl *supérieur* . . . on call to this one man only.

Motion picture agents sometimes start a girl downhill if she has roundish heels already. Because so many girls want to get into movies and television, a constant stream of hopefuls winds through an agent's office. If he is important enough to be able to get a girl in to see a going-concern movie or television producer, he may not be much interested in girls himself—past the age or doesn't want the trouble—but may be able to further two careers, his and hers, by suggesting she play up to the potential employer. After the interview the agent will call the producer and say, "She really went for you, Joe . . . she'd like to see you again, maybe in the evening." (Why should movie producers be any less susceptible to whopping lies that flatter their egos than other men?) To the girl the agent says, "If you play your cards right and are really nice when this guy takes you to dinner . . . something may come of it."

Whichever way the evening goes, the agent is not paid off in cash, of course, and neither is the girl—usually. If she gets the part, however, her career may be started and her agent will receive commissions.

This isn't to say that dozens of girls don't get jobs in movies and television on the strength of their talent, charm and beauty alone. (*Then* could come the propositioning, because the girl is more or less the producer's protégé and he may feel entitled. She may feel he's entitled, too, what with the next movie to be cast and all.) I'm also not saying that girls who are "procured" for a movie producer (or even an industrialist) don't eventually, despite their tattered virtue, become movie stars. More girls, however, are apt to be catapulted into call-girling (or one of the variations such as party-girling) after having dined too frequently with producers *without* getting the part.

WHAT IS SHE LIKE?

As to the varieties of call girls, there are all kinds—peppermint, fudge ripple, butter pecan. Some call girls are gypsies—no more able to keep appointments and be a success at call-girling than they are at anything else. Some are shrewd and efficient business women. A friend in the public relations division of an ad agency told me he nearly keeled over the other day when a pro got in to see him by presenting a fake business card. Once inside his office door, she briskly announced that she was a call girl and would like to help him in any way she could with clients. If he was thinking in terms of banquets or large meetings, there were many more like her she could recruit, she said. Phil just listened and let her do most of the talking. It's so rare that somebody comes in off the street and offers to lift burdens from a busy man's shoulders that I think he was genuinely touched.

I'm told the most successful calls girls, aside from the fragile young beauties, are good conversationalists, fascinating to the men who go out with them. One of my sources said it was fun and games to watch a haughty call girl out-haughty and upstage an unknowing Park Avenue hostess at whose home she was a guest. (Call girls not infrequently decorate some of the poshest parties and places.)

Another friend was accosted recently by what surely *must* be a new breed of call girl. Rex was driving home along the Sunset Strip late one night in a Maserati convertible. (I have three or four very chic friends!) At a stop light two girls in a Cadillac Fleetwood pulled up on his left. "Why don't we all stop for a drink?" one of them called over to him.

"Afraid it's too late for me," Rex told them.

"Well at least let's stop for a minute and get acquainted," the girl on his side said. "We'll give you our phone number and you can telephone some time."

Both cars pulled to the curb at the next block, Rex wrote down the girls' numbers and called one of them a few weeks later. She explained that she was a pro but had found him enormously attractive and would love to see him. He went to her house in Beverly Hills—or technically, her parents' house—at eleven one morning.

The "old folks" were in Palm Springs. The girl took him to her room overlooking the pool. Its walls were cluttered with college banners, corners piled with skis, tennis rackets and golf clubs and the bed innocently populated with stuffed animals. The daughter of a hideously wealthy, invincibly "stable" Beverly Hills family was a pro at the creaking age of eighteen. (I never did understand teen-agers!)

Some call girls lead multiple lives. A Los Angeles police officer, married to a friend of mine, told me of picking up a fairly famous actress in a raid at a downtown hotel. She had succeeded in business because of her acting as well as her looks (still *is* succeeding) but there she was with ten other party or call girls.

There's the case of Gloria Y. At twenty-six, Gloria is a computer operator at one of America's ten largest industrial plants. Her looks are "just passable" at work. She wears mousy skirts and blouses, flat heels and no make-up. Her salary is $79.70 a week gross. By night the mouse skirts and blouses are exchanged for veils, bangles and beads, and a spectacular figure is revealed. The scrubbed face grows heavy-lidded under bushels of make-up. Little Gloria metamorphosizes into Little Egypt, an accomplished belly dancer. Culling customers from the cabaret patrons, Gloria is also a call girl. She never mixes her daytime job with her nighttime work. The computer job is her security for the future when she'll be too old to dance or play. The belly-dancing is her real love, but the work isn't steady. The occasional paid date is her way of having expensive baubles.

DO THEY LIKE THE WORK?

You can't say categorically that *all* call girls hate what they're doing and want *out*.

Twenty-year-old Anita told me, "I was first seduced when I was twelve and I loved it. I've been with one man or another ever since, and I can honestly say I couldn't live without them or what they do. Sometimes I feel like a fraud taking money for something I enjoy so much."

That's one point of view, although not the one most widely held.

Barbara said she felt a kind of satisfaction in being able to give *pleasure* to men . . . in being needed so intensely. She considers her call-girl life a search for love!

Although the four girls I talked to didn't seem particularly hostile toward men or eager to exploit them, maybe the feelings were there and I just couldn't detect them. (I don't admit this very often of course, but I'm really *not* a psychiatrist.) Apparently many call girls *do* hate men (Dr. Greenwald says they do) and are perpetually frigid. They also often prefer girls. The fact that men want to *degrade* them, not just *enjoy* them, might upset a girl's usual sunny attitude toward the opposite sex.

At best a call girl probably doesn't *mind* the act of love (because if she did, she wouldn't be physically able to be in business). Barbara, who has been a pro for twelve years, said that something happened to her perhaps every sixth or eighth time. "If you tried to reach a climax each time and you're seeing eight or ten customers a day," she said, "you'd *collapse*."

"When you meet a man you think you might fall in love with and possibly marry," I asked, "do you try to keep him from knowing about your work?"

"It's a temptation," Colleen said, "but how can you bring it off? You can't give up your income while you decide if you really were meant for each other—and he decides whether he wants to marry you. If he's already married, he'll be even longer deciding. You have to keep working, and that means you are busy nights and can only see him at the last minute after no business dates have come through. Any guy is going to ask questions about *that* kind of setup. Usually you tell him in the beginning to avoid hurting him later or avoid his being abusive when he finds out."

Customers do fall in love with the girls occasionally, but it isn't always desirable for the girls. What they want is a steady customer, not somebody who is going to be a pest and moon about and not want them to see anybody else. Of course, as you have probably already figured out for yourself, the professional life of a call girl can't last forever. Her best-paid years are before she is twenty-five. Until the age of thirty-five she can do reasonably well financially if she takes care of herself. Hardly anybody lasts past forty.

Some call girls knock off occasionally, or let's say *curtail,* to become kept by one man. Many of them can't stand the monotony, however.

Call girls *do* get married, some as often as three and four times. The marriage may or may not take them out of the trade. Sometimes a girl makes enough money to retire, become respectable and begin a new life in another town. In that case she usually changes the color and style of her hair along with her name—and sometimes her nose, teeth and chin to go with them.

THE CALL GIRL'S CUSTOMERS

Suppose a girl has gone astray and become a call girl by virtue (if you can call it that) of associating with evil friends, wanting to make money but not having the self-respect and drive to do it some other way. How does she get a steady flow of customers?

Keeping up her gross sales, if you'll pardon the expression, takes all her time. There is no central booking agency to send her on assignments. She can't be listed in the yellow pages. She's an independent operator who must show initiative.

Several of the girls act as madams, going out on assignments themselves as well as getting customers for friends who pay them a commission. There are also the shadowy men who procure (often working also as race-track touts, bookies and bartenders). For arranging a date, they receive up to 50 per cent of the girl's fee. Cabdrivers, elevator operators, clerks and bellhops in hotels also get the supply and demand together, taking part of the proceeds. The procurers I talked to did not take a fee from customers *or* girls, because they were "high-class" businessmen whose only reward was in making people happy (they said) and in storing up good will with their customers and prospects.

At the procuring rates charged, a girl naturally likes to stay away from the procurers as much as possible and arrange her own dates. Once a pro is established, much of her business comes from referrals. A satisfied customer not only returns but also recommends her to friends. (It's all unspeakably sharing . . . like giving *your* good little dressmaker's name to a pal, I suppose.) To get the ball rolling, a girl may say to a customer, "If your friends are as nice as you are, I'm sure I'd enjoy meeting them too. I hope you'll have some of them call me." If business is slow, a girl may call up customers she hasn't seen for a while to stir up some action. Some call girls have interesting pictures of themselves on display in a local photographer's studio, and admirers are given their phone numbers. The photographer's fee for taking the pictures and showcasing them might be an occasional free date with the girl herself.

Unless a girl is an official madam, she doesn't often give a girl friend's telephone number to one of her own customers. Each girl guards her clientele jealously. Occasionally a customer may ask her to get a date for a friend, which she will do—but the girl she calls is supposed to reciprocate by including *her* on a double-date.

Couldn't a call girl operate out of an office? It seems so logical that I asked that question. After all, the men *are* there, and she would seem so respectable as a bookkeeper or file clerk while checking out prospects.

Dumb! Norma patiently explained the girl would work her way straight through the office in about ten days and then where would she be? Out on the street probably, men being the gossips they are. Cocktail-waitressing, she said, would be a much better arena for a call girl. Having to work like a beast in *any* regular job, however, would defeat some of the purposes of call-girling in the first place . . . the irregular hours, a relaxed life (!) and freedom from eye-strain bending over pesky machines.

Even if call girls don't work out of offices, however, they certainly are—as we've mentioned earlier—part *of* the business world and therefore part of *Sex and the Office.*

WHO CALLS CALL GIRLS IN OFFICES?

From everything I've been able to glean on the subject, about as often as a supply clerk orders up carbon paper or the caterers come to service the coffee machine, somebody in an office orders the services of a call girl delivered to someone in another office. The girl is sent as a bribe, payment for a favor expected or received, or as an inducement toward getting an order or contract. Sometimes the girl is delivered as a good-will ambassadress. Of course she isn't just wrapped up in cellophane and sent over like a bon voyage present. The recipient has to indicate that he'd *like* such a present and sometimes requests it (her).

Aside from the expense, if they were to foot the bill themselves, many men prefer, for psychological reasons, to have the girl be a "gift." I guess it's like chocolates. You wouldn't dream of buying a pound of mocha creams for *yourself,* but if somebody *gives* you a box, you hide them in your desk and nibble greedily.

This is a business situation in which a call girl might be introduced: One food-store chain in a city does most of the business. One man in the chain places most of the orders. How is he going to decide which macaroni to give extra shelf space to and possibly promote when *all* macaroni is good—and if you've seen one you've seen them all? If the chain-store buyer should say to a macaroni salesman, "Joe, you must know some swinging girls," the salesman might not be inclined to spit in his eye. (Listen, I don't mean to pick on macaroni. I'm just using it as an example. The salesman of *any* product that looks, acts, tastes, smells and feels a great deal like the competitor's *could* find himself considering the "intrinsic" advantages of calling in a call girl.)

Here's a similar situation: A purchasing agent lets contracts for hundreds of thousands of dollars in airplane parts. (Talk about *macaroni* all looking alike!) The airplane parts salesman who's able to interest the agent in a girl may possibly just endow his own airplane parts with that *je ne sais quoi!*

A man who is in a position to request a call girl from a number of different suppliers may spread his demands around the group so that nobody is stuck with the tab more than three or four times a year.

Other possible call-girls-in-business setups are these:

A struggling independent movie company wants its pictures to be publicized favorably in national magazines. When a magazine editor comes to Hollywood, the *second* thing he is offered is dinner at Chasen's.

The advertising manager of a distillery has *everything* to say about whether the company's present advertising agency will be retained. If redheads and blondes around the clock would help the ad manager feel disinclined to make a change right now, he may be offered them (particularly if this is the agency's one big account).

Sometimes a man just "falls into" a call-girl situation. A client wants a date for the evening and the fixer-upper is instructed to get a date for himself and come along. Obviously no gosling junior executive is going to be trusted with such an assignment—nor would he try to instigate such an evening. Only a seasoned pro would know how far his company would go.

One major public relations firm in New York makes it simple for the clients to indulge. It retains ten call girls, one more glamorous than the next, according to insiders, for the exclusive use of clients —no questions answered or asked. At five every afternoon the girls check in to get their assignments. By midnight all of them are hard at work. Their "salary" is part of the sizable fee the client pays to be represented by the firm in the first place.

It probably sounds by now as though I think *all* companies use call girls the way Santa staffs his factory at the North Pole with helpers. I'm sure nothing could be further from the truth. Most companies do without call girls very nicely. Only certain frantic firms include them as part of their regular business operation. Only certain men find the getting or the giving of a call girl necessary or even palatable.

DOES HE OR DOESN'T HE?

Which businessmen do and which don't . . . call call girls?

It's been said that men in glamour businesses, such as movies, television, advertising or photography, aren't so sexy-girl starved as men in heavy industry. My private survey (I'll never reveal my sources, so relax, sources!) says this is nonsense. A man is never immune to *more* beautiful girls even if a flock is nesting around him already.

Some sexperts say the less adept and more ill-at-ease a man is with women, the more frequently he resorts to call girls. The sexpert—an inordinately handsome and successful man—with whom I checked this theory out was adamant. "If I'm going to make love to any woman besides my wife," he said, "it's going to be a professional. Fewer risks. No emotional involvement. No family troubles. The girls don't get pregnant. They're honest and willing and also the most beautiful in the world. Men are such jerks to insist the girls be in love with them . . . that it has to be romantic. For the most part they're probably just too stingy to spend the fifty or hundred dollars."

Colleen said her best customers were good family men. They were utterly loyal and devoted and wouldn't dream of getting involved with anybody their wives might find out about or meet socially. Nevertheless, when wives sometimes become "mamas"— stop being sexy and start treating their husbands like one of the children—*naturally* the poor men have to do *something*.

There doesn't seem to be an infallible rule for detecting what kind of man consorts with call girls. And you know what . . . I don't think it matters. All you need to comprehend is that this sort of thing goes on. (It's possible you don't even need to comprehend *that*, but I took the position that you do and now you know.)

The call girl, though enormously attractive to certain men, is not really competition for you. She's an entirely different thing. (And since *she* doesn't enjoy sex, I think *he* overpays *horrendously* for what he gets.) Regardless of the numbers of men who stray to her, there are still plenty of men left for you at the office.

Now we must move on to *another* group of girls who, although far removed from the last group, *still* do not have your advantages. They don't get to fraternize with men all day or do any of the other pleasureable things you do, because you see, the poor darlings are stuck under their thatch, tile and mansard roofs at *home*.

Out of the goodness of our hearts, we are going to put ourselves into a philanthropic mood and go over there to see if we can figure out some way to get these girls to join us.

CHAPTER 17

COME BACK LITTLE
WIVES, WIDOWS, DIVORCEES

Now wives (and that includes past wives, present wives and wives thoughtlessly left strewn about by the departed), *will* you agree the work world can be shimmery? Challenging? Sexy? (Excluding the professional variety discussed in the last chapter.) Will you agree that you're silly to be letting others make off with the spoils—grown-up companionship, money, recognition—while you stand there with your grocery list? Will you admit that you're simply mule-headed?

No, I suppose you won't admit anything of the kind. You're convinced that holding a paid job may be all right for *other* femmes but you prefer straightening up the pad, stitching up the tea towels, baking up the beans . . . to say nothing of golfing up the green, bidding up the no-trumps and who knows . . . maybe toting up your wins at Santa Anita.

Sometimes I think I've failed you utterly! I haven't gotten through! Don't you understand that while you are cheerily being

Nora in the doll's house, some doll in an *office* may be thinking about your very own husband—or one you plan to acquire—as part of *her* profit-sharing plan?

Don't you see that by working you could have it *all*? Hire somebody *else* to do the household drudgery, keep your dainty mitts on the creative stuff if you like (gourmet cooking and decorating), continue to golf and no-trump for recreation, and be more exciting to your *husband* (or to that someone you have in mind for the future in case you're a divorcee or widow).

I could almost give *up*. You're not listening! Tell you what I'm going to do. Rather than harangue you any further about the joys of working, I'm going to reveal exactly how two wives and mothers who work (real girls, of course) manage to give everyone in the family his full share of love and attention and have a delicious grown-up life as well. Since I'm not a working mother myself, having never been a mother, the only honest thing to do, I felt, was secure some qualified people to talk to you. Two case histories do not a Gallup Poll make, but the testimonials you're going to hear will certainly show what can be accomplished. Once we get going, the girls will do most of the talking, and I'm just going to sit and crochet or something.

Christine and Sally might be considered unlikely women to hold the jobs they have. They each have young children. Their husbands are "old-fashioned," masculine, good providers. The girls are not driven, selfish, "career" types. Yet each says her job makes her feel more alive and more richly fulfilled. Christine, mother of seven (including two sets of twins), told me, "Maybe it's my Catholic upbringing showing through, but I was taught that you are honor-bound to make fullest use of your potential. If you have a talent or flair, you develop it . . . show God you are grateful." Sally says, "I started working accidentally, but now I couldn't give it up."

Sally is twenty-eight, peach-skinned, dark-haired and nobody's hips, including a matador's, look better in skinny pants. Sally is executive secretary to a famous furniture designer and her husband's an engineer with one of the world's great airspace companies. They have two boys, aged seven and two, and Sally figures they own about one-sixteenth of their pretty house. In the next few pages you'll read her story, in her own words.

HEAVEN OFTEN HELPS
THE WORKING GIRL

My husband has an excellent job. Most of the other engineers' wives stay home. Why do I work? [This is Sally speaking.]

It began with my *having* to work when Carl was an engineering student. I toiled long and hard in those years which we now refer to fondly as "our darkest hour." I wasn't a whiz and my first job wasn't too good. I had to keep reminding myself all the time that what I was doing was important to our future. During that slavery period, a good friend kept telling me, "Don't feel sorry for yourself, Sally dear. You may be the sole support of a student husband *now* but, believe me, when Carl is through school and you don't need to work anymore, you'll find yourself doing exactly what you're doing now because you enjoy it."

She couldn't have been more right. Carl was graduated. I got a degree too—P.H.T. (Pushing Hubby Through)—signed by the dean of the engineering college in official recognition of my efforts. I was very proud. But after Carl got a good job—engineers usually do—I wasn't about to stop working even though by now I was a working *mother*. The decision to continue was simplified by one important aspect of my job. My boss at this time (I'd had several jobs by now) was an impatient, difficult, demanding, quick-witted, fast-moving executive, for whom I worked at all times at top speed. Nevertheless, he had a genuine regard for my family situation. He knew I had a husband, a child and home life and always made it possible for me to do justice to them.

Many bosses *profess* to love and appreciate their secretaries but actually believe the girl has no interest in life outside the office—and ought *not* to have. Leave those bosses to the single girls who really don't have much of an outside life, I say. There are plenty of bosses who prove their love and appreciation by respecting your personal situation. For example Mr. B. (my boss during this period) let me start late and take a long lunch hour so that I could run home and visit with my boys. He knew I would work twice as hard the rest of the time out of appreciation for these motherly privileges —and I did. In return for his understanding, he had my deepest loyalty and respect, from which stems the greatest efficiency and support a secretary can ever give a boss.

I'd say, then, the first requirement for a working mother is to find a man who is interested in you and your little brood and to whom you can give complete efficiency and devotion in return. (Sounds like quite an order, but there are such men.) The second requirement is: Never travel any great distance to a job.

While Carl was still in school we rented a little house just five minutes from my office, and the house we finally bought is twelve minutes away. Living close by means an anguished mother can get home in an emergency in minutes, and the lady who's caring for your children has the reassurance of knowing you're near. You can also run home to spend many lunch hours with the little folk. Most important, you can usually be home before your husband in the evening, so that he seldom has to experience that dismal business of being alone in the house around dinnertime, feeling neglected but compelled to start the potatoes! I've always made a habit of setting the table the minute I get in the door because it gives a welcome-home feeling to Carl. That table setting—pretty place mats, silver and wineglasses—says that you are just as prepared for his home-coming as you would be if you'd stayed home all day.

Not everybody agrees with me, but I don't think the husband of a working wife should *ever* do domestic chores. They rob him of his manliness and diminish his role as master. Carl has never helped with dishes, errands or marketing, and I've never encouraged him to. I'm so grateful he doesn't object to my working that I feel one way I can repay him is by spoiling him at home—just as he'd be spoiled if I were there all day.

Seems odd, but the busiest working girls often turn out to be the most efficient housewives. They don't have time for the coffee klatches and endless telephone gossip that never helped *anybody* keep a better house. They're well-organized. Housework to them is something to get over with, not expand to fill lonely hours or build up to make them feel what they're doing is important.

As to how a husband fares when you work, there are many reasons to support the idea that he's the winner, not the loser. A working wife is twice as eager to please the man because of her secret guilt—she enjoys her job more than housework! I cook Carl a big farm breakfast with two kinds of meat every morning. When you work yourself, you understand a man's mood better at the end of the day when he gets home. He can have a quiet moment with a newspaper and a drink instead of a barrage of questions from his bored little wife who hasn't had any adult conversation all day.

And this lucky man seldom comes home to a slob who is too pooped to pretty herself up. She works in a world of men, so the business girl never lets up on her grooming or wardrobe. Even though *you're* pooped *too,* it would never occur to you to scrub off your make-up and shimmy into a Mother Hubbard after work. You get out of your office clothes—but into a sexy sweater or blouse and Capris or hostess skirt.

THE CHILDREN

Carl Junior—whom we call Skip—and John Quincy have never known me as anything but a working mother, so they've never begged me to stay home. A friend of mine with five children once said, "Sally, I don't think it's the *amount* of time you spend with your children that counts, it's the quality of the time." I think that about wraps it up. Because Carl and I both work, we rarely go out evenings during the week. That time is devoted to the boys. They may go to bed a little later and get up later than other children but they still get their twelve hours' sleep, as advocated by Dr. Spock. We plan family activities for weekends and, I confess, are forever late for all our social gatherings because we don't like to leave before the children are in bed. The housekeeper we have now said that Carl and I spend less time away from the kids than any other parents she has ever worked for, and she has only worked for mothers who stayed home before.

I don't think I've ever missed any of Skip's school activities that required a parent to be present, again thanks to bosses who've had a genuine regard for my "mother's role." It's always kind of interesting to note the difference between the rest of the mamas and me on parents' visiting day. Ninety per cent of the girls show up in sweaters and scruffy pants because they can't be bothered to dress up in the daytime, even for a school occasion. Skip, though he's only seven, always seems very proud of his high-heeled, slick-chick mother.

I do my share for the PTA but stay out of their gab fests. In the meetings I've attended, I'd say most of the business could have been decided in about ten minutes—except that the girls like to argue and debate even the most trivial stuff.

As for the emotional effect my working has on Skip and John Quincy, teachers and other parents tell me the kids seem happy and normal. (I hate the phrase "well-adjusted.") I think the boys are great. Carl thinks they're great. But it's good to hear it from somebody else. Treated like children they *are*. Spoiled they are *not*.

I've heard nonworking mothers say that by bedtime some days they're ready to chloroform the children and jump out the window themselves. I cheerfully admit I'm tired to the breaking point *too* when the boys are cranky or sick, but I do think you have more tolerance with them when you have daily hours away from one another. It improves the "quality of the time" you're together. Lots of mothers manage this separation with club meetings, bowling, golf, bridge, anything to get *out*—and I don't see how anybody can blame them for wanting a break. The trouble is the girls wind up spending more time on this *nonsense* stuff than if they worked, and they aren't so careful about the quality of the time they spend with their children.

HOUSEHOLD HELP

It takes some doing to find the right household help when you are a career-girl mother but hiring anybody for *any* particular job is not necessarily simple. Do you know how many girls a man interviews looking for a secretary? Maybe twenty. It's not that there's any shortage of household helpers, far from it. You just have to find the person who fits into *your* home and who's going to be happy with you.

When I first started working and Carl was in school, we had very little money, of course, so I thought it would be cheaper to depend on friends, aunts, grandmothers, sisters, stepmothers and foster parents to baby-sit for a while. It didn't work out very well, so I finally put an ad in the paper. To my amazement the phone rang nonstop all weekend. I saw about two dozen unsuitables, but from that whole mob I found the Rock-of-Gibraltar Englishwoman who stayed with us for four and a half years. She used to arrive at eight-forty-five every morning, stay until five-forty-five, take care of baby Skip, do all the laundry and ironing, start dinner for me—and all for thirty dollars a week. This was in the second biggest city in the country, too, where wages are supposed to be high. Mrs. Marcussen left us only when we moved to a neighborhood that had no public transportation.

We pay our present live-in housekeeper one hundred and fifty dollars a month plus her social security and provide her with everything right down to Kleenex. She has a pleasant bedroom and bath and is completely satisfied with her salary—says she doesn't know many people who have one hundred and fifty dollars free and clear every month. I also hire a cleaning woman for a day every other week (eleven dollars) to do the heavy work. Almost any top secretary can make one hundred dollars a week, so working is still profitable even if you pay a housekeeper.

WHAT DOES MY HUSBAND REALLY THINK?

I've given my version of what it's like to be a wife and mother and work. What are my husband's views?

I guess it's safe to speak for Carl, because we've certainly discussed the subject often enough. Carl believes a man gets into real trouble when he tries to force his wife to do *anything* simply because *he* wants it. When he says, "Your place is home with the children," but she secretly yearns to be out in the world, she can grow to hate him, her home and very possibly even resent the children. How much wiser, Carl says, to let your wife *try* something on the outside if she wants to, even encourage her to. If it's wrong, she'll discover it herself and come right home. If it's right for her, Carl thinks the husband is the winner. "I'd much rather have a working wife doing something constructive that she really likes and bringing in money," Carl says, "than spending us blind on her shopping sprees because she's hostile."

It works the other way too, of course. When a husband tells a wife she *must* find a job because they can't manage on his income, she pretty soon starts thinking she married a failure. It's quite human to resent any situation that somebody forces you into. Carl has always said, "If you want to work, *work*. If you want to stay home, stay home." That way, you see, I can't whine too much about my life, because I've had a choice.

Carl, I know, likes being married to somebody other men enjoy talking to. Recently we were at a gathering of his office buddies and I was the only working wife. Naturally I kept rather still on the subject. Well, the girls talked at great length—of course we were all on our side of the room—about how the checkstand boys tried to do them out of the right number of green stamps. They explained in exquisite detail the bylaws and machinations of their baby-sitting club, then branched out into linoleum waxing and finally got to pediatricians. Honestly, I felt just like a single woman crashing a married women's party . . . there, save for the happy accident of having once had to help a husband get through school, went I. When Carl and I were at home that night, I felt as ravishing as a single woman again.

Recently we entertained a top Detroit executive and his suburban wife. I wish I had a tape recording of that conversation. The woman giggled nonstop, drank nonstop and talked nonstop about her children, their private school, her house, her religion, her relatives. She told her complete repertoire of religious jokes, children's bright sayings, and funny household crises. She obviously hadn't the slightest idea what her husband did for a living and no interest in his work whatsoever. I thought about her a great deal the next day and came to this conclusion: The only women who can survive complete and utter domesticity as a way of life and retain their sanity must be one of two extremes—either terribly simple (like the Detroit executive's wife) or terribly intelligent.

The truly uncomplicated ones would be miserable with a job and need no more mental stimulus than that provided by their offspring. I'm not being derogatory about this group. They usually are the most contented of women—excellent cooks, warm and reliable mothers, accomplished home-furnishers and dressmakers. They know nothing of the outside world and how it works. It was invented for other people. In a sense they are as innocent and protected as their children.

The other extreme, the really brilliant women, keep themselves current by reading and studying practically everything in sight— so that it doesn't matter a bit whether they are in the working world. They are usually more intellectual and technically smarter than girls who work, sometimes smarter than their husbands. By taking the trouble and making use of their time, they stay hip and keep up with their husbands and everybody else just beautifully.

Between these two extremes, however, lies a vast number of women of average intelligence just like myself. And I believe, more often than not, *these* women are discontented at home, though they hide it under layers and layers of rationalization. They are not—or I should say *we* are not—brilliant or self-starting enough to be absolute whizbangs regardless of domestic drudgery. We need an office or a job to bring out the best that's in us and keep us alert.

Perhaps it sounds as though I protest too much. I really am willing to let other girls stay home if they wish, but I can't help believing we working mothers have the best of two worlds. Domestically I have the wondrous enchantment of a good husband and two darling little boys—and I ardently believe that having beautiful babies dwarfs all else that a woman can do in life—yet I get to leave the domestic drudgery to hired help. In the professional world, there's the exciting tempo I love, the friendship of fabulous people I'd never get to know any other way, the feeling of being part of the highly complex, scientific, expanding society we live in. I must confess that if I didn't belong in this exciting working world I would tend to be lethargic to the point of delinquency. I just don't have the resources of the brilliant women I spoke of earlier to keep myself charged up and involved without the outside stimulus of boss, office, responsibilities, pay check, office pals and all that. I need and want the extra push.

AND YOU THINK YOU'RE BUSY!

Christine perhaps doesn't have everything quite so well organized as Sally, but she has seven children—two sets of boy twins, two girls and a teen-age son—to Sally's two. When you hear her story, I think you'll agree she is an amazing example of what can be accomplished by one determined lady. Chris manages a nine-room house ("which we can't afford but have to have"), looks after the lives of nine people—if you count Chris and her husband—is one of the women's editors of one of California's top five newspapers— and does it all without paid household help. Don't you feel like a sloth!

At thirty-nine, Christine is a warm, giving, energetic woman. She's also emotional. ("I'm not above locking myself in the bathroom to weep up a storm when things are really bad," she says.) Her husband, to whom Chris has been married for seventeen years, manages an export-import office. Her own job, which sounds impressive and *is,* started in a quiet, unplanned way. This is Christine's story:

I just kind of plopped into it [Chris says]. The "old" twins were eighteen months old, and we had three older children. I'd worked on my high school and junior college newspapers and done PR work in the WAVES, but never held a job. By the time I was married and the mother of five kids, my writing was confined to notes to the milkman and letters home to mother. About every three months I'd get so nauseated with the junk that women's magazines published that I'd decide I could do better, and I'd write for a couple of hours. Then I'd remember my ironing or the kids would get home from school, and that would end that. During that time I was press chairman for a school mothers' club and also for the Mothers of Twins Club—yes, there *is* such a club.

A club press chairman isn't exactly Pierre Salinger. She mostly gets meeting notices into the paper. Nevertheless, the copy I turned in caught the fancy of one of the society editors, and she prodded her managing editor into inviting me to lunch. This was highly unusual, because most women's editors wish club ladies would all get diphtheria. The managing editor did indeed take me to lunch and offered me a job as a "stringer"—somebody who writes free lance at "space rates," which is virtually the same thing as writing for love. What the M.E. actually said was that I could have a whack at one assignment to see how I did. I managed to turn out a smashing good story because I had a smashing good subject: a three-year-old girl brought back from the dead by open-heart massage.

From that time on for four years I was a "stringer" for the paper, doing my stories from home. It could have happened to any club lady, presumably. I didn't seek out the job. During those years of "stringing," I had no expense account, no mileage allowance and I was paid a whopping thirty cents an inch. Sometimes a feature that I drove for, stood for, talked for and sweated over would bring a cool three dollars.

But there were fringe benefits. I wasn't "just a housewife" any longer, and since the paper was understaffed—what newspaper isn't—I got to interview such important people as Eleanor Roosevelt and John F. Kennedy. I kept reminding myself that there were people who would write for *nothing* just to see their work in print, and that I at least was getting paid something. It was kind of fun to go running around saying, "I'm Christine McPhearson from the *Globe Democrat*," attending press cocktail parties and the like.

TWINS STRIKE AGAIN

After three years on this job I noticed that I seemed to be losing my rather trim twenty-five-inch waistline. I visited an obstetrician, who peered, poked and said "My God, Chris, you look as if you're about four months along."

With this much certainty of pregnancy, I knew it had to be twins again. You just can't confuse a twin-type pregnancy with a loner. The babies were born ten days before Christmas, and when Tom came to me in the hospital I cried an ocean. We could afford seven children like we could afford diamond tiaras, but I was a mighty happy woman.

The paper refused to hear of my quitting merely because I had two new babies—very positive-thinking newspaper. I nursed the new arrivals with a baby on one arm and a pencil in the other hand, and when the snack bar closed, I turned to the typewriter. Six months ago another newspaper asked me to come and see them about a job. They'd asked three times before and I'd always staunchly refused, because the Democrat understood me and my family and how I had to work. This time, however, I agreed at least to go and talk to them.

We couldn't resist each other. Tom advised me to take the job if I wanted it, and I did. One of the reasons I could accept was that a well-educated Cuban refugee family had just moved in down the street. Their eldest son was at our house one night and announced that his mother, aunt and grandmother were home all day with nothing to do—did I know of any children they could care for. *Did* I?! I trotted over there and lined these lovely women up. They love my babies—kiss all three of us when we arrive in the morning— and reluctantly give the twins up when the older children come to get them after school. I pay the Cuevas a dollar an hour and am secure in leaving the babies there any time that I need to.

The first week on the new job I lost eight pounds—this paper was pretty big-time stuff—but after turning out some pages and hearing genuine compliments, I gained the eight pounds back (curses!). I now work two full days a week in the newspaper office and do the rest of the work at home. My two weekly pages are supposed to deal with women's stuff, but I convinced the managing editor that women care about more than brunches and buffets. Now the features often deal with property taxes, politics, child-raising, the high cost of dying, blindness and so forth.

Though our paper is the giant in the area, we have wild competition—four dailies and nine weeklies—and I'm really challenged. I also have to run like a rabbit to get everything done. A photographer who is impossible on his best days but wildly talented helps me, and our personalities click. I probably work twelve hours apiece on Tuesdays and Fridays, set up pictures and organize stories in between.

NO PLACE LIKE THIS HOME

Meanwhile, back at the ranch, how do I manage with that brood?

On my two work days away from home, the older children take off for school, delivering the babies to the neighbors on the way. I do the breakfast dishes, pick up the bedrooms and leave for the paper. Since Tuesday is a late-work day, I usually start dinner the night before. And Tuesday afternoons the children will find this sort of note when they get home from school:

Dear Kids:

Soonest home, get the babies.

Spaghetti sauce in pan in refrigerator. Girls, you know what to do—garlic bread, salad, etc.

Friday will be a big, fat allowance day for all so make me proud to-day. Peggy, parcel out jobs. The house needs vacuuming, dusting and sweeping. Clothes in dryer have to be folded and put away. Stay off phone till work finished.

Nickey, do your homework, eat and collect on paper route. Thursday is the 5th and you have to turn money in.

Terry and Tim [seven-year-old twins] no FIGHTS!

Ellen, don't be silly and slow everybody up.

I love you all.

Mother

Tuesday I will probably stay at the paper until eight or nine in the evening and get home deliciously exhausted. Everyone will have eaten and Tom will have the four twins in bed. The house will be reasonably neat and there'll be fresh coffee on.

Fridays I get home from the office by five P.M. and take four or five of the kids grocery-shopping. Then I'll probably see Peggy off on a date, Nickey off to a dance and possibly Ellen off to spend the night with a girl friend. Tom and I putter in the kitchen, get the twins to bed in shifts, and then I tackle the rest of my newspaper work to meet the Saturday-morning deadline. Sometimes I finish at midnight, more often it's two in the morning. Tom delivers my envelope to the newspaper, brings home a pizza, and we yak until three or so.

Saturdays the "page make-up man" from the paper is on the phone by eight in the morning at the *latest*. When we get through doping things out, the kids and I tackle the house which, by this time, looks like *after* the fall of the Roman Empire. Nickey surfs on Saturday mornings, but his jobs wait for him until he gets home. Peggy and I argue, both feeling pretty abused by this time what with her school work and chores and my four hours' sleep and chores, but around two in the afternoon we go shopping together and giggle over goofy hats and so forth. Teen-age girls are very consoling. They are people by now, and usually you can see glimmerings of the kind of adult they'll be.

They're all good kids. Nickey irons his own shirts and chinos. Peggy does her own ironing, sews beautifully and makes everything in her wardrobe. The three older children do up their own rooms. I help the younger ones. The babies are the only ones who make messes that other people pick up.

No family with seven children runs harmoniously for longer than ten-minute stretches. Personalities clash all over the place. Tom and I try to ignore the little things, yell over the big issues. With the teen-agers, restrictions on going out and using the phone are our most potent weapons. I'm not above swatting one of the kids when I get riled. What pleasure to go to work!

As for my husband, I love that man desperately. He's kind and gentle. He's honest. He's hard-working. He understands me and never goes to pieces. He worries out loud only on payday when his salary is shot before the pile of bills is even halved. But he comes home to say, "I saw the best-looking dress in Henshey's window. It would look good on you. Go try it on."

Tom doesn't resent my working. We both like the money I earn, and he's proud of my being able to earn it. He feels I have been blessed with a special talent, a gift to be used. The family appreciates that nobody has ever had to tiptoe around saying "Sh! Mother's writing!" My office at home is on the old service porch. The desk Tom built for me hides sacks of onions and potatoes. It's next to the kitchen, near the ever-running washer and dryer and off the hall from a bathroom. It isn't private, but I can keep track of things.

I wouldn't say the children are out-and-out proud because their mother writes. They're proud of the new sweater mother's money buys. If a boy friend should mention to Peggy that his father likes a feature I did, Peggy's delighted. When a teacher recommends an article to the class for study and asks, "Ellen, did your mother write this?" Ellen's pleased.

I love pretty furniture and eating out, but our luxuries for the time being are seven kids. I feel rich looking at them, though I often can't help noticing they need shoes. I've just gotten a twenty-dollar-a-week raise from the paper, bless them, and I didn't ask for it. It was just there. They're the type of people who know I'm working hard, and they are willing to pay for it. Maybe they're unusual, but I worked like a dog the first six months and I guess they noticed.

As to what the neighbors say about my working, I tell the catty ones who imply I'm neglecting my family that I don't coffee-klatch, bowl, play bridge or golf. Most women I know spend more time doing those things than I do on the job. There are the "friends," of course who wait for you to slip—when you say, "I wish I could get to cleaning out the linen closet," *they* say, "Well, when mothers go to work in an office . . ." their voices trailing off as though they'd just mentioned an unmentionable disease. I've learned to recognize and discount the signs of jealousy because I have left the kitchen sink and it's still headquarters for them. I stoically resist mentioning that my being a part-time career girl may just *possibly* have kept me from visiting *their* psychiatrists.

When you have a husband you're nutty about, seven children you dote upon, a job that gives you all kinds of satisfaction and wonderful moments, it's hard to take your detractors very seriously.

WHAT KIND OF NUT ARE YOU?

Working and wifing at the same time may not be for everybody (although I don't concede that). I did want to show you how these attractive man- and family-loving women manage to lead double lives successfully and happily. They say they don't have *drive*—only *desire*—to live up to the best that's in them.

If you're at all interested in doing what they do—or something like it—I think we could put down these rules for wives, widows and divorcees with children who would like to get back into the sexy tides of office life:

1. If you want to work—or have the legitimate excuse of work to keep you away from home all day—there is nothing to feel guilty about *provided* you give your husband (if you have one) and children a good amount of attention when you are with them. Possibly you should baby them *more* than if you weren't working.

2. Don't look for support and encouragement in your go-back-to-work plans from nonworking mothers. They will probably resent your leaving their ranks and will try to pin that tired, antiquated, "unnatural mother" label on you.

3. Explain to your husband, if he doesn't already understand, that you will be a better companion, more adoring wife and loving mother if you are allowed to take a job. Besides, the money is lovely—even if there's only a tiny speck left over after you've paid the household help and bought the extra clothes you'll need.

4. You can't have *everything* you had in your non-working days. All-day shopping forays, long, boring lunches with six to eight girls, endless telephone gossip are some of the things that will have to go. You'll *love* being without them. To save more time still, you'll learn to order by telephone—sheets, towels and cases from the white sale, birthday and wedding presents—nearly everything can be charged, wrapped and sent, even groceries.

5. In deciding what to hunt for in the way of a job, decide what *kind of work* would make you happiest if you could do *anything* you wanted. Then look for any job that will bring you close—even if it isn't the most exciting assignment. Don't overlook secretarial work as a chance to get *in*. There are virtually *no* unemployed competent secretaries in a big city. (And you can learn passable shorthand in six months at night school, passable typing in six weeks.)

6. Don't be apologetic about being out of your twenties. A man may tell the personnel office to send him a cutiepie with a thirty-

eight bust measurement, but he usually settles for less. A woman over thirty-five (age, that is) who is chic and cute and prompt and quiet and energetic can become the love of a businessman's life.

7. To *find* the job, check around among your working friends. Ask husbands. Tell everybody you're determined to go back to work and see what ideas they have. Go and visit employment agencies. The want-ad sections of the newspapers are loaded with job offers, many without age limits. The jobs are not glamorous in the beginning, but you can get in and work your way up.

8. Find a boss who'll appreciate your home situation. Give him a full measure of devotion, efficiency and hard work in return.

9. Work in an office as close to your home as possible.

10. Pat yourself on the back regularly. You *are* a very smart girl.

LANDING INSTRUCTIONS

O<small>UR PLANE</small> is now on the ground. You can unfasten your pink alligator seat belt and take off your jeweled goggles. The jet engines have been turned off, the stewardess has given us back our wraps and we're free to leave the ship.

I'm going to miss you, though I wouldn't be surprised if you're glad to get out of my clutches. As your office tour conductor I realize I've poked, prodded and exhorted you to see everything *my* way. Perhaps it sounds as though I think *all* women should work in the offices we've just visited.

That's *almost* what I think—with one or two exceptions. For example, I wouldn't dream of taking a Bona Fide Nester out of her nest. Of course, to qualify as a Bona Fide Nester in my book, you have to prefer your hands in hot soapy dishwater to having them kissed by your firm's creamy representative from South America. A true Nester also prefers masquerading as a Bengal tiger and snarling through an imaginary jungle while her squealing moppet safari stalks her to being bagged by a charming male co-worker for lunch at the Pump Room. Just because you're *afraid* to try your wings outside the nest doesn't make you a Bona Fide Nester, however.

True Silent Partners probably shouldn't work either. A woman who regularly sends her husband down to the soap company with her brilliant sales strategy is not going to be any better off selling men's furnishings. Her husband won't profit, either. However, just saying, "How was it today, honey?" and listening with one ear while you continue to puzzle how your friend Betty the Wizard got that showy angel-cake from only two boxes of cake mix isn't being a real Silent Partner.

Aside from these types—and you'll notice invalids and Spanish-American war widows are not getting off the hook—I believe most women—married or single, mothers or childless, grandmothers or ingénues—are better off working at least *some* of the time.

Positive emanations tell me I am *not* going to be elected mayor on this platform, but then I wasn't planning to run!

It's interesting to me how many seemingly bright people sincerely believe that a "hooked" career girl is incurably ill—a bloodthirsty wolverine who goes down to the office every day to see if there are any new jugular veins to be tasted. Many teachers, lecturers, ministers, psychiatrists, mothers, husbands and Dr. Spock think that holding *any* kind of job gets a wife and mother clean out of whack with Nature's Plan. (Dr. Spock doesn't absolutely forbid a mother to work, but by the time she's examined her motives as thoroughly as Dr. Spock would like, what girl is guilt-free enough to answer the ad? Dr. Spock assures a girl, however, that with proper counseling and soul-searching she can usually talk herself out of that nasty old compulsive need to work.)

Husbands and Dr. Spock strike me as downright *enthusiastic* about wives working, however, compared to a certain group of wives themselves. Suggest that a job might improve their lot and they curl their toes tight around the radiator pipes and shriek that they'll never be taken alive!

Loads of women who work don't seem to like it either! When a single girl marries well, she drops from the office like an overripe apple from a tree. The single ones who *don't* marry wail heart-rendingly for somebody to carry *them* off. The married ones still working wish the somebody they *did* marry would hurry and make tycoon and whisk them away. Even girls reasonably content with their jobs are always scheming about what it would be like to do something Really Important, like rolling bandages for Albert Schweitzer.

I don't believe for a moment that a full-time job gets women out of whack with Nature's Plan. True, I've never been a mother, but then neither has Dr. Spock. Work doesn't seem to have destroyed over fifty million women in Russia, about one million women in Sweden and nearly *twenty-four* million women *or* their children in the United States. Some women seem to need to be with their children or in sight of them every waking hour, but there's no evidence that children (other than infants) need to be with their mothers.

As for a husband glooming up when his wife goes back to a job, no wonder! It isn't *Nature's* Plan that's getting all mucked up. Where is he going to find any more eighteen-hour-a-day household help that doesn't get paid and can't strike? (A housewife who manages to sneak away to a job usually works about half as hard and half as many hours as she does at home.)

As a working girl yourself, perhaps you feel I've exaggerated the glories of offices and lain very sneaky-low about the bad things! (You're *in* an office and you know the life there isn't always a gondola ride through picturesque Venice.)

Don't worry. I'm the first to admit that not *all* offices are pleasure cruises. There are plenty of dull, grimy, drab, boring, sticky little gopher pits a girl can work in, and *I've worked in them!*

Not *all* girls who stay home are dull—I admit that, too. And not all girls who work become vital, exciting personalities. Offices are *full* of drones! However, there's always the *possibility* you'll become a more alive, interesting person if you work. It's likely your very best bet! And from dull grimy offices you simply drain off the good and move on!

Whether their job is good or bad, women in offices never have to search for their *identity* and wonder who they *are*. They *know* who they are and nobody lets them forget it. They are the bookkeeper, the secretary, the receptionist, the model, the actress, the nurse, the technician, the salesgirl, the executive—and people need them and depend on them and reward them.

I'm *proud* of being a career woman and would argue with my last wolverine's breath that a job gives a woman the best of all possible worlds.

Maybe I wouldn't love offices so much if I hadn't been involved in nineteen of them in the past twenty-three years. *Some* people are nutty about hominy grits because during their formative years they hardly ever ate anything else.

Maybe it's nostalgia. (I'm home from the office now getting this book written.) I understand inmates who leave Sing Sing after twenty years sometimes scuff around outside the place whimpering to get back in.

Vanished fringe benefits may be bugging me. Have you ever tried carrying on a world-wide correspondence with only a small cache of *three's* left over from a 1956 mailroom robbery?

Pure masochism may make me miss those machete-brandishings by new managements and dagger practice by the girls. I know for a fact that at the finish of a pain-wracked love affair you can, incredibly, wish the novocaine were out of your system and you were back in there getting beaten black and blue again.

If I'd married sooner and had a real, full-blown emotional experience with slip-covering or buttermilk biscuits . . .

If . . . if . . . if! But honestly, I don't believe *any* of those circumstances accounts for my enthusiasm for the office. I loved being a working girl a mere ten years after I became one. (Any time before that is too soon to say whether you like it, because they always give the beginners such scruffy things to do.)

I miss the office desperately. I haven't tasted a good jugular vein all year. Tell me, dear, are they just as delicious as ever?

A FINANCIAL LITERARY NOTE
FROM THE ORIGINAL PUBLISHER

IT IS CUSTOMARY *for authors of books requiring research to append at this point pages of chapter notes or, at the very least, an impressive bibliography.*

Monumental research went into the preparation of Sex and the Office, *but it was simply not the sort that is usually pursued in a library. Like Mrs. Brown's previous book,* Sex and the Single Girl, *this book is based largely on her own experiences and those of her many friends. Specifically, Mrs. Brown has drawn on her "lives" in nineteen offices, embellished with field trips into those areas that were somewhat too exotic to have fallen within even a remarkably wide range of personal experience.*

We felt her account of Sex and the Office *would not be complete without revealing some of this source material, however, so we asked Mrs. Brown to gather together her early "notes"—bibliography, biography or whatever—for this book. She did, and we were delighted.*

Then the page-counters and cost-watchers came to us in alarm. Mrs. Brown had had a lot to say about sexy office life, and the book had grown. The budget wouldn't allow all those extra pages of notes—they would have to go. Sadly we reread them, feeling more and more certain that they should stay. A dilemma.

282

The solution, like all solutions, was a compromise: small type. So if you're as bright-eyed as we think you are, and if you're really interested in how this book (and this author) got to be the way they are, the following pages will be a breeze, and a fresh and amusing one at that. (Actually, we've just been thumbing through a few paperback books in our office, and we've concluded that small type must really be less of an annoyance than we had thought, since millions read them without ill effect.)

And really, even if you do have to squint a bit, we assure you that this particular bibliography will be well worth it.

BERNARD GEIS

THE PERILS OF LITTLE HELEN

M Y OWN OFFICE LIFE began when I was a little tyke of eighteen —flat-chested, pale, acne-skinned, terrified and convinced of one thing only: working in an office was practically the most gruesome thing that could happen to a woman. If there had been anything else I could have done I certainly *would* have, but there *wasn't* anything. I had only a business college education and that not yet completed. The school got me a part-time job for six dollars a week in a radio station so that I could continue to pay my tuition.

Every day after school I would arrive at radio station KHJ in Hollywood, California, to tabulate the mail for a breakfast show called "Rise and Shine." The emcee, Mr. Wilson, announced birthdays, wedding anniversaries and other sentimental occasions on this show, and it was my business to glean from the mail who wanted what remembered and where the present was hidden, and to pick up any gooey messages listeners wanted delivered on the show. I would type this information on three-by-five cards for Mr. Wilson to read from on the air while pretending to consult the actual letter. "Well, well, well!" Mr. Wilson would exclaim. "Little Deborah Jean Dallyrumple over in Gardena is having a fourth birthday! Let's see. It says here if Deborah Jean will go look out in the garage in Daddy's tool chest, she'll find something her little heart has been beating for."

Whether I went astray in trying to decode some of the handwriting, or whether I looked up from the typewriter too often, or whether I was trying to destroy Mr. Wilson outright (he had a temper like a rattlesnake), I don't know, but at least half the time I would get the information from one letter mingled in with that of a different letter. The child Mr. Wilson sent racing out to look in Daddy's tool chest for her present would unearth nothing more interesting than Daddy's secret cache of Old Granddad, while her own precious gift lay unclaimed upstairs under sister Evelyn's bed. Meanwhile, whoever was supposed to be looking in the tool chest Mr. Wilson would have dispatched to a tree house, or to a Shetland pony's feeding trough, or to sister Evelyn's bed when she didn't have a sister Evelyn.

Those first jobs . . . honestly!

Mr. Wilson was never closer to a stroke than when he had innocently announced, reading from one of my cards, "Well, listen here, twin brother and sister Barbara and Barry Biedenfelder of Monrovia, aged nine, are celebrating their fourth wedding anni . . . (gradual slowing of pace) . . . versary and . . . expecting . . . a . . . *BABY?!*"

Mercifully Mr. Wilson never saw me. He was up rising and shining about four every morning (no *wonder* he had a temper) and was long gone from the station when I arrived in the afternoon. His engineers reported faithfully, however, how Mr. Wilson had turned white, then scarlet and finally gone into big purple blotches as still another birthday child's mother called in to say he had *bungled* everything.

THE SUNNY SIDE

Mr. Wilson's tantrums and my hating secretarial work notwithstanding, the job had its compensations. The place was loaded with men. I've never *seen* so many men in one company with so few corresponding females to louse things up. There were announcers, engineers, newscasters, musicians, writers, sound men and producers in the back building (where I was); executives, salesmen and program directors in the front building. I was too young to appreciate the older men in their thirties, and I wasn't quite as comely as Scarlett O'Hara, but nothing could *entirely* spoil the fun.

When I came in from school every afternoon, some of the men would be playing a dandy game called "Scuttle." The Scuttle rules were simple to get the hang of. All announcers and engineers who weren't busy at one particular time would select a secretary or file girl, chase her up and down the halls, through the music library and back to the announcing booths, catch her and take her panties off. Once the panties were off, the girl could put them back on again if she wished. Nothing wicked ever happened. De-pantying was the sole object of the game. While all this was going on, the girl herself usually shrieked, screamed, flailed, blushed, threatened and pretended to faint, but to my knowledge no scuttler was ever reported to the front office. As a matter of fact, the girls wore their prettiest panties to work. There was some retaliatory action about mid-August. Four secretaries ambushed the head scuttler while he was announcing "Captain Midnight" on a forty-two-station hook-up and took his pants off.

Lest it sound as though I was scuttled regularly those summer afternoons, I have to admit, alas, I was never scuttled at all. Sometimes I would look up hopefully from my typewriter to see three or four scuttlers skulking in the doorway mulling it over, but the decision was always the same—too young, too pale, too flat-chested and all those other things I mentioned earlier. Clearly I was un-scuttleable. (Now, really, was your first job anything like that?!)

THE WONDERFUL TELETYPE MACHINE

At the end of six months Mr. Wilson had had about all he could take, so he got me kicked upstairs to the regular secretarial staff of KHJ. Mr. Wilson could sell anybody anything. He told them I could type like a robot, so they let me fill in for girls who were ill or on vacation.

One afternoon I had to send a teletype. I'd never sent a teletype before, and as everybody knows, teletype keys are lightweight and scatterbrained and always clicking off things you never said. This happened to be a serious message giving all stations of the regional network program changes for the day, and for two lines I got along fine: 1:00 TO 2:00 P.M. DAVE ROSE ENSEMBLE, I clickety-clacked impeccably. 2:00 TO 2:15 RICHFIELD NEWS, 2:15 TO 2:30 NORMA YOUNG HOMEMAKERS CLUB. The next instruction read 2:30 TO 3:00 ALL STATIONS FILL. That meant the network had nothing for them and the individual stations could put in whatever they wished. I wrote 2:30 TO 3:00 ALL STATIONS correctly, then took my hands off the keys, presumably to proofread. When I put them back on, I got the right hand one space to the left, so instead of resting on J-K-L-semi-colon, those fingers were on H-J-K-L, and everything else on that side of the board was loused up too. The letter I became U, L became K, and so forth. A perfectly innocent little word like "fill" came out quite shocking. (Try it yourself. You'll see what I mean.)

For a pale, flat-chested little tyke of eighteen, I certainly stirred up some excitement around there that afternoon with my typo. Bakersfield flashed back immediately, KEEN IDEA. NEED HELP WITH YOUNGER GIRLS. San Francisco called in, AFRA ACTRESSES DEMANDING MORE THAN SCALE. San Diego reported, STATION MANAGER UNABLE PERFORM, HUNG OVER. The regular teletype operator was back at her desk with a temperature of 102 the next morning.

It all seems so gay in retrospect. Actually it's apt to be the contrary when you're that young and that innocent. Sometimes your best-meant efforts backfire. One of my assignments was to put an Alka-Seltzer tablet into an envelope twice a day and staple it to the script of the Alka-Seltzer news program. When the announcer did the commercial and said, "Listen to it fizz," he would drop the real Alka-Seltzer into a Dixie cup of water, and the Alka-Seltzer would fizz raucously—on my good days. (You'd think they would have developed a depth charge or something for these occasions, but radio was quaintly honest in those days.)

I had a lovely inspiration. Why not test the product beforehand and use only a super-fizzy tablet? I tested several, found a real noise-maker, extracted it from the testing water and dried it off for the program. It did start to fizz loud and clear on the air—but only for a second. It was more like a pop, then cathedral-like silence while the newscaster hot-footed it back to the mike.

SQUIRRELS, DEER AND ENGINEERS

During my Alka-Seltzer stint I was madly in love with a young pianist named Skitch Henderson who played with the studio orchestra. I would have been *happy* to be scuttled by him, but no such luck. He never knew I was alive, although I used to pad around after him quite a lot.

Things did get rather sexy for two weeks late in the summer, though. The regular secretary at KHJ's television transmitter went on vacation and I was sent up to replace her. I even got excused from school to handle the assignment.

The KHJ transmitter looked down on everything in the city, and it was very woodsy up there. The deer and squirrels used to mosey around the swimming pool and come right up to the front door to be fed. *They* were tame, but the engineers were something *else* again. They didn't look wolfy, with their tall white foreheads and luminous white gazes, but aside from the head wizard, who knew about all kinds of inventions except girls, a grabbier bunch I never met.

The trouble may have stemmed from the nature of KHJ's programming. The only things being telecast in those days were the fights on Friday and wrestling matches on Monday. That left Tuesday, Wednesday and Thursday with nothing much for the men to do but sit around and practice hammerlocks and right crosses and speculate about their secretary.

Since I didn't have a car, the five of them took turns driving me up the mountain to work in the morning and back down again at night. I hated to do anything to hurt their feelings or impede science—KHJ *was* the only television station in town—but it really was a scramble. On the way up, I would roll down the window on my side and get as far out as I *could*. The only thing that saved me coming down was that the wizard always left the station last and stopped to investigate parked cars or anything that looked suspicious on his private road. Since the driver always had to keep the car in motion, and that took *one* hand, I had at least a fighting chance.

Well, that was my first dear little job. My word, we're only through *one*—there are *eighteen* to go. I'll rush-rush. I just want you to know I'm *qualified* to write about offices.

THE TALENT AGENCY

Job No. 2 was in the Beverly Hills headquarters of Music Corporation of America, then a talent agency of great influence. (I had finished school and was now a secretary full-time.) In case you're not familiar with what talent agencies do, they find jobs in movies, television, night clubs and theaters for actors, singers, writers and comedians, for which the performers pay them 10 per cent of their salaries. Most performers are not very good at ferreting out jobs for themselves, unless the jobs come looking for them. The sought-after people always work anyway. Jack Lemmon can always get a job. Jack Orange (I hope there isn't *really* someone with that name) can't *give* his services away, and an agency doesn't help him much either—but he always signs up. It's part of the game.

At that time MCA represented Betty Grable, Bette Davis, Paulette Goddard, Dick Powell, Errol Flynn, Alfred Hitchcock, Edgar Bergen, Joan Crawford and many other top stars and bands. I was just twenty and filling out—almost 28-18-28 by then. The furniture hooked me as it did every other young innocent who walked through the door. One good sink up to your knees in those carpets, one good blink at the center-hallway chandelier and delicate antique furniture, and you figured this must be the place (the fact that other companies were paying *money* notwithstanding). The MCA building looked so much like a Georgian mansion that tourists used to pile up at the front door and wait to be shown through.

There was nothing Georgian about the secretarial pool from which all secretaries flowed, however. It had everything but a rock castle and snails to give it verisimilitude. The executives who swam through even had a fishy look about them, what with being pale green. (Too much time in night clubs, maybe.) My boss, who was head of the band department, ran to light mustard and looked *sensational* in pink shirts.

A really warm-blooded girl wouldn't hold a man's skin tone against him, but these men weren't really interested in girls . . . in *us* girls, anyway. Occasionally, we would all wear red dresses or pink sweaters on the same day to see if anybody out there had a pulse beat, but no one ever reacted. They just rapped on the glass of our pool—like when it's time to feed the guppies—if they wanted anything.

Sometimes we sneaked down to MCA's posh little theater in the viscera of the building to eat our lunches and take naps on Mr. Jules Stein's yellow, skin-like leather couches. Mr. Stein was president of MCA. He would have had the place sealed off like Tutankhamen's Tomb with us *in* it if he'd known. It gives me a little thrill of pleasure just to think about it to this day.

Once a year we secretaries were fished out of our pool for an outing at the Shipstad and Johnson Ice Follies in the Pan-Pacific Auditorium. The Follies were a client, so the bigger the audience the better. "Bring a date, girls," the company spokesman would say. Now that sort of order can cause a girl to have a heart attack, as any working girl knows. We were all eager to show our bosses how attractive we were to other men, but the *war* was on (yes, I *am* over twenty-two), and there was nobody to show them with but fathers, baby brothers and people with collapsed lungs. (Don't ask me how the MCA men stayed out—perhaps it was their sea-green color.) Of course the MCA men never attended the show with us anyway, so I don't know what we were in such a flap about.

I will say some of MCA's male clients did their best to make up for the agents. Rudy Vallee asked me to dinner at his house one night. That sounded all right—it was a big house, and I was sure I could fade into the crowd. Then he told me what to wear: Black high-heeled pumps, sheer black stockings, any dress at all so long as it was black and sexy. "Put your hair on top of your head," he said.

"Who's going to be there?" I asked. (I thought maybe a Metro-Goldwyn-Mayer talent scout or something.)

"Just us, my dear," he said.

I didn't go, but now I sort of wish I *had*.

One day a famous movie star invited me to have breakfast with him the *following* day, after which he said he would drive me to work in Beverly Hills. (Wake up now . . . another sexy little incident for you.) It seemed an odd time to have a date, but food was food. Besides, he was most attractive. I ordered the sandhog breakfast—large orange juice, waffles, blueberry syrup, bacon and cold milk. I was starting on a Danish (dessert) when my date said we must be going. He'd only had coffee and had had quite a wait already. He then proceeded to drive me to MCA by practically the same route the KHJ engineers used to take to get up that mountain to the transmitter. A *very* good thing I'd had breakfast. A girl needs strength.

I took being fired from MCA with *reasonable* grace, and I don't think the firing had anything to do with my alienating MCA clients. It had something to do with what MCA called "not working out," a miserable expression you may hear used in connection with your *own* work some day, heaven forbid. Unfortunately, MCA neglected to tell *me* I wasn't working out, and I trained my own replacement for three weeks under the impression I was helping the new girl learn the ropes. Naturally I didn't weep when Attorney General Robert Kennedy closed the talent division of MCA down many years later.

JOBS THREE THROUGH SEVENTEEN

After a few shabby part-time involvements, I was hired by Eddie Cantor's gag writers, some of whose best gags were wasted in the elevator of the Hollywood Roosevelt Hotel. The shortest, fattest of the four would take out a roll of bills as we rode up to the office, squint at me and say, "How much you say it was, Myrtle, fifteen or twenty?" That broke up everybody in the elevator except me.

If one of the four writers thought of a gag *he* was insane about but the other three didn't think was funny, they would yell for me across the room. "Gurley!" (What can you do if that's your last name?) "Come over here! Is this or isn't it funny? A guy says to his mother-in-law . . ." If I *laughed* I was in trouble, and if I *didn't* laugh I was in *worse* trouble.

The publicity office which took me in a little later at least had *girls* in it, but I didn't get on well in publicity. (This is job seven—I'm skipping along.) My boss sensibly traded me to a young attorney friend whose secretary hated *legal* work. I hated legal work *too* when I found out about it, but a girl has to *eat*.

You learn a little something from each job. In a law office I learned that if a junior partner is gazing out the window at the girls in their *any* kind of dresses, you may *not* ask him to proofread something with you. He is *thinking*. If you interrupt him he may report you to the office manager. Also, when you're told to type a conformed copy, that doesn't mean just type the same words as in the original. It means everything has to come out the same distance from the top and bottom and you must try to duplicate the old erasures and smudge marks too if you can. Nine depositions too *late* I learned this.

The man I worked for was a darling . . . at *last*. My very first day on the job, at the *height* of rationing, he gave me ten pounds of bacon. I had one great big bacon orgy for eight days.

Mr. Paul Ziffren was also smart (he later became head of the Democratic Party in California), and he taught me several very smart things. If you want somebody to think you're lying, for instance, just tell the truth, he said. They'll say, "Where were you last night?" You answer, "I was so drunk I had to sleep in the back of my car." They will then say, "Come on now, where were you *really*?"

Who knows who left whom? I was *finding* myself.

COMEDIANS, SINATRA AND JUNGLE BEASTS

I learned something from each of the jobs that followed, and they continued to follow in rapid succession. With Abbott and Costello (I was secretary for their radio show) I learned how it felt to be very, very popular! They often did their weekly show at an army camp, and sometimes singer Connie Haines and I would be the only girls on the entire base for the day.

With Jack Carson I learned how to tell a joke to a comedian. Before the warm-up for his radio show, I would tell him a new joke I'd heard. It wouldn't have sounded funny from me if it had been the season's laugh riot, but Mr. Carson needed only the bare bones. "Yeh, yeh, yeh . . . radio announcer gets the hiccoughs . . . yeh, yeh," he would say, then go out and tell the story so that it really *was* funny. It made me feel funny, too.

I got to see Frank Sinatra about fifteen glorious minutes a week in my next job. I worked for the firm which packaged his radio show and took the payroll checks over for him to sign (during which time I gazed on him like a praying mantis examining her next grasshopper). I learned that if you get hold of an absolutely fabulous eleven-by-fourteen picture of a man and put it under his nose, he will autograph it for you. "To Helen," Frank wrote. "Thanks for *everything*." For years I have let it be understood among friends that *everything* applied to far more than just handing him payroll checks. But, since I have sworn to tell *you* only the truth . . .

I next made a movie with Frank Buck, cast mostly with snakes. It was two months in production, one for each customer who came to see it. I don't know whether I learned anything on that job, although I felt I was gaining in favor with man and possibly with God. We worked in Mae West's old bungalow, which was kind of sexy, I guess. I don't recall learning any valuable lessons, but the production company probably learned that in casting their next picture they should use *people*.

Next came a brief sojourn with three more talent agencies. Somehow a girl could *always* get a job there. At the William Morris Agency my typographical errors tended to be more southern than pornographic, and instead of getting me fired, they seemed to *solidify* my position. When I wrote "chile" for child, or "Satiday" for Saturday, Mr. W., a literary agent, would crumple up at his desk and have trouble getting his breath. An Irish-type booboo—"I forgot me (instead of my) brief case," tore him apart completely. I would warily wait out these bursts of mirth expecting them to turn to rage, but he was genuinely tickled.

I moved on to the *Daily News*, Los Angeles' one Democratic newspaper, and might possibly have made out all right if it hadn't been for the weather. The first afternoon I was there, my new boss got around to taking a good look at his new No. 2 girl (me) and sent word out by his No. 1 girl that at the *Daily News all young women wore stockings*. (It was the middle of July, for heaven's sake, and no time to be putting things *on*.)

Job fifteen was with producer Howard Hawks' brother Bill, a nice man who was "writing a book." Mr. Hawks taught me that when somebody says he's writing a book, he hasn't necessarily got around to it and possibly never will. I worked in Mr. Hawks' home and, although I never took one word of dictation, I think it made him feel closer to his goal to have a secretary around.

He had fascinating friends. Actress Arline Judge was his best girl. Miss Judge had married at different times *both* the Topping brothers, and she was so rich that I wondered if she had left anything for Sonja Henie and Lana Turner. While rubbing the philodendron leaves with whole milk—my only official duty—I would listen shamelessly as Arline told Mr. Hawks what she had said to the children that morning. "Now Dan Topping," Arline would have said to her eleven-year-old, "if that woman (his new stepmother) *says* anything to you, you just hit her over the head with her skates."

Actor Walter Pidgeon was another visitor, and he was a dear. My roommate Barbara and I both got a virus while I was working for Mr. Hawks, and Mr. Pidgeon telephoned to see if we needed anything to pull through. The only things Barbara and I could handle just then were boiled potatoes and weak tea, but we made a grocery list of several pages, including steak, Scotch, and other staples. Mr. Pidgeon graciously paid for them and sent them over.

Job sixteen was so dismal I won't even try to recall. I don't know *why* I skipped around so much, I really don't. Still looking for but not finding the real *me*, I suppose. An employment agency got me my seventeenth assignment—we're almost through the *heap*. I was by now their steadiest customer, and this time they placed me as secretary to a wealthy builder. He was *so* rich that his two young children each had a nurse, and each nurse had a maid. It was absolutely ridiculous.

Mr. Winston (which was *almost* his name) hated Communists (Commies), Catholics, ostentation (our office furniture was late William McKinley), Roosevelt (even though the man had graciously obliged him by dying), noise of any kind before lunchtime, and Jews. He hated all these things pretty vehemently, but most of all he hated Jews. It was really kind of pathetic, because the poor darling had, incredibly, constructed a motion picture studio with many sound stages right in the heart of Hollywood, not realizing until it was built that the entertainment business was *larded* with his least favorite people. (Mr. W. had led a sheltered life.)

Maybe Mr. W. had problems, but things were looking rather brighter for me. All I had to do for eighty-five dollars a week (when every other secretary in town was making forty) was keep things quieted down (the rustle of carbon paper was too much before noon) until Mr. W.'s hangover began to subside, take scattered dictation and guard the office from undesirables who might try to rent sound stages. (You can imagine who *that* meant.) The rest of the time I was free to eat and read. I went straight through the Melrose Lending Library and about thirty pounds of peanuts in three weeks.

Mr. W. adored gossip, particularly if the subjects were in trouble. He didn't have to know the people—he found just any kind of trouble anybody was getting into soothing. I never bothered with the facts but embroidered the simple plights of friends into a rich tapestry of woe. I got to be rather accomplished.

In return for the gossip Mr. W. told me about people he had ruined —and you can imagine who *they* were—how he drove them right out of New York State and sometimes all the way out of the country with just the clothes on their backs.

Since he was so good at ruining people, I thought there might be something he could do about our landlady. Ever since Barbara and I had put forty-two beer bottles out in back of the apartment one night—one of our beaux was a bit of a drinker—she'd considered us undesirable tenants and was conducting a vendetta against us.

"Do you have rats?" Mr. W. asked.

"Not that I've ever seen," I said.

"Don't you ever hear anything running around in the walls?" Mr. W. demanded.

"Yes," I said, "but we always just assumed it was Mrs. Tuttle."

"Keep an eye out for rats," Mr. W. advised. "I could sic the health department on Mrs. Tuttle if you have rats and scare hell out of her while I check into who holds the trust deed on the place."

Clearly the man wasn't *all* bad.

Around five o'clock every day Mr. W. would break out the Haig & Haig Pinch Bottle, one or two other quiet employees would be asked to join us, and cocktail hour would begin. We drank the Scotch out of paper cups with a splash of water. (Glasses and ice would have been too noisy.) Around six every night I would go home crocked.

Despite the fact that I was becoming an alcoholic, the money on this job was too good for me not to try to stay employed. I was doing nicely too—mouse-quiet, a dedicated gossip, hadn't rented a sound stage to anybody—desirable *or* undesirable. My one big problem in making good was in learning to hate Jews. I couldn't tell who was *Jewish*. Mother never told me I was different. In Little Rock where I grew up everybody was too busy with lynchings and all that to get around to Jews. In my whole life I don't think I'd ever heard of anti-Semitism (obviously I never read a newspaper) and in one or two of my former jobs I had apparently been the only gentile on the place, but had never realized we weren't all peas in a pod, racially speaking. This lack of perception about my co-workers Mr. W. found not only unbelievable but morally irresponsible.

My roommate Barbara, who was half-Jewish, tried to help. Like me, she was convinced this was too good a job to go the way of all my others.

"See my eyes," Barbara would say. "Jewish eyes are sort of big and brown and terribly sad."

"Your eyes are blue and little and mean," I said, "and you look perfectly happy."

We decided we needed outsiders to practice on, and wherever we went, Barbara would scout Jews and I would study them. I explained to Mr. W. that Barbara was helping me with my problem and that, although she really could have been *more* help if she'd been all Jewish she *had* unselfishly produced some full-blooded friends for observation. His reaction was percussive.

"My God," he said. "My God! My own secretary in a hotbed of them! This is what comes from not having had you investigated." (He peered at me to see if by some monstrous error he could have made a mistake about me.) "I just never dreamed the agency would send me a . . . a . . . a . . . *Jew*-lover!"

Because of my first-rate gossip perhaps, or maybe because I *was* mouse-quiet, Mr. W. decided to save me from the ovens. But despite our reconciliation, Mr. W. was never quite himself again. He sold the studio to a savings and loan company at a personal loss of nearly half a million dollars—only a year before a burgeoning television industry made studio space so rare he could probably have made *four* million on his property.

Well, let's see . . . that was job seventeen, and there are only *two* more.

You would think I'd be blackballed after the number of bosses I had sent either to psychiatrists, bankruptcy or monasteries, but it doesn't work out that way. You can be a butterfly, a gadabout, a kook, a moth, a migrant or a dilettante; you can be fired, cursed, turned out in wolf-packed black forests or deposited in deepest snow drifts—if you keep working long enough and try enough different jobs, you'll eventually find one to which you can safely give your heart. My eighteenth was like that.

THE AD AGENCY

One Saturday morning just after my twenty-fifth birthday I went to an advertising agency, Foote, Cone & Belding, to be interviewed by their board chairman for a job as his secretary. I wasn't impressed with the job *or* his title. Downtown Los Angeles? That was someplace to drive through to get to Palm Springs. Advertising? I was fresh from the exciting world of entertainment, whether I'd rented any sound stages or not.

Mr. Belding's office was as black as Carlsbad Caverns except for one sliver of lamp light. It was a high-ceilinged old thing with brown suede draperies, now drawn. He was behind his desk, and behind *him* was a painting of two Neanderthal fellows doing battle in a misty glen. Each held a spiked club in his *one* hand and, so far as I could see, their other hands weren't anywhere in the picture, although they must have been lying around on a rock or under a bush. All each man had on one side was a jagged stump which was bleeding wildly. An animal carcass lay between the two fighters, and there was blood all over the place. A plaque under the picture said, "The Ad Game." (Mr. Cone made Mr. Belding take the picture down when he saw it.)

The other walls of the office were strewn with autographed pictures of Harry Truman, Konrad Adenauer, Herbert Hoover, Dwight Eisenhower —*that* crowd—mixed in with pictures of girls rinsing out undies, girls making tuna sandwiches, girls waxing linoleum. (They were using client products, I learned later.) There was also an American flag in one corner, brown overstuffed couches, three mounted Kietsal birds and costumes from Guatemala under glass. It looked like the Field Museum.

Mr. Belding himself looked like Lionel Barrymore sprung from his wheelchair—balding, lean, lion-like and quite handsome, despite having only one good eye. (That's why the draperies were drawn, he said.) During the interview I never knew whether I was looking into Mr. Belding's good eye or Mr. Belding's *other* eye; it was impossible to look into both of them at the same time.) We sat there in a widening pool of silence. I'd stopped feeling so cavalier about the job already and was numb with fright.

"I'm out of town a good bit," Mr. Belding said finally, probably to cheer me up.

"I have excellent contacts with all the airlines," I said, never having booked a ticket in my life.

Mr. Belding said the company didn't usually have much trouble with reservations. He was a member of United's Hundred Thousand Mile Club, an American Admiral, a TWA Ambassador and TWA was a client.

About eight minutes later I was out in the sunlight again, blinking like a mole. The following Monday Mr. Belding's secretary, who was leaving to get married, telephoned to say I had the job.

Now *this* was a sexy office, and here was a sexy job, although I didn't know it in the beginning because I was drowning. (You'll find this is often the way it is in the beginning with a good job.) Miss Cunningham, my teacher, was thirty years old. She was a whirlwind, tweedy, fantastic with figures, lovey-dovey with stock quotations . . . a really dreadful girl, you know, and how I was supposed to *follow* somebody like that I couldn't imagine! I was dying to get rid of her at the same time I was dying at the thought of getting along without her. Every morning she would take the stopper out of my head and pour in so much information I would bubble up like Drano in a clogged sink. I was supposed to memorize account executives and supervisors and the accounts they worked on, copywriters and art directors, departments and what went on in them, clients' names and titles, clients of other Foote, Cone & Belding offices, Foote, Cone & Belding brass in other cities, Mr. Belding's partners and their families and Mr. Belding's two families—one by his first wife, Eunice, and another by his second wife, Alice. They each had children, grandchildren, brothers, sisters, mothers, cats, dogs, birds and servants. It was clearly impossible.

Mr. Belding kept springing *new* characters on me. He'd have me call his ranch in San Diego, then he'd take the phone and say, "Put Sarge on." (The foreman? The cook?) Then he would say, "Hello, Sargie? Hi, Sargie! Did you catch any nice gophers today?" It couldn't have been Eunice or Alice—their names weren't Sargie, and besides, whoever was on the other end was howling like a wolf.

I soaked up my daily briefings from Miss Cunningham and girded myself for the time when it would be Lionel Barrymore and me alone together. When the day came in two weeks, it wasn't so much like drowning, after all. It was more like being in a French railway station in a movie when they take the spy off the train—absolute bedlam. Phones rang, callers called, conferences convened, the mail poured in, campaigns coagulated, clients were coddled, civic activities got sandwiched in along with the problems of mothers, wives, children, grandchildren, and pets.

Mr. Belding turned out to be a nut about punctuality. There were just two morning buses I could take to get to work on time—one that got me there thirty minutes early and one that got me there thirty minutes late. That meant there was really only *one* bus I could take. While the moon was still out, I would whip out of my nightgown and into a dress. While the big red Pacific Palisades monster roared its way downtown I took out my curlers, made up my face, doused on cologne and, when there was any time left, went back to sleep. When Mr. Belding charged into the office around eight-twenty, forty-five minutes before anybody else arrived, he would find his secretary in her posture chair, unconscious but *there*.

"You here?" he would growl. "*This* time of morning?"

I refrained from giving him the Shepherd Mead line, "Oh, is it morning, sir?" but I did produce my, "Wouldn't have it any other way working for *you,* sir," smile, which kept me out of trouble until the office opened.

My first week without a keeper Mr. Belding asked me to send a bunch of ballpoint pens to Mr. Albert Lasker in La Quinta, a California desert resort. Mr. Lasker was Mr. Belding's benefactor and he liked to keep him informed on new products developed by clients. I wrapped up a whole mad assortment of pens, not saving out even one for me because I had decided never to steal from Mr. Belding. Then I sent them off to La Kenta, California. Who knew Indian? I spelled things the way they sounded.

In about three weeks we got the whole mad assortment back, of course. "I can't understand it," Mr. Belding said. "We never got anything back from La Quinta before. Let me see the package." I showed him the wrappings. "My God," he said, "you'd think Mary Cunningham would know how to spell La Quinta by now."

"You certainly would," I said.

Mr. Lasker left La Quinta presently to spend a few days at his ranch in Arizona, from which he planned to take the Super Chief back to Chicago. Before leaving town he asked me to get him a virginal drawing room to step into in Phoenix—he didn't want anybody to have been in the space when he boarded. He was so awfully pleasant and smiling, how did *I* know he'd handed me the messiest transportation problem of all time?

"Why *can't* somebody use the drawing room from Los Angeles to Phoenix?" Santa Fe wanted to know.

"Because Mr. Lasker wants the room to be virginal," I said.

Sante Fe explained that since several hundred, possibly thousand, people had used the room in the past ten years, what difference would two *more* make if they'd be gone when Mr. Lasker got on? They wouldn't hear of letting a drawing room go empty from Los Angeles to Phoenix, and Mr. Lasker, who was perfectly willing to pay for the room all the way from Los Angeles, wouldn't *hear* of other people using the room.

I offered Mr. Belding my solution. I would get on the train in Los Angeles and occupy the drawing room, sitting in one corner so as not to disturb anything, then pop off the train in Phoenix and disappear. Mr. Lasker would never even know I'd been aboard. Mr. Belding didn't think it was a bad idea, but before agreeing called the railroad himself. They relented.

The same week our tallest client and one of the most important, Mr. Philip Liebmann, President of Rheingold Breweries, wanted to go to New York, also by train. Mr. Liebmann didn't want an *empty* room. He wanted *two* rooms—one for him and one for his feet. (Apparently adjoining bedrooms could be opened up and Mr. Liebmann's feet could be stuck into one of them.) Of course Santa Fe wasn't any more going to let me have a bedroom for Mr. Liebmann's feet than they were going to give me an untouched drawing room for Mr. Lasker.

When I broke the news to him, Mr. Liebmann was hurt. "I am a tall man, Miss Gurley," he said. "Do you honestly want me to sleep with my knees under my chin all the way to Chicago—curled up in the fetal position, Miss Gurley—for two thousand, two hundred and twenty-three miles? Think of it . . . my curvature of the spine on your conscience."

Mr. Belding made some phone calls and I was saved again.

The next six months were filled with adventures. I mention them only to show how anybody can change from a dumb broad into a career girl if she stays with it. For instance:

1. I gave a funeral for about six hundred people.

2. I arranged a dinner party for the Rheingold group at the Hollywood Brown Derby. Thirteen guests were invited (which was my fault?), but Mr. Liebmann was superstitious and refused to sit down to dinner, so they had to get the Brown Derby cashier to come over and eat with them.

3. I answered Mr. Belding's private phone maybe two dozen times until Mr. Cone or Mr. Foote—I don't know which one—finally got tired of asking how the weather was out there and asked Mr. Belding to restrain me from lifting the receiver. He'd already explained this was his *private* phone, but it always sounded so lonesome ringing there all by itself.

4. I locked myself out in the hall in a swimsuit. Several garments had been left in Mr. Belding's office after a Cole of California creative meeting, and I just slipped into one after everybody had gone home. There was no full-length mirror in Mr. Belding's office so I flitted down the hall to the ladies' room to see how ravishing I looked, shutting his office door behind me because my clothes and purse were in there. It locked tight and I had to ring for the elevator man, who stopped off with a load of people from the eighth floor. (I think they kind of liked having an ad agency in the building; you never knew what you were going to find out in the hall at six-thirty waiting for the elevator.)

5. I lost a letter from Charles Luckman, President of Lever Brothers, another client, before Mr. Belding ever saw it. I never saw him unhappier.

6. I picked Mr. Belding up at the Lockheed Air Terminal one day in my thirteen-year-old Buick station wagon because we couldn't get word of his arrival to Mrs. Belding, who had his car and driver. (Mr. Cone and Mr. Foote insisted that Mr. Belding have a driver because of his eye. Since he could only see out of *one* he figured only one side of the road needed to be considered in making motoring decisions.)

We got a ticket first thing going through an I-said-yellow-they-said-red signal light. When the policeman asked for my car registration and I said I didn't have it with me, Mr. Belding said nonsense, everybody keeps his car registration in the car, and it was probably in the glove compartment. He started hauling out silk stockings, one-of-a-kind gloves, a half pint of brandy I was literally taking to a sick friend and a bra of ancient vintage I was going to buy elastic for. Then he gave up and let me get the ticket.

7. I tried to locate Mr. Belding's old Lord & Thomas proof file of favorite ads. The first time he requested it I took the place apart. After

I'd done everything but dismantle the air conditioning without success, Mr. Belding said, "It's in the building somewhere," gazing down the hall with his Treasure of the Sierra Madre look. "I saw it about four years ago."

When the request came up again, which it did regularly, I always dropped everything, went to "look" and came back to my desk forty minutes later carefully smudged, dishevelled and hungry. "The file was last seen in the vicinity of the Union Oil account group's office," I said. "And I'm concentrating my next efforts there."

"Splendid," Mr. Belding said. "Splendid."

8. I walked my paddies off looking for a piece of genuine cuneiform writing with an advertising message on it which Mr. Belding could use in making speeches to advertising groups. On checking with the County Museum I found that most cuneiform writing was located on slabs weighing roughly seven hundred pounds, priceless, and not available for purchase by civilians even if they could get it carted away. Dawson's Book Store finally located a small rock with hieroglyphics on it they *swore* were in the cuneiform period, give or take a few thousand years, and it only cost fourteen dollars. The message was something about fat cows being for sale and Mr. Belding accepted that as an advertising pitch.

9. I let somebody in Mr. Belding's office who sold him two dozen terrible ties. Since he had no sales resistance whatever, the purchase was *my* fault.

10. I turned away a man looking for a job—a far more serious offense. Mr. Belding felt that anyone out of work is usually in shock and must always be seen.

11. Swept out six or seven nuts who refused to leave the waiting room until the company hired them. It was a well-known fact that Mr. B. got taken on as a mailroom boy at Lord & Thomas (later Foote, Cone & Belding) by using these same high-handed tactics, and it handicapped us severely in unloading people who were trying to do the same thing.

12. I tracked down Toni Twins for "Which Twin Has" ads. This was my one non-secretarial assignment and I took it very big.

13. I arranged a cocktail party for visiting members of the Swiss Watch Federation, a client, while Mr. Belding was out of town. None of them spoke English and none of us spoke French or German. I dragged in a Berlitz instructor who held the account while the staff drank up the booze.

14. I signed for documents from Mr. Howard Hughes (Hughes Tool, Hughes Aircraft, RKO Pictures and TWA were clients) when my boss was out of town. The courier would ask that we go into an office, shut the door and affix a wax seal to the envelope to be broken only by Mr. Belding. Naturally I volunteered to be put to death for watching.

Mr. Hughes sometimes visited the office late at night, but I never saw him. He and the head of the motion picture department would study Jane Russell's cleavage hours on end to determine just how many inches more a blouse could slip off and still be considered on. (*The Outlaw* was being re-released and the agency was doing ads.) Depending on the outcome of the nightly conferences, the artist would move the blouse up or down a quarter of an inch the next day.

This happened too:

1. The agency resigned the fourteen-million-dollar Lucky Strike account because it was giving Mr. Foote a nervous breakdown. After the account was resigned, Mr. Foote had a nervous breakdown anyway.

2. Some of the staff were brainwave-tested by a group of brainwave specialists to determine their worth to the company. (You never *know* what a company is going to come up with to prove they made a mistake about hiring you.) These people ran an electrical current through your head, and it was very impressive. First they brainwaved the mailroom boy, who was a protégé of the office manager, and he came out somewhat smarter than Bertrand Russell. Then Mr. Belding and the office manager volunteered, and they came out only a notch below the mailroom boy. Then somebody suggested the brainwavers give the test to two unidentified employees. The most quiveringly sensitive art director in the place was diagnosed as unperceptive and qualified to do only simple manual labor. The account supervisor who held four million dollars worth of oil-company billing came out slightly better than a Jukes. The "geniuses" adored their scores, but consented to have the brainwavers packed off for the general good.

3. Mr. Ade Pelletier, president of the Purex Corporation, a client, drank a glass of Purex at a banquet to show stockholders how mild the product was, then he had his stomach pumped backstage after dinner. I know I would have fallen in love with Mr. Pelletier if we'd ever met.

4. A husky young mailroom boy (not the genius) went off his rocker, swooped up a frail, elderly employee and carried her around the office until they made him put her down.

5. An agency executive handed down Smock's Law on the Strangely Sexual Yearnings Advertising Men Experience During a Severe Hangover. "Your body feels so terrible it knows it's going to die," Mr. Smock said, "and wants to procreate before passing on."

6. The head switchboard operator had a dinner date with a publisher's representative, and while in the ladies' room of the restaurant, her upper plate fell out. She accidentally flushed it down the toilet and didn't have nerve enough to go back to the table. Her companion may still be waiting.

7. Mr. Belding spent most of the night in a TWA hangar under the impression he was on his way to Chicago. He had crawled into his berth and gone to sleep when the crew discovered engine trouble. They finally grounded the plane, thought they got everybody off, taxied into the hanger and discovered Mr. Belding, a sound sleeper, four hours later. "Here already?" he wanted to know. He wasn't happy to find he was just where he'd started.

It was exciting to work for an important man. (And that's the kind every girl should have after being a competent secretary for a while.) I took dictation in the back of a limousine to and from airports. Sometimes I would be sent for by Mr. Belding's driver and limousine to bring myself and the mail to Santa Barbara or San Diego where Mr. Belding was just coming in from the boat races. I found it very romantic slipping along in the night under a fur lap robe like Marie Walewska being spirited out of Poland to Napoleon.

One Saturday my boss gave me to General Omar Bradley, then Chairman of the Joint Chiefs of Staff, as a burnt secretarial offering when the General came to California to make a speech. Mr. Belding also gave the General his car and driver (William and I were kind of a package). The General, a quiet charmer, really didn't need any secretarial help, so I had lunch with his two aides, later to become generals too, at the hotel pool. A third aide, a Naval lieutenant, holed up to work on the General's speech, Around three-thirty he came down to the pool waving the speech and asked if I would make a clean copy for the General. "Are you mad," his friends asked him. "This lovely creature type a speech? She wouldn't know where to find the space bar." The writer sensibly turned the manuscript over to the public stenographer.

Ye gods, you've probably deserted me—not one out-and-out really full-*fledged* sexy incident in a dozen paragraphs!

On to sexy incidents . . .

The office Don Juan at Foote, Cone & Belding had his hooks into me practically before I had my hat and coat off.

D.J.'s have to work fast, because they've usually already gobbled up everything in the office and are starving for a new arrival, while the earlier victims are poised to warn the new arrival about the D.J. If the new girls gets the idea that he's a cross between Bluebeard and the Boston strangler, he's through before he starts.

There wasn't any excuse in the world for me, however. I had been warned by no less an authority than old Pete's *wife*. She and I had worked together in another office, and when she heard I was going down there with *him*, she said, "Watch out for old Pete. He has the appetite of a tapeworm." (They were working out the terms of a divorce.) I had a drink with old Pete one day after work. Several other people were with us, and he was catching a plane to San Francisco—what could be safer? The next night I found Pete on my doorstep. "I came home a day early," he said. "I had to see you. I think I'm falling in love with you."

A Don Juan, no matter what else you say about him, is no time-waster. Pete suggested we drive to Santa Barbara for dinner. It was just dusk, and I shifted into something shifty for the journey. During cocktails he declared finally, firmly and positively he *was* in love with me. (I already mentioned a D.J. is decisive.) We chatted about our office friends during dinner but not much. Two miles out of Santa Barbara on the drive home old Pete made another decision and turned the car into a motel. Under the burning neon he said, "I wish I could stop this, but it's too late."

For *him* maybe. He got out of the car and stalked off to the innkeeper. I slid over to the driver's seat, put the car in "drive" and drove off to Los Angeles.

This quick-thinking saved me from the demolition corps all of four hours. Around dawn old Pete was on my doorstep again, this time with a taxi driver to negotiate a loan of thirty-four dollars. (If you're going to delay a Don Juan in the pursuit of happiness, all I can say is you'd better be rich.)

From that day on I was done for—in love . . . in pain . . . in ecstasy . . . and in for the inevitable. Our *l'amour* had been *toujours* for only three weeks when one of the girls in the office and I stayed late to address Mr. Belding's Christmas cards. She was an even newer arrival than I. Old Pete took us both to dinner several nights in a row and in the dimly lit restaurant it was hard to tell which girl friend had the boy friend.

In time-honored Don Juan tradition we broke up just before Christmas.

I bound up my wounds with a young Swiss chap (good heavens, I hope this isn't boring you) who was studying advertising at our office. Freddy was about as tall as I, darkly, devilishly foreign-looking, bushy-eyebrowed, gutteral-sounding and not without charm. Freddy handed out Swiss watches for tips (I never got one, since I wasn't a waitress) and on his way West had bought a cow at auction in New Orleans because nobody wanted her. He brought her to Los Angeles and found her a good home.

Mr. Belding took quite a fancy to Freddy, so I decided that our friendship should be kept secret, lest Mr. Belding think I was making off with his staff one by one. There was another reason. Freddy looked like an anarchist. His suits were not only belted in the back and double-breasted, his trouser legs were *square*. His beard came out so furiously about noon he just *looked* like the one whose hotel room you should search *first* in case of a bomb scare. He was very cooperative about the secrecy thing and we did everything but meet like trolls under bridges for dates.

Sometime later Freddy was the embarrassed one. He had become madly successful in his own agency in Zurich and had returned to Los Angeles on SAS' historic first flight over the Pole. I picked him up at the airport, and I couldn't believe it *was* Freddy in his homburg and navy pinstripe. We got into Appletrees, my antique station wagon with the natural wood sides and composition roof. The roof was so thin by then that when the sun shone brightly, the back end of the car looked like a greenhouse inside. After a good hard rain all Appletrees' doors would fly open and flap about during the drive. I finally had taken to tying all of them to the car with pieces of rope, except for the one on the driver's side. That door I just held shut under my left arm as I drove. Freddy didn't balk at crawling under the driver's seat so as not to disturb his own roped-up door, but he winced when they had to haul his luggage out through the window at the Sheraton Town House.

One of my office romances was with Jack Dempsey, who was then endorsing a client's product, Bulldog Beer. Mr. Dempsey couldn't pronounce beer. When he said it it came out burrrrrr, and it was the happiest mispronunciation that ever happened to a client. After hearing his radio commercials, people would come into a bar and say, "Gimme a bottle of Bulldog Buuurrrrrrrr." By the time they got through laughing and decided what they *really* wanted, the Bulldog was there.

Some people thought Mr. Dempsey and me such an unlikely couple that we probably used an interpreter to talk to each other. It's true Mr. Dempsey *did* bring a friend along on a good many of our dates—an ingratiating chap named Willie. This gave *him* somebody to talk to. I didn't have a lot to say anyway. We usually went to a night club or the fights where nobody needed to talk.

At the height of our friendship Mr. Dempsey flew to New York to see about a labor dispute in his restaurant, and while there he got engaged to a rich widow. The engagement lasted only two weeks, but I was dreadfully upset. I *did* think he might have mentioned the widow before. Mr. Dempsey sent me a cheesecake in an effort to make up—I'm pathological about cheesecake—but our friendship was never the same again to me.

The longest-in-my-life beau at Foote, Cone & Belding was a Don Juan *supérieur* who worked for another agency. (How any one girl can become involved with *two* Don Juans so close together I don't know, but it does get them *over* with, like childhood diseases.) Allen liked to play a little game called "Who Do You Love?" An answer like "You, darling," branded you a total idiot. You were supposed to say "John Foster Dulles," so Allen could say "He's too reactionary," or "Leonard Bernstein," "His hair is too bushy," or "Krishna Menon," "He's too occult," or "Mike di Salle," "He's too roly-poly." The more obscure the personality, the more points you got. Judge Crater was my biggest hit. He was "too disappearing!" The trouble was that in order to give Allen this chance to show off his knowledge of who was who by making his snappy comeback, *I* had to know the characters too. Getting ready for a date meant cramming with *U.S. News and World Report, Time, Life* and maybe *The Saturday Review.*

I suffered during this romance like a purebred little masochist. If things were going *reasonably* well, I couldn't stand it and would sneak a look at Allen's address book . . . a big fat looseleaf thing whole sections could be added to. I could check who was new by the color of ink and have a nice quiet nervous breakdown. The girls of my general tenure were in purple. Blue and green were a newer vintage.

When this romance was at its unhappiest, I asked Mr. Belding for a week off to go to Mexico to recover. He said it was a very good idea and that while I was away perhaps this fellow would miss me and come to his senses. Darling Mr. Belding.

It *might* have happened that way, only Allen went with me. I felt terribly guilty the whole time, because I was supposed to be in Mexico with a girl friend and we kept running into Mr. Belding's friends. First I spotted two clients at the airport at the same time they spotted me. Introductions all around. At the Del Prado Hotel in Mexico City I crashed head-on into the head fund-raiser for Mr. Belding's most cherished philanthropy. More introductions. It was nerve-wracking.

Having used up my week's vacation to get away from Allen without getting away from him, I now had to take the cure at the office. This, however, is as good a place as I've ever found to forget a man.

PUSSYFOOTING TO THE TOP

Would you believe it—we're almost up to my eighteenth job, and there's only one more to go.

When Mr. Belding was out of town—which was often—I spent most of each day compiling a long, gossipy letter to him. Mrs. Belding read them and thought I had such a breezy style she prodded her husband into letting me try writing copy on one of the accounts. No man in his right mind wants to give up a good secretary, but Mr. Belding was a sweetheart. He made the Sunkist Orange account supervisor give me an assignment. "Lady, a big shipment of juicy navels has just arrived in your city," ten out of my fourteen commercials began, and it only took me fourteen days to write them. You couldn't say only Sunkist navel oranges had navels, because God had given *all* navel oranges navels. You *could* say that if they bore the Sunkist trademark it was a very lucky thing for *you*, and I said that *lots*. Some of the commercials were actually used in Albany and Schenectady, where they were up to their navels in Sunkist oranges.

I remained Mr. Belding's secretary three more years, writing copy only when Albany and Schenectady were under orange juice again. The association might have gone on like that forever if I hadn't entered a contest in *Glamour* Magazine called "Ten Girls With Taste." (It was one of the things I did to get over Allen.) One of the questions was, "What is your ambition?" I didn't really have any except to continue to be Mr. Belding's secretary. Knowing *Glamour* wouldn't want to have anything to do with a slug, I said I'd like to be a copywriter. It was hideously embarrassing when the magazine printed some of the winners' ambitions. There I was, sounding like the ambition-ridden girl I wasn't. But Mr. Belding took me at my printed word—I wasn't really consulted —and gave me a little office with my name on the door. I became a copywriter.

MOVE OVER, BABY

Writing copy in an advertising agency is quite sexy because you get to fraternize with a lot of men. (I was the only girl among eight writers and six art directors.) You can yappety-yap away at them all during business hours, and nobody thinks you aren't attending to business. You can also flirt lethally while pretending to be arguing about a headline. Deciding between "Our batteries stay fresh" and "Our batteries charge longer" can have you leaning over a man's desk all morning.

My client was the Catalina Swimsuit account, and when ads were photographed I usually went along. (Copywriters were encouraged to know all phases of ad preparation.) One of the choice locations for photographing swimsuits was a lonely cove at Malibu that you couldn't even get close to by car. We would park a mile away and pack in with cameras, reflectors, girls, fins, film, picnic baskets and bourbon in the misty dawn to catch the sun's first rays. Why it always had to be a misty dawn and the sun's first rays I never understood, but no photographer or art director I ever met cared a hoot about moonlight or bright sun.

One day we shot three mermaids on a rock several yards out in the Pacific in a *foggy* dawn. The sun never showed at all, and the surf was very frisky. I can see the mermaids now in their long flaxen wigs, clasping lyres and lutes to their mermaid bosoms, trying not to fall off the rock on their mermaid fannies and have their mermaid tails pounded off in the surf. They looked very sweet and mermaidenly, except that they were turning blue. The photographer would haul them back in every so often, hand them a Dixie cup of bourbon and send them back to the rock, hoping for an improvement in skin tone. I can still hear him bellowing across the surf to the mermaid who couldn't swim and kept inching toward center rock: "You're spoiling this setup, baby, now *move over!* God dammit, baby, move OVER!"

The spring William Randolph Hearst's San Simeon ranch was opened to the public we decided it was just the place to photograph the Catalina collection. However, just because San Simeon welcomed the public on carefully-supervised tours didn't necessarily mean that an enterprising swimsuit company could immortalize its wares beside the Neptune Pool or on the stairs of La Casa Grande. Our art director finally got permission by giving Mr. William Randolph Hearst Jr.'s office the impression our little group would be photographing a story for one of his magazines—*Harper's Bazaar*. It's true our swimsuits would be in the pages of the *Bazaar*, but we just omitted to say they would be in the advertising pages.

San Simeon, as any vistor knows, is not really possible. Castles there are with turrets and towers and drawbridges—but with lapis-lazuli-lined *swimming* pools and subterranean Egyptian *baths?* Mr. Hearst is said to have spent a million dollars a year on treasures for San Simeon from 1919 to near the time he died in 1951, but almost any woman looking at the place would say he got a bargain. I thought it made Versailles look a little tacky.

Visitors were allowed through the castle from 8:42 A.M. to 5:12 P.M., and even with our *Harper's Bazaar* credentials we were only permitted to photograph before the crowds arrived and after they went home. We had to hustle. The models arose at 4:00 A.M. to put on their make-up. The rest of us staggered out at 5:00 and drove to the bottom of the castle, where San Simeon guards met us and led us up the mountain once guarded by Mr. Hearst's cougars, lions and tigers. If we were on time, it was pitch dark.

Equipping for Malibu was like packing lunch compared to the junk we moved in around the Neptune Pool. It was huff, puff, puff, huff, and it all had to be set up before the sun came up if we were to catch the ever-loving misty dawn. At sunrise the models flitted from pillar to pillar, embraced stone gargoyles and climbed in and out of sarcophagi while the cameras click-clicked, then shimmied into new swimsuits and started over again. When the sun was high and visitors' hour upon us, we halted dead, the models turned off their smiles and collapsed, we repacked everything and guards led us down the mountain again. Then we drove back to the hotel to sleep like vampires until afternoon, hopped once more out of the sack and raced back to the castle for twilight. How can anybody say working is always the same old thing?

During our third afternoon of shooting, the Hearst family checked into the bungalow reserved for their special use next to the castle. The bungalow couldn't compare to the castle—just a little feudal hideaway that slept about seventy-five. Mr. Hearst, his wife and two young sons came down to swim in the Neptune Pool and to ask how the photography was going. Fine, we said, just fine. Then Mr. Hearst wanted to know whether Nancy White was back from Europe. I was the only one who had ever heard of his editor-in-chief at the *Bazaar*, but I hadn't even known she was gone. "She isn't home yet," I said. (I didn't want Mr. Hearst chasing off to his bungalow to call her up), "but she's having a marvelous time and *adores* the Fabianis."

This seemed to satisfy him. "Use the pool," Mr. Hearst said. He really was affable and sweet. The models had to be restrained from jumping in in their new Catalina Masterpieces, but we happened to have other suits along.

The late Humphrey Bogart also let us photograph aboard his yacht, the *Santana*. We know who put him up to it. In return for her husband's wearing a Catalina sport shirt in the picture (he refused to part with his own pants), Mrs. Bogart (Lauren Bacall) was invited to select all the Catalina merchandise she wanted for herself and her children. The agency doesn't know how many carloads of sweaters and swimsuits she took out of there, but the Catalina shipping clerks reported *she* was there most of the day and *they* were there most of the night. Getting Mr. Bogart was a coup, however. He was the perfect male image for the men's stuff, and Mrs. Bogart in *anybody's* merchandise was a dream ad walking.

Foote, Cone & Belding presently gave me to Catalina Swimsuits in a gift-wrapped package so that I could tour the country for the company. (I don't know why bosses were always giving me to somebody else—they *said* I could learn more about the client's product that way.) I accompanied minor celebrities on a Catalina promotion tour of major department stores.

Florence Chadwick was my first charge—a very nice lady, indeed. Olympic diving star Pat McCormick was the second. The next year Catalina sent me out with the reigning Miss Universe, Hillevi Rombin of Upsala, Sweden. You have your definition of a pill, I have mine. Hillevi was not only sweet, funny, gorgeous and poised as a swan, she also spoke five languages. How could you love a girl like that (if you were another girl)? When there were men in the same room, I felt as though I'd become part of the furniture. The only time I was noticed was when some man wanted to take Hillevi to show her Milwaukee or Duluth—then I'd be asked if she could go. I was always inclined to let the child see Milwaukee and Duluth—goodness knows when she'd be back again, and a chaperone left in the hotel might become more visible without her little charge under-foot. Hillevi never wanted to go, however.

Hillevi was vain but forthright. If she wanted to look at herself she never stole a glance in the elevator door or sneaked peeks at store-window reflections. She would pause at the mirror, take a good, long, slow, languorous, all-encompassing look and announce, "Ah loooooooooooook lak a spoke."

"What, Hillevi dear?" Her vocabulary was good, but it didn't always jibe with her train of thought.

"A Halllloweeeeeeeeen spoke!" Hillevi said triumphantly. This was a hint that we should cut out all this fashion-show nonsense and get out in the sun where a bathing beauty belonged.

Hillevi had one tiny flaw which nearly endeared her to me. She was a candy sneak of almost criminal proportions. If I let her out of my sight in the May Company or Whelan's drugstore, she came back with enough chocolate-covered marshmallows to short the Easter bunny that year. Hillevi was supposed to stay wand-slender as the star of our swim-suit fashion shows, but I never scolded. Let the child have her fun! A fat Miss Universe—how marvelous! But no matter how many marsh-mallows she packed away, nothing seemed to happen to her startling proportions.

HELEN'S OTHER AD AGENCY

Travel is fun and profitable, but I returned to my desk in Los Angeles and eventually began to write very good copy. I was written about in trade magazines and started to win little awards. Then, during my tenth summer with Foote, Cone & Belding (you can be so *faithful* when you're happy), another Los Angeles agency named Kenyon & Eckhardt ac-quired the four-million-dollar Max Factor account and needed to staff up with girl writers in a hurry. I was a logical acquisition.

Of course, there is nothing in the world so attractive to a company as someone who doesn't need *them.* (This works in love too.) All summer long Kenyon & Eckhardt kept upping their job offer until it was getting ridiculous. What kind of coward *am* I, I began to wonder. In taking this new job I would hardly be putting in with a band of gypsies. One thing that disturbed me was the reputation of Max Factor's ad manager. He was said to put agency people in jars like lightning bugs and squeeze out their lights. I decided to go check out the squeezer myself.

Mr. Gross received me cordially. He was dapper, crew-cut, shortish, rounded, neat, wore hornrimmed glasses and couldn't possibly be a mon-ster, I decided. When I asked him about the monster rumors he said, oh yes, *those*—possibly they got started because he was *firm* with people, but he was also very *loyal.* His key people stayed with him forever. (I never found this to be untrue as long as I knew him, but the people who qualified as "key" got down to a precious few.) Mr. Gross and I chatted for about an hour, and he seemed eager to have me go to work for his advertising agency. When they got the salary up to double the one I was making, I took the job.

Mr. Gross, as it turned out, didn't put people in jars and snuff out their lights. He shell-shocked them. Though I hadn't noticed a single gun around the place during my interview, whenever a group of us went to call on Mr. Gross we never knew whether we would be fired on by a short-barrel Luger or a Smith & Wesson revolver. "Got a new gun," Mr. Gross would announce in the middle of a spring shade presentation. Then he would point it straight at the account executive's head and fire. We just had to trust that he would *continue* to use blanks.

On special days we would be bombarded with "it"—a shotgun that fired three woolly purple and yellow snakes with springs inside to make them expand the moment they were free of the gun barrel. With a big, woolly, yellow and purple snake flying at you, it is hard to remember your name, rank or the color of the shade promotion.

Two other female writers also worked on the account. I adored them personally, but sibling rivalry ran high. One played it child-like and bubbly. She would get so excited about every new product you thought she was going to *eat* the Green Jade eye shadow instead of write about it. They adored her. The second girl was a pretty, sunny, ex-farm girl who could make roses bloom in the snow. Between them those bitches had grabbed of *all* the great client-pleasing qualities and left me with nothing to wear but femme fatale or lady tycoon. I was too blabbermouthy for one and too short on leadership for the second. *My* big moments came at rifle practice, however.

The more scared you were when Mr. Gross fired off a gun, the better he liked it. Well, the girls just weren't in my league hysterics-wise. They were normal, run-of-the-mill girl-screamers—but I was superb. Loud noises unhinged me anyway, and snakes! Whatever came at me out of Mr. Gross's gun barrel—snakes, noise or butterflies—I would go entirely to pieces and wander about looking glassy-eyed for minutes. Mr. Gross grew pleased and expansive.

We worked awfully hard on this account. During rush season, which was all four seasons, anybody who left before midnight was chicken. Thanksgiving Day, Memorial Day and *always* on Sunday a girl found herself on the floor of an art director's office trying to figure out a new way to show a girl looking radiant. (Surrounding her with flames was too hot. Having her emerge from a flower was too floral. Showing "before-and-after" pictures was too real. Max Factor never admitted girls who used their products were ever birds to begin with.) One Sunday we had a three-hour meeting to decide whether the headline should be "Eight Obstacles to Beauty" or "*The* Eight Obstacles to Beauty."

There were many things we couldn't say for Max Factor, such as suggesting that a product did what it was *supposed* to do. For instance, we couldn't say that a matte-finish make-up gave a matte finish, because that might frighten girls who liked a glowing schoolgirl look. We

couldn't say Max Factor's glowing schoolgirl make-up produced a glowing schoolgirl look, either, because this might frighten away girls who
wanted a matte finish. If Max Factor had a glorious new product—say an
iridescent lipstick—it was Pussyfoot Time. We couldn't *say* it was
phosphorescent in case somebody preferred a regular lipstick, but if we
didn't say it, millions in research money would have been wasted. If
things got *too* frustrating, we could always drop empty beer cans out the
window and try to hit somebody waiting for the bus at Hollywood and
Vine.

I calculate that during my years on the Max Factor account I personally thought up nine thousand, two hundred and seventy-four names for
make-up, eye shadow, nail enamel, skin cleansers, hair-spray and perfume. Everyone else in the agency thought up at least as many. We had
enough names to start our own language. The exercise was academic,
really. Max Factor usually had a name all picked out before they gave
us these assignments, and the idea was to see how close the agency could
come to guessing *their* name.

Would you like to play the name game as it's played for money in an
ad agency? Okay, let's name a lipstick.

Write down every pink, red or orange color you can think of. Never
mind what color the lipstick is actually going to *be*, that has nothing to
do with it. Ready? Carmine, scarlet, flame, cherry, blush, shocking, camel-
lia, peppermint, ruby, garnet, damask, vermillion, mauve, coral, tangerine
and magenta will do to start. Now write down all the fruits, flowers,
jewels, vegetables, birds, zodiac signs, cities, dances, gods, goddesses,
fabrics, spices, seasons, weather conditions, emotions, wild animals and
terms of endearment you can think of. Skip wines and spirits. No cosmetics manufacturer will ever admit that anybody who uses *his* products
tipples. Avoid colonial uprisings, too. Swahili Red and Viet-nasturtium
will go over like wrought-iron kites. Now if you have really gone about
this conscientiously, you will have exhausted the dictionary, the en-
cyclopedia, the thesaurus and seven or eight friends, and it will be five
days later. (The friends usually have terrible ideas, but they can make
coffee for you.)

Now for the fun—you simply mix and match! Watermelon Madness,
Count-Down Red, Ginger-Peachy Grapefruit, Blueberry Kisses, Tiger
Sapphire, Venus de Pink, Kabuki Peach, Orange Olé, Heart of a Stranger,
and on and on.

What am I *doing!* First thing I know *you'll* be writing copy. Don't
look to me for instruction about writing television commercials, though. I
wasn't too great at it. I had one with a girl taking her hair to the psychiatrist to find out why it hated her, and another with Mr. Acne tracking
down kids at high school to break out on. I was told that you're supposed
to try to sell the client's product, not take it off the market.

That was my last office job—so far. Staying in that particular office
meant outlasting nine creative directors and four office managers, and
when you have a thirteen of *anything,* naturally some of them don't *like*
you. Being out of favor occasionally is nothing to pound your temples

about, however. Any working girl comes up against squirrels as well as divine lions and tigers and deer in her jobs. My four years at Kenyon & Eckhardt were most rewarding in many ways, and during some of that time I was Los Angeles' highest-paid advertising woman. I'd doubtless still be in an advertising agency or an office *somewhere*, but while I was at K & E I fell really out of favor with one of the nine creative directors, and, having nothing to do, I wrote a book. It turned out to be so successful that it called for *another* book, and I'm just now finishing that one, which you are just now finishing *reading* (if you can follow *that* bit of time juggling you're probably ready for Einstein). It's hard to write books and carry on in an office too. I carry on in my office at home of course, but believe me, that isn't the same kind of carrying-on at all.

But you—you can still carry on in your *office*-office, you lucky girl!